Hand Book of Ice Cream Technology and Formulae

Hand Book of Ice Cream Technology and Formulae

Written By

EIRI Board of Consultants & Engineers

ENGINEERS INDIA RESEARCH INSTITUTE
4449, Nai Sarak, Main Road, Delhi - 110006 (India)
Ph: +91-11-23918117, 23916431, 45120361, 23947058, 64727385
* E-Mail: eiribooks@yahoo.com & eiriprojects@gmail.com
*Website: www.eiriindia.org & www.industrialprojectreports.com

PRINTED & PUBLISHED BY

ENGINEERS INDIA RESEARCH INSTITUTE

4449, Nai Sarak, Main Road, Delhi - 110006 (India)
Ph: +91-11-23918117, 23916431, 45120361, 23947058, 64727385
* E-Mail: eiribooks@yahoo.com & eiriprojects@gmail.com
*Website: www.eiriindia.org & www.industrialprojectreports.com

Sole Distributor:

EIRI PROJECT CONSULTANTS AND PUBLISHERS
4/54 Roop Nagar, Delhi-110007

2nd Revised & Enlarged Edition

ISBN: 9788186732700

Printed in New Delhi (INDIA)

₹ 750/-

Printed & Published by Sudhir Gupta for "Engineers India Research Institute", 4449 Nai Sarak, Main Road, New Delhi -110006

Preface

Ice-creams of many varieties, flavours and in different forms (cones, cups, slices, bulk packing, candies, etc) are served round the year and demand is going up year after year. Possibly the most popular mode of serving is in cones as it is neat & clean, easy to store and there is no disposal need. With continuous increase in sale of ice-creams, demand for cones is increasing. It is a mass consumption item.

Ice-cream cones are prepared from wheat & corn flour and they are eaten along with the icecream. Pre-determined quantity of ice-cream is automatically filled in each cone. Cones are not only convenient but there is no residual waste as well. They are of different colours and flavours. This is a very common product and can be produced all over the country. Nearness to urban market should be the main guiding factor.

The book "**Hand Book of Ice Cream Technology and Formulae**" covers almost all the basic and advanced details to setup own Ice Cream Industry. The book covers *Introduction, Nutritional value and Classification of Ice Cream, Composition and Properties of Ice Cream Mixes, Raw Materials used to produce Ice Cream, Manufacturing Process, Ice Cream Freezing, Ice Cream Mix Calculations, Packaging of Ice Cream, Frozen Dairy Products and Formulations, Ice Cream Varieties, Novelties and Specials, Ices and Sherbets, Laboratory Tests, Cost and Merchandising, Plant Economics of Ice Cream Stabilizer, Plant Economics of Ice Cream & Ice-Candy, Plant Economics of Instant Ice Cream Mix, Plant Economics of Ice Cream of Different Flavours, Plant Economics of Cone for Softy Ice Cream, Plant Economics of Ice Cold Flavour Tea, Suppliers of Plant & Machineries, Suppliers of Raw Materials etc.*

Frankly speaking - the book is also quite indispensable for those who have also setup their industry.

The primary objective of the book is to facilitate the entrepreneurs in understanding the importance of setting up unit of ice cream cones. This book will serve as guidance to the entrepreneurs on starting up such a new project and basic technical knowledge for setting up such a facility.

EIRI Board of Consultants & Engineers

CONTENTS AND SUBJECT INDEX

CHAPTERS	PAGE NO.

Chapter 1

Introduction

Ice cream is a frozen dairy product made by freezing a mix with agitation, to incorporate air and ensure uniformity of consistency. The ingredients used in the preparation of the mix are milk and milk products, sugar, dextrose, corn syrup in dry or liquid form, water or other optional ingredients with or without egg or egg products. Harmless flavouring, colour and stabilizer or emulsifier are added in small quantities.

Ice cream and related products are generally classified as frozen desserts which include ice cream, frozen confection, ice milk, sherbets, water ice, and mellorine and parevine-type products.

In India, the Prevention of Food Adulteration (PFA), rules, 1955 defines ice cream as the frozen product obtained from cow or buffalo milk or a combination thereof, or from cow and/or other milk product, with or without the addition of cane sugar, dextrose, liquid glucose and dried liquid glucose, eggs, fruits juices,preserved fruits, nuts, chocolate, edible flavours and permitted food colours. It may contain permitted stabilizers and emulsifiers, not exceeding 0.5% by weight . The mixture shall be suitably heated before freezing . The product shall contain not less than 10% milk fat, 3.5% protein, and 36% total solids except that when any of the aforesaid preparations contain fruits or nuts or both, the content of milk fat shall not be less than 8% by weight. Starch may be added to a maximum extent of 5.0% under a declaration on the label as specified in sub-rule (2) of Rule 43. The standards for ice cream also apply to soft-serve ice cream and kulfi. In case of ice cream, where the chocolate or like covering portion forms a separate layer, only the ice cream portion should conform to the standards of ice cream.

The composition of ice cream varies in different regions and different markets. Generally, a good ice cream contains 12% fat 11% milk solids not fat (MSNF), 15% sugar, 0.3% stabilizer and emulsifier, and 38.3% total solids.

Ice cream, is a complex formulation consisting of a foam which contains air dispersed as small cell in a partially frozen continuous phase. The liquid phase solidified fat globules, mild proteins, insoluble salts, stabilizers of colloidal dimension, and sugars and soluble salts in solution. The finished product consists of liquid, air, and solid., and constitutes a three- phase system.

Ice cream is a highly palatable and nutritious food. One serving of a good ice cream of average composition (100 g) supplies approximately 200 cal, 4g protein, 0.13g calcium, 0.105 g phosphorus, 0.1 mg iron, 490 IU Vitamin A, 0.38 mg thiamine, and 0.24 mg riboflavin.

Frozen custard is a product similar to ice cream, except that it contains egg ingredients, and as per US food laws should contain not less than 1.4% by weight of egg yolk solids for plain flavours, and 1.1 % for bulky flavours. It is marketed either as a soft frozen or as a hardened product.

Ice milk, according to PFA Rules (1955) should contain not more than 2% milk fat, not less than 3.5% protein, not more than 0.5% stabilizer and emulsifier and not less than 20% total solids.

Sherbet is made of fruits and fruit juices, sugar, stabilizer and a small amount of milk product. An edible acid such as citric acid is added to produce a tart flavour.

Frozen confections include stick novelites and fancy-moulded items.

Mellorine-type products, which are similar to ice cream, have suitable vegetable or animal fat instead of butter fat. The vegetable fat can include coconut, cottenseed, soybean or other plant fat.

Peruvine-type products do not have any dairy ingredient and are similar to ice cream in all other respects.

Water ices are similar to fruit sherbets except that they do not contain any milk ingredient.

Chapter 1-A

Nutritional Value and Classification of Ice cream

NUTRITIONAL VALUE

There are five forms of energy, viz. Chemical, mechanical, thermal, solar and electrical. According to the principle of the conservation of energy, all living creatures can neither create nor destroy energy, but can only transform it. Green plants, in the presence of sunlight, manufacture their own food from simple inorganic materials like H_2O,CO_2. SO_4 and NH_3.This process, known as photosynthesis, converts solar energy into chemical energy which is stored by plants. Animals obtain energy from food which is derived directly or indirectly from plants. Energy, produced by food, is used for three functions— to maintain the tissues of the body, to perform mechanical work and for growth.

In human beings, the conversion of chemical energy into mechanical energy can be compared to an engine with a measurable thermodynamic efficiency. A maximum of 25% of the energy in food can be converted into mechanical work. Thus man is as efficient as a good internal combustion engine, and more efficiently than most steam engines. Of the proteins of other organic substances or for the osmotic pumps which maintain the differences in electrolyte concentration between intra and extra cellular fluids.

The conversion of energy present in food into heat helps maintain the temperature of the body. With adequate chilling, under cold environmental conditions, even little muscular activity produces enough heat to maintain body temperature. When hard mechanical work is done, extra heat generated is eliminated by swearing which helps maintain normal body temperature.

Energy Content of Food

The heat of combustion of a foodstuff can be measured by exposing it a high pressure of oxygen, and igniting it with a small electric current. The heat of combustion of carbohydrates, protein and fat is given in Table 1.1 (At water and Benedict, 1899). In animals, fat and carbohydrates are oxidized completely to water and carbon dioxide whilst the oxidation of proteins is never complete. Uric acid, creatinine and urea, which and derived from protein, are excreted in the urine. Many studies have shown that urince contains unoxidized material equivalent to 7.9 kcal/g (33.1 kJ) of nitrogen or 1.25 kcal/g (5.23 kJ) of protein oxidized by the body. Therefore, 1.25 kcal/g (5.23kt) should be subtracted from the heat of combustion of protein. Atwater and Benedict carried out extensive studies on human subjects for determining the energy value of foods. They concluded, after allowing for losses in digestion and metabolism, that, 92% of protein, 95% of fat and 99% of carbohydrate were normally absorbed. This constitutes the basis for Atwater factors for the available energy of protein, fat and carbohydrate (Table 1.1). Southgate and Durnin confirmed the validity of Atwater factors for most practical purposes. Generally the energy values of diets are calculated from food tables. The tables give the content of protein, carbohydrate and fat as determined by chemical analyses. The energy value of the food is calculated by multiplying these figures by the Atwater factors or some variant of them.

Tabel 1.1 The Heat of Combustion and the Available Energy in the Three Proximate Principles in a Mixed Diet

	Heat of Combustion		Loss in urine		Availability	Atwater Factors	
	kJ/g	kcal/g	kJ/g	kcal/g	%	kJ/g	kcal/g
Protein							
Meat	22.4	5.35	5.23	1.25	92	17	4
Egg	23.4	5.58					
Fat							
Butter	38.2	9.12					
Animal fat	39.2	9.37	-	-	95	37	9
Carbohydrate							
Starch	17.2	4.12					
Glucose	15.5	3.69	-	-	99	16	4
Ethyl alcohol	29.7	7.10	Trace		100	29	7

The energy requirements of individuals are dependent on body size and composition, age, physical activity, climate and environment. A high intake is recommended for growth in childhood, adolescence, and during pregnancy and lactation.

The nutritive value of a food is generally expressed in terms of nutrients-water, protein, carbohydrate, fat, vitamins and minerals.

The nutritional value of ice cream depends on the food value of the ingredients from which it is made. The dairy ingredients used in its manufacture contain the constituents of milk in different amounts. Ice cream contains about four times as much carbohydrate, three to four times as much fat and about 12-16% more protein than does milk. Fruits, nuts, eggs, when added, contribute significantly to its nutritive value. However, like milk, ice cream is not a good source of iron and vitamin C.

Ice cream is an excellent source of food energy. Since all its constituents are completely assimilated, it is a highly desirable food for growing children and for adults who want to increase weight. When consumed in moderation as one of the regular foods, it can be used to advantage in a reducing diet.

Caloric content of Ice cream and Related Products

The amount of energy derived from milk carbohydrate, fats and protein is as follows:

1g of protein yields about 4.27 cal, 1 g of carbohydrates yield about 3.87 cal, 1 g of fat yields about 8.79 cal. These values represent the amount of energy released from the food nutrient as calories. Thus, proteins and carbohydrates have about the same energy value per gram while fats are 2.25 times as rich in energy.

The lactose content of milk solids not fat (MSNF) is about 52%, and the protein content of MSNF is about 36%.

The total caloric value of ice cream depends on

(i) The percentage of protein including milk protein or any other source of protein that is present in nuts, eggs or stabilizers,

(ii) The percentage of carbohydrates including lactose, added sweeteners and sugars that is present in fruit or flavouring, and

(iii) The percentage of fat from any source including emulsifier, egg, cocoa, nuts, etc., that is present in the mix.

The caloric value of 100 g of vanilla ice cream containing 12% fat, 11% MSNF, 15% sugar and 0.5% stabilizer- emulsifier (having approx. 70% monodiglycerides and 30% indigestible hudrocolloids) can be calculated as follows:

Carbohydrated (15 + 11 x 0.52) x 3.87	=	80.18
Fat (12 + 0.5 x 0.7) x 8.79	=	108.55
Protein (11 x 0.36) x 4.27	=	16.91
Total calories		205.64

Minerals or vitamins, which do not furnish appreciable amounts of energy, have not been considered in the calculation.

The caloric value of a serving of ice cream varies with the components of the mix, overrun and weight of the mix per litre. Thus, while determining the caloric value of ice cream it is necessary to determine the exact weight of the product.

Protein content of Ice Cream

Proteins are essential components of protoplasm of each living cell. Proteins in the diet supply the amino acids required for the growth of infants and children, and for the maintenance. The newly born human infant probably needs five times as much protein as the adult per unit of weight. Values for proteins in four common foods (Passmore and Eastwood, 1986) are given in table 1.2.

The milk proteins in ice cream have high biological value. They contain all the essential amino acids and are important source of lysine and tryptophan (Table 1.2).

Table 1.2 Content of Essential Amino acids in Protein (mg Amino Acid/g Protein)

	Hen's Egg	Cow's milk	Beef muscle	Wheat flour
Isoleucine	54	47	53	42
Leucine	86	95	82	71
Lysine	70	78	87	20
Methionine and cystine	57	33	38	31
Phenylalanine and tyrosine	93	102	75	70
Threonine	47	44	43	28
Tryptophan	17	14	12	11
Valine	66	64	55	42

Milk proteins also have high chemical quality and high Net Protein Utilization (NPU) values. The chemical quality of a protein is determined by comparing its amino acid content with that of hen's protein which is recommended as a reference protein. It is difficult to obtain NPU values using man as the test animal, but relatively easy using the rat. Since the results of two species agree sufficiently well, the values obtained with rats can be applied to human diets. The chemical score and net protein utilization of some common foods are given in Table 1.3.

Table 1.3 The Chemical Score and NPU of some Common Foods

Protein	Chemical Score	NPU determined on children	NPU determined on rats
Maise	49	36	52
Millet	63	43	44
Rice	67	63	59
Wheat	53	49	48
Soya	74	67	65
Whole egg	100	87	94
Human milk	100	94	87
Cow's milk	95	81	82

The assimilation of milk protein is 5-6% higher than that of other proteins. Ice cream has a high concentration of milk solids not fat, which represents 34-36% milk protein.

The protein content is determined by the total nitrogen content in the food by the Kjeldahl method, and multiplying the value found by 6.25 or other appropriate factor. For milk proteins, the conversion factor is 6.38.

Milk Fat Content of Ice Cream

Fats are a rich source of energy. These are present in foodstuffs and storage depots of most animals, mainly in the form of triglycerides. Milk fats have both saponifiable and non-saponifiable matter. The saponifiable fraction includes the glycerides (mainly triglycerides), phospholipids and other esters, such as those of cholesterol and minor acid components. Glycerides are compounds in which one, two or three fatty acid molecules are combined by means of ester linkages with glycerol. Thus, mono, di and triglycerides contain one, two and three molecules of fatty acid respectively. When only one fatty acid is present, the glycerides are known as simple glycerides; if different fatty acids are present, they are called mixed glycerides. On saponification, fatty acids are released from glycerol. The non-saponifiable fraction includes cholesterol and related sterols, the fat soluble vitamins, A, D, E and K and traced of other minor components. Milk fat contributed significantly to the nutritive value of milk and milk products. It is a rich source of energy, serves as a carrier of fat soluble vitamins A, D, E and K, and contains a significant amount of essential fatty acids-linoleic and arachidonic acids.

Carbohydrates

Carbohydrates provide significant amount of energy in all human diets. These are synthesized by plants from carbon dioxide and water with the liberation of oxygen under the influence of sunlight. The chief products are the sugars which are a convenient source of energy for the cells. Starch is formed by polymerization of sugars and stored in large amounts in seed grains and root vegetables. The polysaccharide glycogen formed in animals is present in small amounts. Most human diets contain substantial amount of polysaccharide starch.

Starch and the sugars are broken down into simple sugars, monosaccharides by enzymed and absorbed in the small intestine. Gums, pectin, cellulose and hemicellulose are not digested by the human body. This sugars most commonly used in ice cream are sucrose, corn sugar (contains predominantly glucose or maltose and fructose) and invert sugar which is a mixture of equal amount of fructose and glucose. The sugars from fruits added to ice cream are sucrose, glucose and fructose. Lactose, milk sugar, constitutes about 20% of the total carbohydrate in ice cream.

Sucrose is a disaccharide, and is hydrolyzed into glucose and fructose by the enzyme sucrase in the small intestine.

Maltose is a disaccharide composed of two molecules of glucose, and is formed by the hydrolysis of starch.

Fructose is a monosaccharide found in fruits and vegetables.

Glucose is a monosaccharide found in fruits and vegetables. It is much less sweet than sucrose and fructose.

Lactose is a disaccharide, and is readily hydrolyzed into glucose and galactose. It enhances utilization of calcium and phosphorus in the human body. Additionally, ingestion of higher amount of lactose is conducive to the growth of lactose fermenting Lactobacillus acidophilus, which produces acid condition in the intestine, thereby creating unfavourable conditions for the growth of putrefactive bacteria.

Minerals

The term minerals refer to the various elements required by the body in the form of compounds or their component irons. Most of the minerals are complex salt. Minerals, though needed by the body in smaller amounts than other constituents like fat, carbohydrates and proteins, are essential for growth and performance. Inorganic materials, which are required in relatively high concentrations, are phosphorus, sulphur, calcium, magnesium, sodium and potassium. Other elements which are required in much smaller amounts, but are essential for metabolic processes, are known as trace elements. These are iron, copper, zinc, cobalt, iodine, fluorine, chromium, manganese, molybdenum and selenuim. The inorganic nutrients should be present in a definite proportion in the diet.

Ice cream is a very rich source of essential minerals, especially calcium and phosphorus. Nutritional studies indicate that assimilation of calcium is favoured by higher amounts of lactose in the diet. Apparently, ice cream is beneficial in the assimilation of calcium in the diets of growing children and adults as it is rich in lactose. The calcium content of milk and ice cream are 0.118 and 0.132 g/ 100 g, respectively; the corresponding phosphorus content are 0.093 and 0.105 g/100 g, respectively.

Vitamins

Vitamins are organic substances which are required in small amounts by the body for its metabolism and cannot be synthesized in sufficient quantities by the body. These do not contribute appreciable amount of energy.

Vitamins are classified into two groups: the fat soluble and the water soluble. Vitamins A, D, E and K are fat soluble; the water soluble vitamins are B_1 or thiamine, B_2 or riboflavin, B_3 or niacin, B_5 or pantothenic acid, biotin, folic acid, choline, B_{12} or cyanocobalamin, inositol and C or ascorbic acid.

Fat Soluble Vitamins

Vitamin A : It is essential for growth and also for normal functioning of the retina. Butter fat is a rich source of vitamin A. Its deficiency results in night blindness and follicular keratosis, a skin disorder. Ice cream is its excellent source.

Vitamin D : It facilitates the absorption of calcium and inorganic phosphorus in the blood. Its deficiency leads to depletion of calcium and rickets. Like milk, ice cream has small amount of vitamin D.

Vitamin E : It is found in all cell membranes. It appears to act as an antioxidant for polyunsaturated fatty aids, and prevents a large number of degenerative disorders. However, medical evidence to support this viewpoint is lacking. Ice cream contains an average of 3 mg per kh.

Vitamin K : It is essential for the formation of prothrombin which prevents bleeding by clotting the blood. Its content is very low in ice cream.

Water Soluble Vitamins

Vitamin B_1 (Thiamine) : It is part of the coenzymes essential for proper metabolism and health. Its deficiency causes beriberi which is manifested by loss of appetite, anxiety, exhaustion and irritability. In some cases, it can cause nervous disorders or dilation of the heart.

Vitamin B_2 (Riboflavin) : Ice cream is a fairly good source of riboflavin. Its deficiency can cause lesions of the eye and of the mouth and reddening of the lips.

Vitamin B_6 (Pyridoxine and related compounds) : It is an important coenzyme in the metabolism of amino acids. Its deficiency can cause anaemia and convulsions.

Vitamin B_{12} (Cyanocobalamin and related substances) : It is one of the anaemia preventing vitamins and is unique amongst vitamins, as it is not found in any plants. Its deficiency can produce pernicious anaemia and degeneration of the spinal cord.

Vitamin C (Ascorbic acid) : Ascorbic acid widely distributed in the tissues of all plants and animals. It is abundantly found in fruits, fruit juices and green leafy vegetables. Lack of vitamin C causes scurvy which is manifested by bleeding, swollen gums and haemorrhages of skin.

Ice cream, other than fruit ice cream, has a small amount of this vitamin since milk is not a good source of vitamin C.

On an average, the amount of vitamins B_1, B_2, B_6, B_{12} and C in ice cream is 0.48 mg/ kg, 2.3 mg/kg, 0.68 mg/kg, 0.0047 mg/kg and 3 mg/kg respectively. The nutritional value of ice cream and related products is given in Table 1.4.

Ice cream is considered an ideal food for people suffering from stomach or throat ailments when other foods cannot be taken. There are several reasons to support this view point. Its sweet, pleasant flavour, smooth texture and characteristic coolness make it a highly palatable food. Its high palatability stimulates the flow of digestive juices which enhances digestion. Moreover, homogenization employed in its manufacture makes it easily digestible like homogenized milk, as the fat globules broken into small globules are readily acted upon by the digestive juices.

Table 1.4 Nutritional Value of Commercial Ice Cream and Related Products

Product	Weight (g)	Fat (g)	Protein (g)	Carbohydrates (g)	TotalSolids (g)	Calories
Vanilla ice cream	100	12	4.0	20.7	38.3	204
Mango ice cream	100	10	3.5	21.2	36.3	188
Strawberry ice cream	100	8	3.6	25.8	40.8	194
Chocolate ice cream	100	13.1	3.6	21.8	42.1	221
Saffron Pistachio	100	13.9	4.8	20.5	40.8	225
Ice milk	100	4.0	4.1	23.5	33.5	144
Low calorie ice cream	100	2.0	4.2	20.6	28.9	91
Diabetic ice cream	100	9.0	4.3	13.2	28.6	152
Orange sherbet	100	1.5	1.3	27.3	30.5	124
Lemon sorbet	100	-	-	27.6	29.1	113
Ice lolly	60	-	-	14.1	14.5	54
Chocolate coated ice cream bar	60	10.4	1.8	10.7	23.1	142
Vanilla sandwich Ice cream	50	3.7	3.5	16.6	24.0	115
Milk shake	100	3	3.9	15.7	24.5	104
Frozen yoghurt	100	3.5	4.0	21.7	31.1	135

Ice cream is a palatable, nutritious, healthy and relatively inexpensive food. Perhaps, no other food product has as much food value, attractiveness and appeal as ice cream.

CLASSIFICATION OF ICE CREAM AND RELATED PRODUCTS

The classification of ice cream may be based on commercial terms commonly agreed upon or on regulatory composition requirements, or on flavour labelling standards.

Commercial Grouping of Ice Cream and Related Products

Plain Ice Cream

An ice cream in which the total amount of colour and flavouring ingredients are less than 5% of the volume of the unfrozen ice cream, for example, vanilla, coffee, caramel and maple ice cream.

Chocolate

Ice cream flavoured with cocoa or chocolate.

Fruit

Ice cream containing fruit, with or without additional fruit flavouring or colour. The fruit, such as pineapple, apricot, strawberry, etc. can be fresh, frozen, canned or preserved.

Nut

Ice cream containing nut meats, such as almonds, walnuts, cashew, pistachio, etc. with or without additional flavouring or colour.

Frozen custard- French Ice Cream, French Custard Ice Cream

One or more of the optional egg ingredients permitted are used in such quantity that the total weight of egg yolk solids content is not less than 1.4% of the weight of the finished frozen custard or less that 1.2% for bulky flavoured product.

Confection

Ice cream with appropriate flavouring and particles of candy such as peppermint stick, butter crunch, chocolate chip.

Bisque

Ice cream containing appropriate flavourings, and particles of either grapenuts, macaroons, ginger snaps, sponge cake, or other bakery products.

Puddings

Ice cream containing a genuine amount of mixed fruits, nut meats, and raisins, with or without liquor, spices or eggs. Examples Nesselrode and plum puddings.

Mousse

Whipped cream, plus sugar, colour and flavouring and frozen without further agitation. Sometimes condensed milk is added to give better consistency.

Variegated Ice Cream

A plain vanilla ice cream combined with a syrup such as chocolate, buttersotch, etc., so as to produce a marbled effect in the hardened ice cream.

Fanciful Name Ice Cream

These products usually do not contain single flavour, but the flavour is due to a mixture of several flavouring ingredients.

Neapolitan

Two or more distinct flavours in the same package.

Ice Milk

A product containing 2-7% fat and 12-15% MSNF, sweetened, flavoured, and frozen like ice cream.

Fruit Sherbet

Made of fruit juices, sugar, stabilizer and milk products. It is similar to an ice except that milk, either whole, skim, condensed, or powdered, or ice cream mix is used in place of all or part of the water in an ice.

Ice

Made of fruit juice, sugar and stabilizer, with or without additional fruit acid, colour, flavouring or water and frozen to the consistency of ice cream. Usually contains 28-30% sugar, 20-25% overrun and no dairy products.

Soft Serve Ice Cream or Ice Milk

These products are sold as drawn from the freezer without hardening.

Novelties

These constitute quiescently frozen dairy confections and frozen confections. Novelty item have different shapes, sizes and colours. Some novelty items are Eskimo pies and candy or chocolate coated ice cream bars with or without sticks; ice cream sandwiches, slabs of ice cream pressed between biscuits or cookies and wrapped in wax paper and hardened; fudge and other ice-like mixtures frozen on sticks.

Frappe

An ice, made from a mixture of fruits juices and frozen to a slushy consistency is served as a drink

Granite

Water ice frozen with very little agitation.

Souffle

A sherbet containing egg yolk or whole eggs.

Frozen Yoghurt

Prepared from mix which is cultured with Yoghurt bacteria. Fruits, nuts, and other flavouring materials are added before or after the mix is pasteurized and cultured.

Lacto

This is milk sherbet made from cultured sour milk, butter milk or fermented milk.

Fruit Salad

A mixture of whipped cream and largest pieces of fruits are frozen and served as a salad. Mayonnaise may be added if desired.

Fancy Moulded Ice Cream

Includes ice cream, ices, and sherbets moulded in fancy shapes and composes either or one colour and flavour of ice cream or a combination of colour and flavour, or specially decorated.

This group includes

(a) Brick ice cream in two or more layers, or with fancy centres; (b) Cake pies, long rolls; (c) Cake roll; Ice cream on moist cake, rolled like a jelly roll; (d) Moulds representing fruits, flowers, animals and other objects and designs, and (e) Aufait: Two or more layers of ice cream with pectinized fruits spread thinly between the layers; of the fruits may be stirred gently into the ice cream as it comes from the freezer to give a marbled appearance.

Mellorine-type Products

It is similar to ice cream except that the butterfat has been replaced by a suitable vegetable or animal fat.

Artificially Sweetened Frozen Dairy Foods

These products are made by replacing sweeteners with non sugar, non nutritive artificial sweetneres.

Non Dairy Frozen Dessert

These do not have any dairy ingredients. The composition may be similar to that for ice cream.

Labelling Requirement Grouping

The International Association of Ice cream Manufacturers (IAICM)has grouped ice cream and related products into three categories, depending on the nature of the flavours as follows:

Category 1: Those which contain no artificial flavour.

Category 2: Those which contain both natural and artificial flavour and in which the natural flavours predominate.

Category 3: Those which are flavoured exclusively with artificial flavour or with a combination of natural and artificial flavour in which the artificial flavour predominates.

The IAICM presented a further grouping of products in determing predominance of flavour as follows: (i) Vanilla; (ii) Fruit; a) citrus, b) berry and cherry, c) other fruits; (iii) Nut, (iv) Two or more distinct flavours in the same package; (v) Neapolitan; (vi) Fanciful name ice cream; (vii) Variegated product; (viii) Cherry Vanilla, and (ix) Confectionery.

The standards provide that ice cream may be flavoured with any one of the nine classes of optional flavouring ingredients specified for the above grouping of products. This grouping is necessary to provide information necessary to meet flavour-labelling standards.

Chapter 2

Composition and Properties of Ice Cream Mixes

Composition

Ice Cream is composed of a mixture of food material, such as milk products, sweetening materials, stabilizers, emulsifiers, flavours, or egg products which are referred to as ingredients. The effect of these ingredients upon the finished product is influenced by the constituents of these ingredients. An ice cream mix is the unfrozen blend of the ice cream ingredients, and consists of all the ingredients of ice cream with the exception of air and flavouring materials, i.e., percentage of milk fat, milksolids not fat, sugar, egg yolk solids, stabilizers, emulsifier and total solids. Its composition varies in different markets. It is often difficult for a manufacturer to establish the best composition of ice cream.

In developing a formulation of satisfactory composition, some of the factors which need to be considered are: personal preference of company management or customer demands for flavour, body and texture and colour characteristics of the finished product, i.e., natural or fortified flavour with artificial flavouring; chewy to heavy, higher overrun or more cooling body and texture characteristics. Composition standards are also influenced by demands of customers, volume of operation, quality of ingredients and ingredients costs.

Although the methods of processing and filling influence the characteristics of the mix and the finished product, the effect of constituents, supplied by the ingredients is also important. Therefore, the role of each constituent (fat, MSNF, sweetners, egg solids, stabilizers, emulsifiers, total solids, salts, optional ingredients, flavour and colours) is important in contributing to the characteristics of the ice cream.

The Role of the Constituents

Milk Fat

Milk fat is of major importance in ice cream. It contributes a rich flavour to ice cream, is a good carrier for added flavour compounds and promoted desirable tactual qualities. It is essential to use the correct percentage of milk fat to balance the mix properly as also to satisfy legal standards. Milk fat does not lower the freezing point. It tends to retards the rate of whipping.

High fat content limits consumption, will increase the cost and increase caloric value. Generally, the fat content of a good average ice cream is considered to be 12%. The best source of milk fat is fresh cream. Other sources are frozen creams, plastic, butter, butter oil and condensed milk blends.

Milk Solid Not Fat (MSNF)

MSNF is the solids of skim milk. It includes the protein, the milk sugar lactose and the mineral matter. MSNF is approximately 36.7% protein, 55.5% lactose and 7.8% minerals. It contributes to body and texture, and storage properties. It is inexpensive, high in food value, and adds very little to flavour, except indirectly by improving the body and texture. Lactose supplement the sweet taste largely produced by added sugars. The minerals impart a slightly salty taste which rounds out the flavour of the finished ice cream. The proteins in MSNF make the ice cream more compact and smooth and tent to prevent a weak body and coarse texture. However, excessive amounts of MSNF result in a salty or cooked flavour and soggy or sandy body and texture defect. A sandy body and texture defect is caused by high concentration of lactose. Although statistically it is impossible to state the limit of MSNF that may be used in ice cream mix, the following thumb rule is adopted to calculate the maximum serum solids content. Subtract from 100 the sum of the percentage of all the solids of mix, except MSNF and divide by a factor of 6.4-7.4 depending on whether the turnover is expected to be rapid or slow respectively.

Thus for a mix, having 12%fat, 15% sugar solids and 0.3% stabilizer, the highest percentage of MSNF for expected rapid turnover (consumed within a week) would be

$$100 - \frac{(12 + 15 + 0.3)}{6.4} = \frac{72.7}{6.4} = 11.36$$

Thus as much MSNF should be added as possible without getting the sandiness defect. Too high concentration may impart an objectionable condensed milk flavour.Though MSNF increase viscosity and resistance to melting it lowers the freezing point.

Sweetener Solids

Sweeteners are added to ice cream to enhance palatability as also to improve handing properties.The most common sweetener used in ice cream is cane sugar (sucrose). The sugar is used in liquid or dry form. Of all the sweeteners available, sucrose imparts the most desirable properties. However, many good sugar blends are available. Blends of sucrose with low medium or high conversion corn solids are also used to gain solids and maintain product properties and sweetness.The proportion of sweetening agent to be used alongwith sucrose will depend on:

(i) the total solids content of the mix;
(ii) the desired concentration of sugar in the mix;
(iii) the effect on the properties of the mix, such as viscosity, freezing point and whipping ability, and
(iv) the concentration and relative sweetening power of the sweetening agent itself.

Lack of sweetness produces a flat taste while too much sugar tends to mask desirable flavours. Generally, 14-16% sugar seems most desirable. Sugars increase the viscosity and the total solid concentration of the mix. This improves the body and texture characteristics provide the total solids content does not exceed 40%, or the sugar content does not exceed 16%. Beyond these limits the ice cream tends to become soggy and sticky. The sugars, being in solution, depress the freezing point of the mix. This result in slower freezing and requires a lower temperature for proper hardening.

Egg Yolk Solids

Egg yolk solids are high in food value hut greatly increase the cost of ice cream. They impart a delicate flavour, but even slight off flavours in egg products are easily noticeable in ice cream.

They increase the viscosity, have almost no effect on the freezing point and improve considerably the body and texture characteristics. Egg yolk solids improve whipping ability, and this is attributed to lecithin which exists as a lecithin-protein complex. They can be advantageously used in mixes where the fat is obtained from butter, butter oil or in mixes having low total solids concentration.

Stabilizers

Stabilizers are used to prevent the formation of objectionable large ice crystal in ice cream. They have high water holding capacity which is effective in giving smooth body and texture to the finished product. Besides, they prevent ice crystal formation in storage, give uniformity of product, give desired resistance to melting and improve handling properties. The effect of stabilizer on flavour is indirect. They increase viscosity, have no effect on the freezing point and generally decrease whipping ability. The amount of stabilizers to use varies with its properties, with the solids content of the mix, with the type of processing equipment, and other factors.

Generally, stabilizers are added at the rate of 0.2 to 0.3% of the mix. Stabilizers commonly used are sodium alginate, CMC (Sodium carboxyl methyl cellulose), guar gum, locust bean gum, carrageenan, gelatin and pectin. It is not necessary to age the mix when alginates are used. CMC produces a chewy characteristic in the finished product. Gelatin produces a thin mix and requires an ageing periods. Pectin is used alone or in combination with gums as a sherbet or ice stabilizer. Addition of excessive amount of stabilizers results in soggy or heavy body and high resistance of melting.

Emulsifiers

Emulsifiers are used to produce ice cream a smoother body and texture, to impart dryness and to improve whipping ability of the mix. Emulsifiers extensively used are monoglycerides or diglycerides, sorbitan esters and polyoxyethylene sorbitan esters (polysorbates) and are added at the rate of 0.1 to 0.4% of the finished product. Egg yolk solids are also used as emulsifiers. Excessive amounts of emulsifiers result in ice cream having slow melting characteristics and body and texture defects.

Total Solids

Total solids replace water in the mix and, thereby, increase the viscosity, and improve the body and texture of ice cream. Addition of sweet cream buttermilk solids, dextrin and eggs significantly improves the body and texture of ice cream. However, the total solids content should not be too high; when it is above 40-42% a heavy, soggy product is obtained.

Water and Air

Ice cream is a physico-chemical system having a gas (air) dispersed in a liquid (water), a solid or a mixture of liquid and solid. Thus, a partly frozen emulsion with ice crystals and solidified fat globules embedded in unfrozen water phase constitute a continuous phase. The sauce of water in the ice cream mix is mainly from fluid dairy product or added from the water supply.

The amount of air in ice cream is important because it influences quality, profits and legal standards. In order to maintain quality, it is important to have a uniform amount of air. Studies have been conducted on gases other than air in ice cream. It has been found that addition of finely shredded solid CO_2 to ice cream during the manufacturing process helps in obtaining an improved, very acceptable product.

Flavour and Colour

Flavour is generally considered the most important characteristic of ice cream. The king of flavouring material to be added is influenced by the quality of the ice cream mix since slight off-flavour in it can obscure the delicate flavour of the flavouring material to be added. Local preference of the consumers will determine the type and intensity of flavour to be added. Natural and synthetic flavour substances are available for the flavouring of the ice cream.

Ice cream should have a delicate, attractive colour which can be readily associated with the flavour. Most colours are of chemical origin. Colours are available in liquid or powder form. Most ice cream manufacturers prefer to purchase dry colour since these are more economical and can be dissolved in boiling water as needed.

Chapter 3

Raw Materials used to Produce Ice Cream

The selection of good ingredients is the most important factor in the successful manufacture of ice cream. A clean, fresh, creamy flavour in ice cream is obtained by using products which have been carefully produced and handled. On the contrary, the more the product has been handled and the longer it is held in storage, the less desirable is the flavour and other properties imparted to the ice cream.

SOURCES OF MILK SOLIDS NOT FAT

Milk

Milk is composed of water, milk fat and milk-solids-not-fat (MSNF).The total solids content of milk includes all the constituents of milk except water. The MSNF constituents are those found in skim milk, and include protein, lactose and minerals. These solids are also referred to as skim milk solids and serum solids (SS). The composition of milk varies, as it is influenced by numerous factors. The MSNF content varies with the fat content of milk. In general, the MSNF content of milk at different fat levels can be determined by assuming that there is a variation of 0.4% in MSNF for each percentage change in fat. The average chemical composition of Indian cow milk is distinctly different from that of the European cow. Schneider et all (1948) made a detailed and exhaustive study of the composition of Indian cow and buffalo milk. The average values of major constituents of milk of Red Sindhi, Holstien-Sindhi and country cattle, viz fat, SNF, protein, lactose and ash was 4.97%, 8.46%, 3.18%, 4.59% and 0.74% respectively; the corresponding values for Murrah and Village buffaloes was 7.45%, 9.44%, 3.78%, 4.88% and 0.78% respectively.

The degree of dispersion of the constituents in milk ranges from true solution to a coarse dispersion. Water acts as a dispersion medium for other constituents. Lactose and salts (with the exception of colloidal calcium phosphate) are in true solution; protein occurs in a colloidal state and fat occurs as an emulsion. The fat globules have a layer of colloidal substance on their surface composed of protein and lecithin. This layer is commonly referred to as the fat globule membrance.

Skim Milk

Skim milk is a cheap source of MSNF. It should have a clean flavour and low acidity. Skin milk should be purchased on the basis of a definite MSNF content, in order to guard against dilution with water. A hundred kilograms of skim milk obtained after separation of cow milk will normally contain about 8.7 kg of the MSNF.

Butter Milk

Sweet-cream buttermilk is obtained by churning fresh cream, i.e., cream that would not have developed acidity. Sweet-cream buttermilk increases the whipping ability of the mix and contributes a richness of flavour. The increase in whipping ability is attributed to the presence of lecithin. Generally, 1/5th of the MSNF present in the mix can be supplied by sweet-cream butter milk. Use of larger proportions tend to give a slightly undesirable flavour. The lecithin content of butter milk ranges from 0.1 to 0.2%. In ice cream made with butter, it is especially desirable to use buttermilk, since butter does not contain lecithin.

If a high quality dry butter milk is used, it can supply all the MSNF of the mix without affecting the taste of texture.

Concentrated Skim Milk

Plain concentrated skim milk is used more frequently than any of the other condensed milk products. Since the keeping quality of the condensed skim milk is only a little better than that of cream, the product should be used while fresh and sweet. Concentrated skim milk has 25-35% MSNF.

Sometimes superheated concentrated skim milk is used as it improves whipping ability of the mix, melt-down characteristics and, body and texture of the finished ice cream. Superheated concentrated skim milk is not commonly used as it costs more than the plain concentrated milk. In the West, it is used by manufacturers who omit the use of stabilizers in ice cream.

Sweetened Condensed Milk

Both sweetened condensed whole milk and skim milk are used as a concentrated source of MSNF. Sweetened condensed whole milk contains on an average 9% fat, 22% MSNF and 42% sugar. Sweetened condensed skim milk contains 0.50% fat, 30% MSNF and 42% sugar.

Sweetened condensed milk should be smooth and free from 'sandiness'. The defect of 'sandiness' is caused by the crystallization of milk sugar lactose into large crystals.

Skimmed Milk Powder

Skimmed milk powder is the most commonly used concentrated source of MSNF. The powder manufactured by the spray process is very commonly used by ice cream manufacturers. The powder should have fine flavour, light colour, be free from darkened particles and have good solubility. 'Instant' powders made by modern spray drying techniques are also available, and these have the ability to disperse easily and quickly in water without forming lumps.

Skimmed milk powder has 96-97% MSNF. Its use in ice cream related products has distinct advantages. It has excellent keeping qualities, and refrigeration is not required. However, it is hygroscopic, and proper protection is necessary to prevent if from absorbing moisture. It has been found to keep best when kept in cool, dry storage and also when packed in tight containers to prevent moisture absorption.

Skimmed milk powder is an economical source of solids. It is a product of uniform composition, and gives minimum variation in quality of the finished ice cream. Skimmed milk powder can be low, medium and high heat types-depending on the temperature to which it has been preheated before drying. Although from the standpoint of flavour, low heat powders are more desirable than high heatones, the mixes in which high heat powders are used, are superior in their whipping properties to heat-shock, body and texture characteristics and melting properties.

Whole Milk Powder

Powdered whole milk is not used widely because it develop off-flavours very rapidly in storage.

Dry whey

Dry whey solids contain the MSNF portion of milk except the casein. Commercial experience has shown that whenever skimmed milk powder is supplied, in part or entirely, to make ice cream, dry whey can be used to replace skimmed milk powder to a point where the lactose to water ratio of the ice cream mix is approximately 9.6: 100. Thus, approximately 20-25% of the MSNF in the mix can be provided by whey solids without objectionable effects on the flavour and with improved body and whipping quality at a reduced cost.

Whey Protein Concentrate

Conventionally produced whey protein concentrate has limited use in ice cream due to its off flavour and processing problems caused by an excessive viscosity and gelation of the mix. However, with partially denatured whey protein concentrate (made by subjecting retentate obtained by ultra filtration to heat treatment), there is increased water binding and increase in viscosity to manageable levels. Moreover, ice cream obtained has improved whipping ability, another texture and creamy mouthfeel.

SOURCES OF FAT

Both butter fat and MSNF contribute to the flavour of ice cream. The butter fat is more important because it imparts a rich and creamy flavour to ice cream. The MSNF has an indirect effect on flavour. The proteins improve the body and texture. The milk sugar contributed to the sweet taste largely produced by added sugars. The milk salts, which carry a slightly salty taste, improve the flavour of the finished ice cream.

Whole Milk

Whole milk is highly desirable source of fat and MSNF. Only milk of a clean flavour with a low acidity of 0.16% or less should be used. A combination of milk and sweet cream is considered to be the best source of fat for ice cream.

Cream

Cream is the most desirable concentrated source of butter fat for use in the mix. A good quality sweet cream imparts a clean, rich creamy flavour to the mix.

Cream should be free from off-flavour and odours. Each purchase should be tested for its fat content, so that the buyer has the assurance that he is receiving the full amount of fat for which he is paying.

Frozen Cream

Frozen cream may be stored by some manufacturers when it is abundantly available at low price during the flush season. Cream intended for storage should be pasteurized at 74-79^{0}C for 15 min to inhibit the development of off-flavours. The cream should not come in contact with utensils of copper, iron and bronze, since these dissolve in the cream producing a tallowy and metallic flavour during storage of the frozen cream. Cream should be stored at -23^0 C, and should not be held for more that six months. Although it is economical to store frozen cream, its flavour is not as good as that of fresh cream. Off-flavours that can develop in frozen cream are fishy, rancid, oily an tallowy flavours. It has been observed that the addition before freezing, of 10% by weight of cane sugar is desirable. The cream has better flavour, melts more quickly and with less fat separation, and also imparts higher whipping ability to the mix.

Plastic Cream

Plastic cream is a highly concentrated source of fat (80% fat), and is similar to butter in consistency at ordinary temperatures. It is prepared by separating cream of a lower fat content (25-35%) using a special separator bowl. Its use can cause "oiling off" and lower whipping ability which is similar to mixes made with frozen cream, butter or butter oil.

Unsalted Butter

It is an important source of fat. It is a comparatively cheap source of fat, has good keeping quality, as it can be stored for months with little deterioration in quality and can be transported at low cost. In case the butter is of good quality, as much as 75% of the fat of the mix can be secured from this source. The unsalted butter should preferably be made from sweet cream. It should be free from off-flavours, like stale, neutralizer, rancid and tallowy.

Reasarch has indicated that the use of butter, instead of cream as a source of fat in ice cream mixes, produces less desirable freezing properties. This is attributed to the absence of lecithin in butter mixes.

Butter Oil (Anhydrous Milk Fat)

Butter oil is sometimes used as source of fat for ice cream. It is prepared by heating cream or butter under vacuum to remove water from the cream or butter, and precipitate the milk solid. Gravity separation and centrifugal methods of manufacture and employed in the butter oil technology. Butter oil can be stored for months at room temperature provided the packaging is not translucent and is gas-light. In chill storage, the shelf life of butter oil is up to one year.

Other Sources of Fat

Concentrated sweetened cream has been used to manufacture ice cream. To the cream containing 76% fat condensed skim milk and sucrose are added. The blend is heated to 93^0 C for 15 sec, cooled to 70^0 C, and flashed into an unheated pan under a vacuum of 65 cm for 1 hr and packed in plastic bags. Studies have indicated that the product has better storage properties than frozen cream or butter. In the western countries, butter fat mix products are also used. These are blends of butter or butter oil with either sucrose alone or a blend of sucrose and skimmed milk powder. Butter fat mix blends can satisfactorily replace 50% of cream.

High-melting point anhydrous milk fat imparts an acceptable flavour and desirable keeping qualities to the ice cream mix.

SOURCES OF SUGARS

Addition of sugar enhances palatability of ice cream. Generally, the desired sugar concentration in ice cream is 13-16% on a sucrose basis. Sweetness in ice cream depends upon the concentration of sugar in the water of the mix, and decreasing the water content of the mix causes an equivalent increase in sweetness. Beside sweetness, sugars are important as an ingredient since physical properties of sugars and their solution affect the freezing point and properties of the mix and also the finished product.

Sugars depress the freezing point of the mix and produce ice cream with smooth body and texture but with low melting resistance and low whipping ability.

Relative Sweetness: Sweetness is influenced by concentration, presence of two or more sugars, presence of other substances and temperature. Since there is no chemical test for sweetness, only the sweetening value of sugars and other substances can be compared with sucrose. Considering the value of sucrose as 100, the sweetening value of sugars and other substances is given in Table 3.1:

Table 3.1 Relative Sweetness of Ice Cream Ingredients

Glucose (Dextrose)	74
Sucrose	100
Fructose (Levulose)	115
Galactose	32
Maltose	32
Rhamnose	32
Lactose	16
Xylose (Wood Sugar)	40
Cyclamate	3000
Acesulfame-K	20000
Saccharin	30000
Aspartame	18000
High conversion corn syrup (62 DE)	60
Intermediate conversion corn syrup (52 DE)	50
Regular conversion corn syrup (42 DE)	42
HFCS (High fructose corn syrup solids) 42%	90
Sorbital	64

*Corn syrup and HFCS (42%) have 77% total solids

Effect on Freezing Point

Sugars do not dissociate in solution, and the freezing point of sugar solution can be calculated from the known concentration of the solution and the molecular weight. For a given weight and volume of the solvent, the effect on the freezing point will be inversely proportional to the molecular weight, i.e., sugars with the low molecular weight will cause the greatest lowering in freezing point, while the sugars with high molecular weights cause the least lowering of freezing point. The molecular weight of some sweetener solids are given in Table 3.2

Table 3.2 Approximate Molecular Weights of Sweetener Solids

Dextrose	180
Fructose	180
Maltose	342
Sucrose	342
Corn syrup Solids (42 DE)	430
Maltodextrin 10 DE	1800

Sucrose

Sucrose is most widely used in ice cream manufacture. It is derived from sugarcane or beetroot. Cane sugar contains approximately 99.9% total solids. It is highly soluble and has a specific gravity of 1.59. Sucrose depresses the freezing point of the mix. It has been found that a 2% increase in the sucrose content of the mix lowers the freezing point by approximately 0.2^{0}C. Sucrose may be used as the sole source of sweetener solids with excellent results. But when it is used as the only source of sugar in ices and sherbets, it crystallizes at the surface. This defect in ices and sherbets is avoided by using 1 part of dextrose to 3.5 part of sucrose.

Corn Sweeteners

Following are the three major sweeteners

(i) refined corn sugar (dextrose), a dry crystalline product;

(ii) dried corn syrup (or corn syrup solids) and

(iii) corn syrup, a liquid.

Dextrose

Dextrose or refined corn sugar is a white crystalline or granular sugar obtained by the hydrolysis of corn starch. It has approximately 99.9% sugar solids. Since it is only about 75% as sweet as sucrose, it requires 1.3 kg of dextrose to obtain the sweetening effect obtained from 1 kg of sucrose. Dextrose causes a lower freezing point than does sucrose because its molecular weight is lower. This effect on the freezing point limits the amounts of dextrose which can be used to about 25% of the total sugar in ice cream. Some workers have recommended the use of dextrose in high fat mixes as it imparts more desirable body, texture and melting characteristics. However, dextrose has a slightly greater tendency than cane or beet sugar to become lumpy when stored in slightly moist air.

Corn Syrup

It is made either by acid hydrolysis or enzyme hydrolysis of corn starch. It does not contain sucrose but has variable amounts of maltose and dextrose with some impurities, depending upon the degree of refining used in its manufacture. It is considered as a source of dextrose. Usually, 105 kg of corn syrup will replace 1 kg of sucrose. Its addition slightly raises the freezing point of the mix (depresses the freezing point less than sucrose). The four major types of corn syrups used in ice cream based on degrees of conversion are:

(i) Low conversion 28-38 DE;

(ii) regular conversion, 38-48 DE;

(iii) Intermediate conversion, 48-58 DE and

(iv) high conversion 58-68 DE. The high conversion syrups are further classified as acid-conversion and acid enzyme syrups depending on the method of manufacture.

Dried Corn Syrup

Dried corn syrup solids are produced by dehydration of corn syrup, and are available either as a white powder or as a granular material. The chemical composition of corn syrup solids is identical with that of the syrup from which they are made. They contain the sugars dextrose and maltose together with dextrins, but usually contain no starch. The dextrins increase the total solids of the mix, and impart a stabilizing effect against coarseness in ice cream. The dextrins also raise the freezing point slightly. These properties give corn syrup solids an advantage over dextrose in sherbets, ices and ice creams of low total solids concentration.

They are white granular solids, and have the same tendency as cane sugar to become lumpy, when exposed to moist air. Usually, corn syrup solids account for not more than 1/4-1/3 of total sweetener in ice cream.

The values used a guide in estimating the freezing point depression of corn sweeteners and other sugars are given below:

Sucrose	=	100
Dextrose	=	186
62 DE	=	115
52 DE	=	96
42 DE	=	80
10 DE	=	21
Fructose	=	192
Lactose	=	100

The dextrose equivalent (DE) is a measure of reducing sugar content calculated as dextose, and expressed as a percentage of the total dry substance. Pure dextrose has a DE of 100. Corn syrups and corn syrup solids are available in the DE range of 28-62.

Invert Sugar

Invert sugar is a mixture of equal parts of glucose and fructose obtained by hydrolysis of sucrose, and is generally in the form of a syrup. Since it is sweeter than sucrose, the inversion process can be adopted at a time of sugar scarcity. However, like dextrose, it depresses the freezing point of the mix, and therefore, should be used to supply not more than 1/3 of the total sugar in the mix.

Honey

The principal constituents of honey are invert sugar, glucose and fructose. It has about 17.5% moisture, 74.5% invert sugar and 82% total carbohydrate content. It is used mainly as a source of flavour to make honey-flavoured ice cream.

Other Sweeteners

Fructose is a white crystalline powder (DL-1 Levulose) having a molecular weight of 180. It has a high sweetening power, and is used as a sweetener in dietetic ice cream.

A maltose syrup containing approximately 45% maltose has been used in ice cream manufacture. It is bland in flavour, and is sweeter than the lower DE syrup.

Malt syrup contains approximately 70% maltose. Malt syrup, malt extra or dried maltose syrup are also used, as these have properties similar to those imparted by maltose. Malt products carry a typical malt flavour, and may impart it to ice cream depending on the usage rates.

Maple sugar contains about 10% moisture, 86% sucrose, and 4% invert sugar, whereas maple syrup has about 45% moisture, 52% sucrose, and 3% invert sugar.

Brown sugar is raw or muscavado sugar obtained from the juice of sugar cane by evaporation and draining of molasses.

Maple sugar and brown sugar contain characteristic flavouring materials which limit their use in ice cream. For example, only 6% of maple sugar in the mix will produce a good maple flavour.

Intense sweeteners, such as aspartame, acesulfame-K, saccharin and cylamates, are used in dietetic preparations. However, these artificial sweeteners are not yet approved in all countries for application in ice cream.

EGG AND EGG PRODUCTS

Fresh eggs are seldom used in ice cream. However, it is necessary to use eggs and egg products in pudding and custard-type ice cream. Fresh eggs can be used in other rich ice cream that are sold at higher than average prices.

Frozen egg yolks and powdered egg yolks are used by some ice cream makers because the egg yolk solids improve the whipping ability of the mix. Usually, this is accomplished by adding 0.5% of egg yolk solids in the mix. Investigations have shown that sweetened egg yolk solids having 10% sugar considerably improve the rate of whipping in mixes in which butter or butter oil is used as main source of fat.

The use of egg yolk solids produce the following beneficial effects:

(i) Firmer ice cream at a given drawing temperature;

(ii) increased rate of whipping especially in slow whipping mixes;

(iii) more uniform overrun while unloading the freezer;

(iv) improved appearance while ice cream is melting;

(v) improved texture , and

(vi) increased food value.

The only disadvantages are the high cost of egg yolks and that they may be slightly off-flavoured.

STABILIZERS AND EMULSIFIERS

The stabilizers are involved in ice cream from the stage of mix processing till storage and distribution of the finished product. In mix processing, their main role is to increase viscosity and homogeneity of the mix. In freezing, they play a secondary role in dryness and stiffness, with little effect on ice crystal size. In the finished product, their effect is maximized. After freezing begins, the concentration of stabilizer becomes progressively greater as the unfrozen serum becomes more and more concentrated as a result of water being removed from the system as ice.

Function of Stabilizers

The basic role of a stabilizer is to reduce the amount of free wate in the mix by binding it as "water of hydration", or by immobilizing it within a gel structure. This is theoretically accomplished by an idel stabilizer (Glicksman, 1963) without reacting or disturbing the physico-chemical equilibrium of the mix components so as to introduce artificial viscosity characteristic in the mix. It is the ability of a small percentage of stabilizer to absorb and hold large amounts of bound-water, produces good body, smooth texture, slow melt-down and heat-shock resistance in the resultant product.

Influence on Ice Crystal Size and Texture

The involvement of stabilizer in promoting smoothness through control of ice crystal size begins after initial freezing and hardening. Before that, the size of the crystals is influenced by lowering of temperature, the number of ice crystals present and agitation. Once the initial size of ice crystals is established by those factors, the role of stabilizer is to stabilizer the size of the ice crystal, that is prevent them from becoming bigger as a result of temperature fluctuation, commonly known as "heat-shock" during distribution and storage.

The deleterious effect of heat-shock on texture can be explained as follows: When the temperature of ice cream, ice melts in an amount which is related directly to the degree of rise in temperature, and the specific temperature range in which the change occurs. The ice crystals, which melt during this temperature rise, must be preserved to promote smoothness. When the temperature decreases, the amount of water that refreezes is the same which melted when there was a rise in temperature. Though the amounts are the same, the water which refreezes does not necessarily involve the same molecules in the same locations as those which melted. Thus, the small crystals which melted do not necessarily recrystallize.

According to the law of physical chemistry, crystallization occurs around the existing crysting crystals. Therefore, in the cooling phase of the "heat-shock", water refreezes to deposit primarily on the existing crystals rather than recreate the previously melted crystals. Consequently, the mean ice crystal size increases each time the temperature fluctuates, and this occurs irrespective of the specific temperatures involved. Since higher temperatures involve more water per unit temperature change, and result in more deleterious effect on texture, it is highly desirable to store ice cream at as low a temperature as possible.

The major role of stabilizer is to preserve the texture, and the mechanism involved is to create a situation where a higher proportion of the water (which changes stage dungin temperature rise) recrystallizes as small ice crystals. This occurs through the formation of a highly viscous or gel-like system which immobilizes the melted water, thereby reducing the degree to which it can migrate to the existing crystals an deposit on them when it refreezes. The net effect is to slow the rate of ice crystal growth whenever heat-shock occurs.

Shape and Body Characteristics

This is a major function at the time the product is drawn, during hardening, and at the time of consumption. It involves the participation of the stabilizer ingredients in the determining the cohesiveness of the product, particularly those aspects which are described as chewy, sticky, weak, gummy, etc.

Retention of Air

As water freezes, the stabilizer and its complexes get concentrated, and these also provide strength to the air cell wall. Therefore, the amount of air, which is incorporated and the degree to which the air cell are stable, is influenced by stabilizers.

Role in Fat Destabilization

There is evidence to suggest that gums interact with protein and other components, thereby affecting the nature of the fat globule membrane and, as a result, fat stability. The degree of stability of fat has a major influence on the body of ice cream. The stiffening effect of emulsifier is directly related to a controlled destabilization of fat globules.

Control of Sandiness

When water is progessively removed as ice during freezing, the dissolved lactose gets concentrated and reaches a state of supersaturation which is sensitive to crystallization. When this occurs, the type of crystals which form are relatively insoluble and have strong resemblance to partilces and sand. Sandiness has also been associated with dextrose crystallization resulting from the incorporation of significant amounts of dextrose through the use of high-fructose corn sweeteners, which are made up of about equal amounts of dextrose and fructose. Dextrose crystals in frozen desserts are distinguished from those of lactose through their higher solubility. Hence, sandiness associated with dextrose crystallizaion is much less persistent than lactose sandiness.

Ice cream is more prone to the development of sandiness when it has relatively high levels of MSNF, and consequently, a high level of lactose to water ratio. Compositional guidelines have been developed to avoid sandiness. Though a high proportion of ice cream today is made in violation of those guidelines, lactose-caused sandiness is rarely seen. This is ascribed to two factors: the widespread use of corn sweeteners and stabilizers like CMC, natural gums, carrageenan, etc. Both these factors probably function in a manner similar to the control of ice crystal size through decreasing the mobility of unfrozen water during heat-shock. The supersaturated state, in which the sugars responsible for sandiness are prone to crystallize in frozen desserts, is reached at temperature associated with high stabilizer concentration. The rheology of the stabilizer system at that concentration, undoubtedly, reduces the mobility of the crystallizing lactose. This encourages the distribution of the crystallising lactose over a large number of small crystals rather than a lesser number of large crystals which can ultimately grow to a size where they can be perceived. Microcrystalline cellulose is particularly effective in this function, probably by providing an additional seeding function which encourages the development of small crystals.

STABILIZERS

The stabilizing agents can be divided into two main groups: the protein and the carbohydrate group. With the exception of milk protein-casein, albumin, globulin and gelatin, all other stabilizers are carbohydrates.

Casein

Casein has a special property, i.e. in a neutral reaction, it has very good heat stability. Thus, sodium caseinate will be able to withstand a heat treatment of upto 140^0 C for several minutes, without precipitation. Albumin and globulin cannot withstand excessive heat treatment well. Usually, heat treatment of globulin solutions result in the formation of sulphydryl groups and their appearance, which in turn, is associated with the ice cream defect normally referred to as "boiled flavour".

Gelatin

Gelatin is derived from the proteins collagen and ossein by hydrolysis. It is prepared from calf skin trimmings, pork skins or bones. After preliminary preparation, according to the raw material used, the prepared stock is heated water, and during this heating the collagen or ossein undergo hydrolysis. As the hydrolysis proceeds, the products formed become water soluble. The broth, so obtained is filtered, concentrated and finally dried. The resulting product is gelatin.

Sodium alginate, guar gum, locust bean gum and sodium carboxy methyl cellulose are the most frequently used primary stabilizers in frozen desserts.

Sodium Alginate

Sodium alginate is a widely used stabilizer. Its basic stabilizing agent algin is extracted from a giant ocean kelp grown on the shores of California and Japan. The basic principle of algin processing is the conversion of the naturally occurring insoluble mixed calcium, magnesium, sodium and potassium salt of alginic acid into a soluble salt such as sodium alginate. The presence of three kinds of polymer segments have been reported. Two segments consist essentially of D-mannuronic and L-guluronic acid units, respectively, whereas, the third segment consists of alternating D-mannuronic acid and L-guluronic acid residues.

One of the most important and useful properties of sodium alginate is its ability to react with calcium salts. This ability to combine with calcium is apparently responsible for the improvement of whipping ability when sodium alginate is added. The removal of calcium tends to prevent fat globule clumping, improving the whipping ability. The commercial product consists of sodium alginate with small amounts of sugar and sodium citrate added to improve its solubility and to standardize its stabilizing properties. A small amount of sodium phosphate is also added to assist its solubility in milk or the ice cream mix.

The three distinct advantages of using sodium alginate are:

(i) It improves the whipping ability,

(ii) It leaves a slightly cleaner flavour in the mouth, and

(iii) It has excellent heat-shock resistance. The main disadvantage of sodium alginate is that it dissolves properly only when added to the mix at about 68-71° C. A slightly smaller amount of sodium alginate is needed to give the same stabilizing effect as gelatin. Usage rates range from 0.2 and 0.3% depending on ice cream composition. However, it has a higher basic cost than the other popular gums, and requires slightly high levels to be effective.

Carrageenan

It is a polysaccharide obtained by extraction from red seaweeds. There are three types of carrageenan, namely kappa, lambda and iota. Both kappa and iota are able to form gel structures, while lambda carrageenan can only be used as a thickening agent. Low concentration (0.01 to 0.02%) of kappa carrageenan forms a weak gel in the ice cream mix, and this prevents whey separartion in ice cream mix having a stabilizer based on guar gum, locust bean gum or CMC.

Guar Gum

Guar Gum is a complex carbohydrate obtained from a legume in India. It contains 1 galactose ring for every 2 mannose rings. Guar gum is readily soluble is cold solutions, and is generally preferred as a stabilizer for mixes which are pasteurized at high temperature for a short period or for continuous pasteurization. However, guar gum is not used alone, since it reacts with protein resulting in the formation of complexes that bring about serum separation. Although guar gum is remarkable for high mix viscosity, it imparts a distinct sliminess. Guar gum, therefore, is used in combination with carrageenan to avoid serum separation and reduce sliminess.

Locust Bean Gum

It contains 1 galactose ring for every 4 mannose units. The aqueous solution of locust bean gum should be boiled first to ensure maximum effect. Like guar gum, it has the disadvantage of precipitating the milk proteins resulting in serum separation. But it functions synergistically with carrageenan, resulting in a very high viscosity of the system. Though guar gum has a chemical structure similar to the locust bean gum, it does not exhibit synergism with carrageenan.

Sodium Carboxy Methyl Cellulose (CMC)

CMC, the trade name for sodium carboxy methyl cellulose, has high water holding capacity and it easily dissolved in the mix. Like guar gum and locust bean gum, it reacts with the protein content of milk, and, therefore has a pronounced tendency to produce "wheying off". It is used in combination with carrageenan. It does not form as firm a gel as gelatin and some of the vegetable stabilizers, but is especially suitable in sherbets and ices.

Pectin

Pectin is a carbohydrate obtained mainly from citrus fruits. It is especially desirable as an ingredient in syrups and fruits used in making rippled effects in ice cream, and is also effectively used in ice and sherbets. It is not a very satisfactory stabilizer for ice cream. Chemically, it is a polymer consisting largely of galacturonic acid, galactose and arabinose.

Agar-Agar

Agar-Agar is extracted from red algae grown in the Pacific coast. It is used in combination with gums or gelatin as a stabilizer in sherbets and ices. Although it has the property to swell and absorb large quantities of water, and thus prevent coarseness in the finished product, it is not easily dispersed in the mix. It is costlier and tends to produce a crumbly body in ice cream.

Xanthan Gum

Xanthan gum is gaining popularity as a stabilizer in frozen desserts. Though it is costly, it has unique characteristics which make it useful. Its ability to function in synergy with locust bean gum, and to a lesser extent guar gum, makes it highly useful as a component in a blend, rather than being used alone. Such blends are particularly useful in water ice and stick ice novelties.

Hydroxypropyl-Methyl Cellulose

This is used primarily in sherbets and ices,where it promotes good whipping properties and a pleasant short texture.

Other Gums

Other gums, such as arabic, tragacanth, karaya or India gum, are substances which exude from the bark of certain trees and plants growing usually in the warmer regions of the earth. They are chiefly used as ingredients in stabilizers for use in ices and sherbets.

Starch

Starch is a carbohydrate polymer synthesized within the plant by the chemical interlinking of hundreds of thousands of individual glucose units to form long chain molecules in the form of starch granules. The 1,4-linkages yield straight chain molicules (called amylose), while the 1, 6-linkages serve as the branching point in the branched chain starch molecules (called amylopectin). The proportion of two types of starch molecules are relatively constant for each species of starch. For example corn starch contains 27% amylose content, potato starch 23% and tapioca starch 17%.

All starches exhibit hydrogen bonding. Starch is insoluble in cold water because the molecular network is bound by hydrogen bonds. When starch suspensions in water are treated, factors such as time, temperature and shear strength exert sufficient calorific energy on the hydrogen bonds weakening it, so that water is absorbed by the granules. However, starch also yields gels that are "starchy", and not smooth and glossy. Therefore, principally pregelatinized starches have been used in instant-type puddings, ice cream and cake mixes. Pregelatinized starches can be dispersed in cold water with agitation to yield pastes, comparable to those obtained by cooking the raw starch. These are prepared from starch slurries that are cooked and dried on heated drums. The dry film is then ground to a fine powder.

Pregelatinized starches yield that are smooth, glossy, non-starchy or pasty, and impart good stability. They also exhibit excellent water binding properties, preventing syneresis. Pregelatinized maize or potato starch have been used alone, or in combination with CMC as stabilizers in ice cream.

Stabilizer Blends

It is not possible to produce ice cream with the desired characteristics by using a single stabilizer. For instance, the short chewy body of ice cream is associated with the use of CMC. Use of guar gum results in ice cream having a gummy body. Sodium alginate produces a light bodied ice cream. Therefore, most ice cream manufacturers use blends of several stabilizer ingredients to achieve the desired characteristics which cannot be provided by a single ingredient. Typical stabilizer combinations are; guar gum and xantham gum; locust bean gum and xanthan gum; locust bean gum and carrageenan; alginates and pectin. For example, to make an ice cream which is somewhat short and chewy, but not to the extent which would be produced by using CMC, it is necessary to select a combination of CMC with alginate or locust bean gum to provide the desired properties.

Blending of colloids can also be done to reduce the cost of the stabilizer. However indiscriminate change in stabilizer composition might prove counter productive since noticeable changes might occur in frozen dessert properties. Thus while selecting a blend of stabilizers, functionality rather than the cost should be the overriding factor.

EMULSIFIERS

Emulsifiers are surfactants which orient at the fat/water interface, with one portion of the molecule- the fat-loving or lipophilic portion attracted to the fat, and another, the water-loving or lipophilic portion attached to the water. The balance between the lipophilic and hydrophilic portions of the molecules of the emulsifier affects the behaviour of the fat system. This balance is commonly referred to as the "hydrophilic-lipophilic balance". Griffin (1949) classified non-ionic emulsifiers on the basis of HLB Number". This number is derived by calculating the proportion of the molecular weight of the emulsifier molecule represented by the hydrophilic portions, and dividing that value by five. In this system, lipophilic emulsifier have low HLB values, whereas hydrophilic emulsifier have high HLB values. Emulsifier having low HLB numbers have a strong fat orientation and are saturated, with high melting point, and high moleculare weight. High HLB number emulsifiers are unsaturated with low melting and low molecular weight and also having a strong affinity to water.

Type of Emulsifiers

The number of emulsifier ingredients commonly used in frozen desserts is less than that of the stabilizer ingredients. Over 90% of the emulsifier ingredients used in the world fall into just two categories: fatty acid esters of glycerol, and ethoxylated esters of sorbitol. Other chemically processed, emulsifier ingredients applied occasionally are: sucrose esters, polyglycerol esters, propylene glycol esters and ethoxylated glyceride esters.

Glycerides—Monoglycerides and Diglycerides (MDG)

These are produced by inter-esterification of glycerol and fatty acid. Stearic acid is commonly used. The mixture contains 40-45%. monoglyceride and an equivalent amount of diglyceride; the remaining amount is triglyceride. The reaction can be forced in the direction of producing more monoglyceride upto a range of 50-55%, but not higher. A monoglyceride has the prerequisite configuration for functioning as an emulsifier. It includes elements which are soluble in fat (the fatty acid), and other configurations which are soluble in water (the portion containing the exposed "OH" groups). The attraction of the long fatty acid chain to fat considerably exceeds the relatively weak attraction of the shorter portion of the molecule to water. As a result, glyceride emulsifiers in general, have relatively low HLB number. In the deglyceride structure, the OH group at the centre is encumbered by the sorrounding fatty acid. Thus, theoretically the diglyceride would appear to have relatively little emulsifier activity. However, empirical observations suggest the possibility that the presence of the diglyceride in the MDG blend enhances its emulsification performance synergistically.

Distilled Monoglyceride

This is produced by separating monoglyceride from the mixture of mono, di and triglyceride by molecular distillation. Distilled monoglyceride contains more than 90% monoglyceride. Since the distillation process does not affect the structure of the monoglyceride involved, the monoglyceride provided by distillation does not differ from the monoglyceride in the MDG mixture. However, the theoretical possibility of replacing MDG emulsifier with a distilled monoglyceride on an equivalent monoglyceride basis is not borne out in practice. This corroborates the empirical observation mentioned earlier that the diglyceride in the MDG blends make some functional contribution. Further, the high cost of molecular distillation makes distilled monoglycerides costlier than the MDG for an equivalent function. Also, distilled monoglycerides have a tendency to gel into particles which are difficult to desperse, when added to aqueous systems. The tendency can be eliminated by reducing the monoglyceride level to about 80%. Most distilled monoglycerides used in frozen desserts are in the form of a dilution of the pure monoglyceride with a hard fat, to an 80% monoglyceride content. This dilution with a non-functional component further adds to the cost of distilled monoglyceride.

The physical form of glyceride emusifiers is determined by the same factors which affect the nature of the component fatty acids, the chain length and the degree of unsaturation of fatty acids present. The complexity of the fatty acid profile will depend on the source of the fatty acid used. These emulsifiers are sometimes referred to in terms of a single fatty acid, such as "glycerol monostearate" or "glycerol monooleate". That terminology refers to the dominance of the fatty acid to which reference is made, not to its exclusive presence in the product. If the fatty acid profile is dominated by long chain, saturated fatty acid such as stearic, the emulsifier will be solid at room temperature. Such emulsifiers are usually reduced to small, free-flowing particles by a process of spray-beading or flaking.

Emulsifiers in which the presence of unsaturated or short chain acids produce lower melting points may be in the form of soft cubes liquids. They can also be put into a free-flowing form by combining them with hard emulsifier or triglyceride fats.

Polysorbates

These are polyoxyethylene derivatives of sorbitan esters. They have a more complex structure than the glyceride emulsifier. The fat-loving portion of the polysorbate molecule is composed of one or more fatty acids. The hydrophilic portion is a complicated structure of sorbitol, a 6-carbon polyol and multiple units of ethylene oxide. The hydrophilic characteristics dominate their structure and functionally giving them a relatively high HLB number. The most frequently used polysorbates are polysorbate 80 (PS 80) and polysorbate 65 (PS 65). Chemically, PS 80 is polyoxyethylene (20) sorbitan monooleate. A typical molecule of this emulsifier contains 20 ethylene oxide units, and one unit of oleic acid. Polysorbate 65 is identified as polyoxyethylene (20) sorbitan tristearate. This shows that it is differentiated from PS 80 by the presence of 3 fatty acid units per molecule and use of stearic acid, a saturated 18-carbon fatty acid. The higher proportion of fatty acid (lipophilic) in the PS 65 molecule, and its greater saturation makes PS 65 less hydrophilic that Ps 80, and gives it a slightly lower HLB number.

PS 80 is a semiviscous liquid at room temperature, and is available per se or diluted with a solvent such as propylene glycol. The strong hydrophilic character of PS 80 is evident from its ability to function effectively, when added to cold mix before freezing. This is particularly true when propylene glycol is used as a diluent. However, the liquid state of PS 80 makes it difficult to preblend with other dry ingredient, particularly stabilizing gums. Also, in the pure liquid state, PS 80 is more susceptible to flavour deterioration as a result of oxidation of the unsaturated oleic acid component. Thus, the most common form in which it is used is in finely divided flaked or beaded-solidified blend with a hard mono and diglycriede (MDG). It is frequently blended with MDG in the ratio of 80/20/MDG/PS 80.

PS 65 is a waxy semi solid material at room temperature. In that form, it is difficult to blend with other ingredients. Therefore, it is usually sold in combination with hard MDG in proportions up to 2/1 MDG/PS 65.

Polyglycerol Easters

These are made by reacting fatty acids with OH groups on the polymerized glycerol in a manner similar to the process used glycerides. Since glycerol units are responsible for the hydrophilicity of this emulsifier, the opportunity to vary the length of the glycerol chain, and to add a larger quantity and variety of fatty acids, makes this emulsifier capable of including an unlimited variety of emulsification properties, spread over a broad HLB range. However, their performance and high cost of production does not match the cost/function properties associated with the glyceride/polysorbate combination.

Fruit Acid Esters

As already mentioned, the hydrophilicity of the emulsifier can be increased by bonding several glycerol molecules before esterification. This increase can also be made by connecting glycerol with a wate soluble acid before the other part of the glycerol is esterified with fatty acid. The acids that have been widely used are fruit acids-tartaric acid, citric acid, etc. Acetic acid and lactic acid can also be utilize. However, when used in ice cream, these products have an undesirable effect, because they contain free water soluble acids which limit to a considerable extent the use of these products.

Ethoxylated Mono and Diglycerides

They are produced by reacting a conventional glyceride easter with ethylene oxide to produce a structure which functions in a similar manner to the polysorbates. This has not yet been used in ice cream on a commercial scale.

Egg Yolk Solids

They contain 8% to 10% phospholipids. They have good emulsifying capability and improve the whipping ability of the mix. Such emulsifying capability results from high level of phopholipids. They are frequently used in puddingand custard-type ice cream.

Functions of Emulsifiers

The emulsifiers used in frozen desserts have primarily two areas of function. Firstly, they provide the basic emulsification required to provide a stable oil-in-water emulsion. Secondly, they supplement basic emulsification by controlling several important frozen dessert properties. These include whipping ability, stiffness and dryness at the freezer, body and texture, melt down characteristics and to some extent, even heat-shock penetration.

The fat in milk or cream is in a naturally emulsified state due to the presence of native phospholipids, including lecithin and milk protein. As homogenization increases the surface of fat considerably, the amount of natural emulsifiers present is inadequate to meet the basic emulsification requirement of ice cream after processing. Therefore, addition of emulsifier is useful in meeting the requirements of basic emulsification. When a significant portion of the fat is derived from ingredients containing free fat, such as butter, butter oil, vegetable fat, or even cream where the natural fat emulsion has been destabilized by freezing or other means, greater quantities of emulsifiers need to be added to fulfil the requirements of basic and supplemental emulsification.

Whipping Ability and Overrun Control

Whipping ability is one of the most important properties of an ice cream mix. It refers to those properties of a mix which determine the rate at which air can be incorporated and the maximum overrun that can be obtained. It is critical that the mix be capable of accepting the air necessary to achieve the desired overrun. It is equally important for the frozen dessert to hold that air up to the point of consumption.

In the batch-freezing of frozen desserts, the amount of incorporated air is affected by the native whipping ability of the mix. A strong interrelationship between drawing temperature and overrun exists under ambient atmospheric conditions. Batch freezing is assuming greater significance as a unit operation in view of the resurgence in store production in recent years. In the continuous freezer, a metered amount of air is whipped under pressure. Thus in the continuous freezing method, we rely less on the native whipping ability of the mix, and more on the control of the whipping process itself in achieving the target overrun. However, despite the ease with which the overrun is controlled in a continuous freezer, the whipping ability of the mix cannot be ignored. Furthermore, whipping ability is important in continuous freezing, when it is desired to achieve a higher overrun or in whipping the products like water ice or low calorie frozen to desserts which have little or no fat. Also, in the routine production the poor whipping ability makes mix more sensitive to variations in the processing conditions. In view of these considerations, whipping ability of the mix is of considerable importance in the manufacture of ice cream.

It has been demonstrated that the agglomeration of fat, which occurs during freezing, provides an element of strength to the aircell wall. However, when this agglomeration proceeds to far, the large fat clumps which form, represent points of weakness in the aircell wall. In practice, most manufactures aim at producing a controlled amount of fat destabilization in the freezer (Berger and White, 1971). Govin and Leeder and PoMin and Leeder found that deemulsification during freezing also increased with the HLB value of emulsifier. PoMin and Leeder suggested that when an emulsifier of low HLB value is used, the emulsifier is firmly associated with the fat globule. During the aeration-agitation-freezing process more of the fat globules retain their identities and minimum deemulsification occurs. When an emulsifier of high HLB value is used, the weaker bound emulsifier is swept off the fat globule causing a coalesecence. Sherman and Kakao and Sherman demonstrated that hydrophilic emulsifier promote structure formation in ice creams through fat coalescence, whereas hydrophobic emulsifiers promote structure formation more through fat clumping during the feezing operation.

Stiffness and Dryness

For proper functioning of the equipment used to package frozen desserts, it is important that the product, as it emerges from the freezer, has characteristics which fall in a narrow range. For instance, for mould-frozen novelties, the product must be soft and slack. Excessive stiffness prevent complete filling of the moulds, leaving undersirable voids when the product is released from the mould. For extruded novelties, the product must be extremely stiff and dry, so that it maintains its shape and surface characteristics during packaging and any intermediate hardening steps. The conventional ice cream must have enough stiffness and dryness so than the product will not "tail" or drag over on to the subsequent package, or on the equipment itself, and yet, be slack enough to fill the package completely. For bulk packaging, the requirements for stiffness are less than for the filling of the smaller containers, but more than for the filling novelty moulds.

The two major factors which affect the degree for stiffness and dryness of a frozen dessert are:

(i) drawing temperature, and

(ii) the state of the fat system.

It is obvious that lower the drawing temperature, stiffer will be the product when it emerges, as more water is converted to ice at the freezer. The drawing temperature alone cannot be depended upon for achieving the desired degree of dryness and stiffness. The behaviour of a frozen dessert, as it emerges from the freezer, is strongly influenced by the fat structure. The dryness and stiffness are related to the state of the fat system which can be manipulated through the use of emulsifiers. The agglomerated fat formed by emulsifiers provides rigidity to the finished product. This rigidity also increases the melting resistance of the frozen desserts. Moreover, the retention of shape is a direct result of the structure contributed by the agglomerated fat. The rigid structure allows small air cells which are formed by continuous agitation to maintain their identity as more and more air is incorporated. Over-agglomeration of the fat can have serious consequences. This is manifested by a greasy mouthfeel in the finished product, and a deposition of churned fat on dasher blades, fillings heads, and other surfaces with which the frozen product comes into contact. In extreme conditions, over-agglomerated or churned fat can cause a loss body and the presence of visible particles of fat. In chocolate-flavoured frozen desserts, cocoa particles are attracted to these fat particles, producing in undesirable, speckled appearance.

While there is a general tendency for the entrancement of useful fat agglameration to be associated with emulsifiers having high HLB numbers, that relationship is by no means absolute. There is a much more direct and useful relationship between fat agglomeration and increasing unsaturation of the fatty acid portion of the molecule (lipophilic, fat loving). For instance, PS 80 and PS 65 at the high end of the HLB range, provide greater dryness than an MDG emulsifier in which the fatty acid profile is dominated by saturated fatty acids. The superiority of PS 80 to PS65 in performance is attributed to the presence of oleic acid (monounsaturated). That greater fat agglomeration is caused by emulsifiers having unsaturated fatty acid is also corroborated by the fact that an MDG product having oleic acid as the dominant fatty acid shows more profound effects than those of PS 65. The same unsaturation, which promoted desirable performance, makes the product sensitive to the development of off-flavour through the oxidation of double bonds. Thus, unsaturated emulsifiers having low-flavour profiles should be selected with caution.

Secondary Effect of Emulsifiers

Emulsifiers enhance contribution of the fat to the creaminess perceived during consumption. This is accomplished through encouraging the development of small air cells, and preserving their integrity by strengthening their cell wall. However, excessive fat agglomeration by emulsifiers results in a product having a soft, slack condition and a coarse texture.

The emulsifier ingredient can play a minor role in providing protection against the effects of the heat-shock of frozen dessert texture. Firstly, a small amount of water, which is bound at the surface of the fat globule, would not be expected to become involved in the dynamic cycling between the frozen and unfrozen state as the temperature of the product fluctuates. Secondly, emulsifiers promote the incorporation of air and increase the number of air cell by effecting a reduction in the size of air cells. When this occurs, the restricted space between the air cells serves to immobilize free water and resist its mobility during heat-shock. This should encourage the preservation of small ice crystals.

The effect of a small amount of emulsifiers on some of the properties of ice cream mix frozen in a batch freezer is given in Table 3.3

Table 3.3 Physical Effects of Emulsifiers

Property	mix having Stabilizer	Mix having Stabilizer + 0.05% Poly-sorbate 80
Surface tension in dynes/cm at 20° C	51.2	49.1
Time to reach 90% overrun in min	19.0	17.5
Average air cell size of ice cream (diameter in microns)	29.1	14.6
Time taken to melt completely 60g ice cream at 30° C	60.0	74.0
Texture comments	Slightly coarse	Smooth

Excessive emulsification of the ice cream mix can cause short body and texture characteristics and slow melting.

Some disadvantages in the use of emulsifiers are: homogenization of the mix is necessary to obtain best results. Some investigators are of the opinion that emulsifiers tend to develop the defect called "shrinkage".

Selection of Stabilizer and Emulsifier

The selection of a suitable stabilizer is influenced by many factors. One of the most important factors is the adaptability of the product to the particular needs of the plant. Other factors that must be considered are;

effect of the product on the properties of the mix, kind of product being manufactured, whether an ageing period is necessary or not, method of processing, the effect on flavour, body and texture characteristics, melting and storage properties of the ice cream. Besides availability, cost and freedom from toxicity also must be considered.

The amount of stabilizer to be used in the ice cream mix is influenced by the fat content of the mix, the total solids content of the mix and the kind of freezer used. Generally, the amount may range from 0.15% to 0.50%.

Incorporation of stabilizer increases mix viscosity, surface tension and whipping time slightly. They have little effect on the flavour of the finished ice cream, produce smoother, more resistant body and texture, and improve storage qualities. According to the Prevention of Food Adulteration Act, 1954, the maximum amount of permitted stabilizers and emusifiers in the mix is 0.5%.

The stabilizers and emulsifiers are incorporated in the mix by mixing with 4 or 5 parts of sugar and adding it before or during the heating process. Algin stabilizers can be suspended in cold water and added to the mix when the mix temperature is 71° C using a hopper and a pump or other special arrangement.

When the batch method of pasteurization is employed, there is mor latitude for the selection of the stabilizer. The stabilizer can be added to the hot or cold mix. In the high temperature short-time process of pasteurization, the stabilizer must be added to the cold mix ingredients which disperse readily at low temperature. The algin, guar and CMC type products are commonly used in this method of processing.

The idela stabilizer should have the following of processing:

(i) disperse readily in water without forming lumps,

(ii) dissolve completely at room temperature,

(iii) should not develop viscosity on standing, and

(iv) must pump easily.

The propreitary stabilizers contain combination of the various stabilizer and emulsifier materials with sugar as a carrier and may contain salts. Generally, these combinations are more effective in producing the desired characteristics than some of the stabilizing materials used individuallly. A further development within the fields of combined emulsifiers and stabilizers is "integrated products", where the individual stabilizer components are suspended in a continuous emulsifier phase. This enables integraated products of find position within the complicated physico-chemical structure of ice cream, where ordinary products would not normally migrate. In the integrated products, each particle is made up of a continuous emulsifier phase in which the stabilizer components are suspended. When the integration process is correctly carried out, other technological advantages are obtained. For instance, the products can be made cold dispersible and thus can be added to the mix at any desired temperature. This is especially useful for continuous mix production whereby the regeneration section of the plate heat-exchanger can be properly utilized, thus giving better heat economy. Furthermore, in the integration process the stabilizer and emulsifier are subjected to severe heat treatment, and this results in achieving high bacteriological standards.

FLAVOURING AND COLORING MATERIALS

The palatability of frozen desserts is largely influenced by flvour. Flavouring materials are sold under many brands and grades. Among the flavouring substances that are commonly used in frozen desserts are vanilla, cocoa, chocolate and coffee, fruits and fruit extracts, nutt, spices and sugar. The selection of flavouring materials is influenced by the quality of the ice cream mix, since slight off-flavours in it may mask the delicate flavour. Local and regional preferences of the consumers is also important since some of the consumers might appreciate the fine and delicate flavours, while others may prefer the strong and harsh ones.

An abundant variety of flavouring substances is provided by nature. However, natural flavouring substances are limited in supply. The synthetic supplements are not only available in unlimited quantities but also economical to use.

Flavour substances (both natural and synthetic) are available mainly in mixtures. Information occurring in the literature about food-flavouring materials is limited, as there is a great degree of secrecy in flavouring technology. The natural flavourings are:

(i) Fruit flavours;
(ii) citrus fruit;
(iii) tropical fruit flavours;
(iv) natural flavours from botanicals;
(v) spices;
(vi) cocoa and chocolate;
(vii) coffee;
(viii) natural flavourings from vanilla beans and
(ix) nuts.

The synthetic flavourings include aromatic chemicals and imitation flavours. Liqueur flavourings consisting of alcohol, whiskey and other distilled beverages, fruit liqueurs, fruit brandy distillate and brandy flavour essence are also included.

There are many flavouring material available for different types of ice cream, but only those materials which impart a delicate and natural flavour are considered to be most satisfactory. Generally, natural flavouring materials impart a delicate pleasing taste, and there is little possibility of over-flavouring even at high concentrations. Imitation flavourings may impart a harsh and objectionable flavour in low concentration.

The smoothness and mellowness of ice cream is influenced by the milk fat-air cell orientation in the freezing process. It seems that when there is an optimum distribution of fat around the air cells, a product with a greater smoothness and full milk fat flavour is obtained. Thus, for an optimum flavour, it is important to have a proper overrun control in relation to the product composition.

The MSNF contributes a slightly cooked as well as salty flavour due to the heat treatment and the natural milk salts present in dairy products supplying this constituent.

Vanilla

Vanilla is the most popular flavour for ice cream. Traditionally, it has been obtained from the fruits of Vanilla fragrance, a plant belonging to the climbing orchid family. The plant is grown in Madagascar, Mexico, Mauritius, the Seychelles, Tahiti, the Comoro Islands, Java, Sri Lanka, the Philippines and parts of Africa. There are three different types of Vanilla fragrans: Bourbon vanilla, Mexican vanilla and Indonesian vanilla. Bourbon vanilla, produced mainly on the Indian ocean island of Madagascar, Reunion, the Comoros and the Sychelles is famous for its delicate, gentle flavour.

The green vanilla beans have virtually no aroma, and their flavour is very different from the one known to consumers. The principle flavouring component vanillin develops gradually during the curing process. The most commonly used method of curing is the "Bourbon" process, during which the beans are immersed in hot wate for a few minutes to stop ripening, destroy the chlorophyll and increase the enzyme activity. The beans are packed into wool-lined crates, covered with blankets and sealed for 24 hours.

During this fermention process, the fruits lose moisture and the development of flavour takes place. Over the next two weeks or so, the beans are dried in the sun and covered with blankets at night to make them "sweat". During this period the beans develop a characteristic dark colour and become more supple. After drying, the beans are kept on racks in well ventilated warehouses. The entire process takes up to six months. The most important aspect of the process is the formation of flavour by vanillin, which constitutes between one and three per cent of the weight of the beans. After curing, the pods are sorted out into various grades.

Vanilla extract is manufactured by dissolving the flavour components of the bean in a solvent consisting of a mixture of alcohol and water and then separating the residue from the liquid.

According to the United States Food and Drug Agency (FDA) standard vanilla extracts must contain 13.35oz (379g) of vanilla beans to a gallon

(3.79 lit.) of 35% alcohol. Thus "two-fold" vanilla contains 26.7 oz of beans. In the metric system, one fold = 100 g of beans in one litre of extract.

Vanillin is the most important of all the components that contribute to the overall flavour profile of vanilla extracts. A good quality vanilla extract has a clean, rich flavour with some woody notes.

There are three types of vanilla flavouring- natural vanilla flavours, nature-identical flavours.

Natural Vanilla Flavour

The flavour components, "solely" or almost, solely" should be derived from the vanilla beans; the remainder may be obtained from other natural sources. A desired profile is obtained by combining the vanilla extract with specific flavour nuances like almond oil, narutal diacetyl, cocoa extracts, natural guaiacol, etc.

Natural Flavour (Not Using the Name Vanilla)

The flavour should be "derived" from natural ingredients only, but these need not originate from the vanilla bean. The vanilla character is obtained by combining vanilla extract with other natural materials.

Natural Identical Flavours

These are based on substances occurring in natural products used for human consumption but manufactured by chemical synthesis. These may contain a certain percentage of natural extracts as well. The use of individual flavouring substances enanles the flavourist a create almost any profile for a specific food application. Moreover they are cheaper than natural flavours and the taste profile can be standardized and kept constant from year to year.

Artifical Flavour

These are based on ethyl vanillin, are economical to use and though have a flavour profile very similar to vanillin, or two to three times as strong as vanillin.

There are over 200 components in the bean which make up the flavour of vanilla and it is now possible to identify them individually. Although vanillin is the major component in a flavour, the profile is determined by other flavours which are present in minute quantities in the bean. Other substances which contribute to a characteristic vanilla flavour are aldehydes, ketones, alcohol, acids, ethers, esters and hydrocarbons. All these flavouring ingredients have to be balanced to produce a profile for a specific purpose. Besides vanillin, the important ingredients for vanilla flavours are heliotropin, guaicol, dihydrocoumarin, diacetyl, lactones, corylone, spices (clove and nutmeg, cinnamon oil), cocoa, hazelnut and bitter almond oil. For instance, heliotropin when added in low doses enhances the vanilla note; guaicol enhances the smoky character in natural vanilla extracts and diacetyl rounds off the profile and imparts a creamy, buttery not at high concentrations.

The most common solvents for compounded vanilla flavour are mixtures based on ethanol, water, triacetin and propylene glycol. The flavour preparations having these solvents do not undergo precipitation, discolouration or separation for long periods of time.

Powdered vanilla flavours are made by spray-drying the liquid flavour with carriers based on gum arabic and maltodextrins. They are fully water soluble and are generally used in instant dessert powders, and ice cream powder blends.

Chocolate and Cocoa

Chocolate and cocoa rank second only to vanilla as flavourings for ice cream. They are obtained from the cacao bean which forms the fruit of the tree, Theobroma cacao growing in tropical regions.

The almond-sized cocoa beans or seeds develop in a large pulpy-20-30 beans to the pod. The ripened pods: rich golden red in colour are cut from the tree, gathered in piles and left to ripen further for about 48 hr, after which they are slashed open, the beans removed and placed in bags to heat and ferment for about 10 days, or until the characteristic flavour and cinnamon red colour develops. The beans are then washed clean of the dried pulp, and dried slowly and sufficiently to prevent mould growth and finally sorted and graded prior to shipment to the manufacturers of cocoa and chocolate.

Processing the Cocoa Beans

The beans are first cleaned mechanically in the factory. They are then roasted to remove the moisture and to bring out the special chocolate flavour and aroma. The roasted beans are then cooled quickly by forced air, and are then run through a winnowing machine, which crushes them into small pieces and separates the shells from the nibs, the seed part, that consists of chocolate and cocoa. The nibs, containing approximately 50% of the fat of the bean are then placed in mills, which reduce them to a liquid by the heat created by the friction of milling. The liquid chocolate produced by the process described above, is know in the grade as chocolate liquor or pure bitter chocolate. This liquor may be cooled in moulds and sold in large slabs or in 200 g packages. It may also be precessed into cocoa.

Dutch Process

In the Dutch process, the beans are treated with certain alkalis at the time of roasting to break up the cell structure. The alkalis counteract the acid taste of natural cocoa, and , thus, bring about fine chocolate flavour, when cocoa is used in the finished product. Another distinct advantage of this process is that it makes cocoa more soluble and also imparts it the desired darker colour. The Dutch process cocoa leaves no bitter taste when used as a flavouring in ice cream.

Concentration of Flavour of Cocoa

As ice cream flavouring cocoa is more concentrated than chocolate liquor because it contains a higher percentage of real chocolate flavour. As mentioned earlier, fat it nearly tasteless and adds very little flavour to the ice cream mix. Thus, 100kg of cocoa contain 78 kg flavour and 22 kg fat; and 100 kg of chocolate liquor contain 48 kg flavour plus 52 kg fat. Apparently, it is more economical for the ice cream manufacturer to use coca rather than chocolate liquor.

Chocolate product used in flavouring ice cream are cocoa (20-25% cocoa fat), chocolate liquor (50-53% fat), cocoa and chocolate liquor blends (36-40% cocoa fat), and chocolate syrups. Some aromatic substances that may be added in small amounts to cocoa to enhance it so aroma are cinnamon, vanillin, air of bitter almond or oil of cloves.

Chocolate Ice Cream

The amount of cocoa or chocolate liquor to be used depends upon consumer preference, strength of flavour, fat content of flavour, colour desired in ice cream, etc. Generally, 4 to 6 kg of chocolate is added to 100 kg of mix. Usually, extra sugar is added to overcome the bitter flavour of the cocoa. Generally, the weight of extra sugar is the same as that of cocoa or chocolate. There is a tendency to flavour chocolate ice cream too highly. However, a better product can be made by reducing the amount of flavour and using, instead, a finer grade of cocoa or chocolate liquor.

Chocolate Syrup

This is prepared by mixing 25 kg cocoa, 30 kg sugar enough water to make 100 kg of finished syrup; 12-18 kg of this syrup is added to 100 kg of mix. The syrup is made in a chocolate kettle or double boiler. The syrup should be heated to the boiling point or heated at 90^0 C for 5 min and then cooled. This method of preparation can be used advantageously by small ice cream manufacturers who can conveniently prepare chocolate ice cream by adding syrup in the freezer.

Chocolate Ice Cream Mix

When it is desired to make an entire batch of chocolate mix, cocoa (or chocolate) and extra sugar and added to the mix, along with the other dry ingredients, before pasteurization. The temperature of pasteurization is sufficient to impart the flavour. When chocolate mix is made by this method, it has better whipping ability than plain mix to which syrup has been added in the freezer. It also has better flavouring, greater uniformity and free of specks.

Freezing of Chocolate Ice Cream

A typical formula for chocolate ice cream of good attributes is: fat 10.5% MSNF 9.7%, sugar 17%, cocoa 3.0%, stabilizer and emulsifier 0.3% and total solids 40.5%. Since the chocolate mix is very viscous, it is difficult to freeze because it whipes slowly. The viscosity may be reduced and the whipping ability improved by adding 1kg of citrate or phosphate or 1,000 kg of the mix.

The flavour of chocolate ice cream is influenced by the chemical and physical changes which occur during the production of cocoa and chocolate. Slight bitterness which might occur, is overcome by adding flavour and slightly reducing the amount of cocoa.

Ice cream should have an attractive colour and should be suggestive of the flavour used. Most of the colours used are chemical in origin. Natural colours are not widely employed since much larger quantities are required to produce the desired hue. Moreover, pH and heating affects the stability of natural colours with the risk that the colour intensity and hue may change. Only colour permitted by local laws and regulations should be used. Maximum levels allowed are specified for individual colours, and in most of the countries total amount of colour permitted is 300 mg/kg of the finished product.

Chapter 4

Manufacturing Process

In order to make ice cream of good quality, it is imperative to select milk products and other ingredients of good quality, and these should be combined to produce ice cream of the desired body with a delicately blended flavour. It is obvious that the mixing of the ingredients in a vat where they are heated to facilitate dissolving, blending and pasteurizing are preceded by the selection of good wholesome ingredients and satisfactory figuring of the mix.

The basic steps of production in manufacturing ice cream are composing the mix, pasteurization, homogenization, cooling, ageing, flavouring and colouring (optional). Freezing, packaging, hardening, storage, loading-out of product, and cleaning of equipments. The flow chart for ice cream processing is shown in Fig. 4.1. A large ice cream plant for the production of 5,000-10,000 litres/hr of various types of ice cream is shown in Fig. 4.2.

The first step of processing is composing the mix. This procedure can range from the small batch operation, where each ingredient is weighed or measured into a pasteurizing vat, to the large automatic continuous operation where many of the ingredients are metered into the batch. Continuous mix-making procedures are quite variable and some such operation can actually be modifications of the batch operation. In the continuous mix-making procedure, the products are blended into the mix in approximately the same order as for batch processing.

Automated and highly mechanized plants are utilized by large-scale manufacturers to reduce the processing cost.

PREPARATION OF THE MIX

Preparation of the mix is a very important process in the manufacturer of ice cream. It involves assembling the ingredients from the storage area to the mix preparation area, Weighing or metering and mixing ingredients, and the pasteurization, homogenization, cooling and storage of mix

Generally four methods are in use for processing mix:

(i) Ingredients in cans and batch pasteurization;

(ii) Ingredients in cans and high temperature-short time pasteurization;

(iii) bulk ingredients and batch pasteurization, and

(iv) bulk ingredients and continuous high temperature-short time pasteurization.

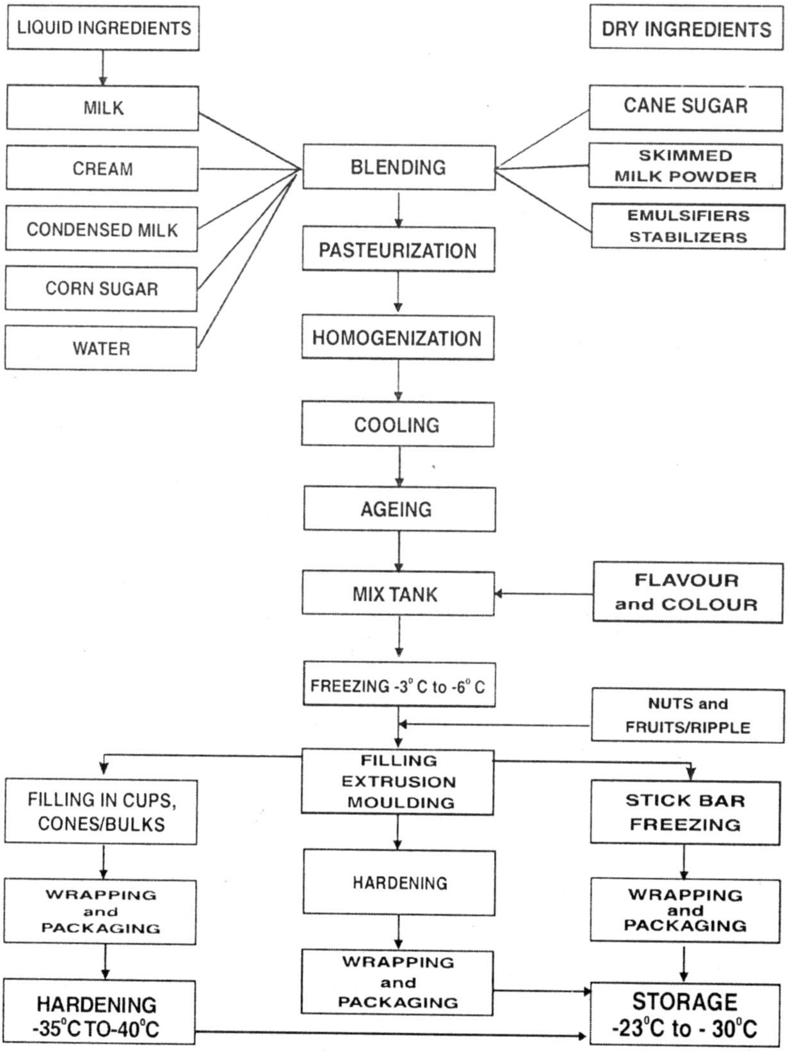

Fig 4.1 Flow chart for ice cream processing

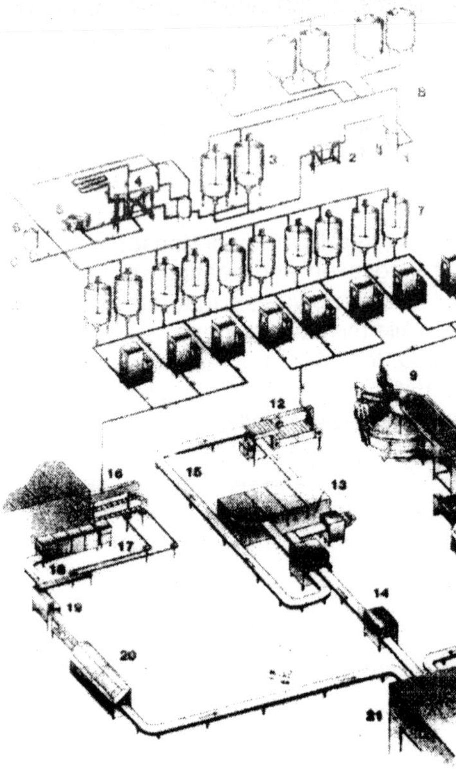

Large ice cream plant for production of 5000-10000 l/h of various types of ice cream.

A Raw material storage

B Dissolving of ingredient and mixing

- 1 Mixing unit
- 2 Plate heat exchanger
- 3 Mixing tanks (at least for continuous processing)

C Pasteurization, homogenization and fat standardization of the mix

- 4 Plate heat exchanger
- 5 Homogeniser
- 6 Tank for AMF or vegetable fat

D Ice cream production plant

- 7 Ageing tanks
- 8 Continuous freezers
- 9 Bar freezer
- 10 Wrapping and stacking unit
- 11 Cartoning unit
- 12 Cup/cone filler
- 13 Hardening tunnel
- 14 Cartoning line
- 15 Return conveyor for empty trays
- 16 Tray tunnel extrude
- 17 Chocolate enrobing unit
- 18 Cooling tunnel
- 19 Wrapping unit
- 20 Cartoning unit
- 21 Cold storage

Fig. 4.2 Large ice cream plant for production of 5,000-10,000 litres/hr of various types of ice cream

All the four methods are commonly used depending upon the size of the plant. The smaller plants (less than 250 thousand gallons per year) generally use the can-and-batch method. The medium-sized plants use the bulk-and-batch pasteurization, or the can-and-HTST pasteurization. The bigger plants (over 1 million gallons per year) use the bulk-and-HTST pateurization method. However, the least-cost method for preparing the mix is the can-and-batch pasteurization method, due to the low cost of equipment involved.

Order of Adding Ingredients

All the liquid ingredients (cream, milk, condensed milk, syrup, etc.) are placed in the vat, and the agitation and heating started at once. The dry ingredients, including skim milk powder, sugar, stabilizer and dried eggs (when used) are added, while the liquid material is agitated and before the temperature reaches 50^0 C. In order to obtain proper suspension without tump formation, the dry material is mixed thoroughly with part of the sugar before slowly adding it to the liquid, or sifting, or otherwise slowly adding these substances to the liquid. Skim milk powder, cocoa, and similar product should be sifted on top of the liquid. This is always done while the agitated liquid is still cool (under 30^0 C). Stabilizer, like CMC and guar gum are added after thoroughly mixing with an equal volume of sugar and before the liquid reached 50^0 C or , it can be sprinkled on the surface of the cold liquid and allowed to soak, before the mixture is heated. Another method is to soak the stabilizer in water and then heat the mixture to completely dissolve the stabilizer. This stabilizer suspension is usually added to warm mix (38-50^0 C). If gelatin is the stabilizer used it can be added in a similar manner. However, sodium alginate should not be added until the temperature of the liquid material has reached at least 66^0 C; it is not allowed to soak, but is stirred up with cold water and immediately dumped into the hot mix. When butter, plastic cream, frozen cream or other frozen products are used, they should be cut into small pieces and added in time to allow complete melting before the pasteurizing temperature is reached. With a few exceptions, the colouring and flavouring are added at the time the mix is frozen.

Pasteurization of the Mix

Pasteurization of mixes is essential because this process destroys all pathogenic bacteria, thereby safeguarding the health of the consumer. Pasteurization requires only slight additional expense since the mix is usually heated to facilitate solution, and since the homogenization process can be accomplished best near the pasteurization temperature.

Pasteurization consists in rapidly heating to a definite temperature, holding at that temperature for a definite minimum of time, and then rapidly cooling to below 5^0 C. Mix pasteurization is required by law and may be accomplished by the batch method, high temperature-short time or other approved procedures.

Table 4.1 Pasteurization Time and Temperatures for Ice Cream Mixes

Batch method	68° C	for not less than 30 min
high temperature short-time	79° C	for not less than 25 sec
Vacreation	90° C	for no apparent holding time (1-3 sec)
Ultra high temperature	135-149° C	few sec

Pasteurization renders the mix

(i) substantially free of pathogenic bacteria;

(ii) brings into the solution and helps in blending the ingredients for the mix;

(iii) improves the flavour;

(iv) improves the keeping quality, and

(v) produces a more uniform product. The methods of pasteurization commonly employed are batch or low temperature-long time (LTLT) and continuous. In a batch system, the heating and holding of the mix are done in the vat used for mixing the ingredients. The mix is then pumped to the homogenizer and from there it passes over a cooler.

Continuous pasteurization can be done with any of the several combination of time and temperature. Continuous pasteurizers consist of series of parallel plates with grooved or waffled surface. Other continuous-flow heat exchangers include tube-in-tube, triple tube and steam injection designs. Incontinuous pasteurization, the cool mix is heated and used as a cooling medium for the hot mix coming from the homogenizer. The principle of regeneration is profitably employed by large factories which use continuous pasteurizers. Continuous pasteurizers have holding tubes which are designed to expose mixes to the minimal temperature for the minimal time, for example, 25 sec when the minimum is 79° C. The holding time is determined by the length and diameter of the tube, rate of the mix flow and the amount of mixing of the fluid in the tube. A high rate of mixing is essential to have the time of flow or each particle of the mix very close to the average flow rate. This is achieved by having trubulent flow conditions. A turbulent flow exists when the Reynolds No. (NRe) exceeds 4,000. However, the International Dairy Federation (IDF) recommends a NRe of >12,000 in the HTST holding tube. High temperature pasteurization of ice cream has several advantages. The reasons are:

(i) greater destruction of bacteria resulting in lower bacterial count in ice cream

(ii) better body and texture;

(iii) better flavour;

(iv) protection against oxidation;

(v) saving of the stabilizer;
(vi) saving of time, labour and space, and
(vii) increased capacity.

Investigations have shown that cooked flavours result above 121°C. Thus, for maximum benefits, the mix should be processed at 99-140°C.

When high temperature pasteurization is employed, stabilizer needed is 25-30% less as compared with that used in batch pasteurization. In high temperature processing, the stabilizers employed usually contain guar gum CMC (Sodium carboxy methyl cellulose), and carrageenan, or algins with additional materials.

Continuous and automatically controlled high temperature units are more economical than batch methods. High temperature pasteurizing system have the following factors of difference:

(i) incorporation of regenerative heating and cooling;
(ii) amount of regeneration utilized;
(iii) adaptability to circulation cleaning;
(iv) ability to maintain long and continuous operation without loss in efficiency;
(v) pressures maintained in equipment which affect pumping efficiencies;
(vi) effectiveness of control which affect the properties of the finished products, and
(vii) adptability to small batches.

Investigations of the HTST equipment by Tobias et al (1995) revealed that the destruction of Micrococcus sp. (MS 102) equivalent to that resulting from laboratory pasteurization at 68°C for 30 min was obtained at 86°C with effective holding times of 0.8 and 3.8 sec., respectively.

From his studies Mitten (1958) found that ultra high temperature (UHT) pasteurization of the ice cream mix assures greater bacterial kill and produces desirable physical and chemical changes of the mix. Mixes processed by the UHT method, generally, had greater water binding characteristics, required less stabilizer, had slightly more dryness when frozen, excellent flavour and greater stability against oxidation. He also stated that for continuously made mixes the stability should disperse readily, be soluble in the cold mix and give the desired stabilizing effect.

Aubuckle and Nisonger studied the effect of high temperature pasteurization of ice cream mix using temperature of 76.6°C, 82.2°C, 87.7°C, and 93.3°C. They reported the temperature of pasteurization had no effect on acidity or pH and little effect on surface tension. As pasteurization temperature increased with the range used, there was a tendency for mix viscosity to decrease and mixes pasteurized at 76.6° and 82.2°C for 15 sec. developed off-flavours during the strorage period. The melting rate was greatest at the lowest pasteurization temperature. There was little effect of pasteurization temperature on the body the texture characteristic. Later studies showed improvement in body and texture at 101.6-104.4°C and again near 126.6°C.

Homogenizing the Mix

The main purpose of homogenization is to make a permanent and uniform suspension of the fat by reducing the size of the fat droplets to a very small diameter, preferably, not more than two microns. Thus, when a mix is properly homogenized, the fat will not rise and form a cream layer. Other advantages derived are, a more uniform ice cream with a smoother texture, improved whipping ability, a shorter ageing period, prevention of churning in the freezer and the use of slightly less stabilizer. It is essential to homogenize the mix when plastic cream, frozen cream, butter and butter oil and oil from vegetable sources are used. A two-stage APV Gaulin homogenizer is shown in Fig. 5.3.

Homogenization is accomplished by forcing the mix through a small orifice under suitable conditions of temperature and pressure, using a positive displacement plunger pump to furnish the pressure. The orifice consists of a valve and seat in which the two adjacent surfaces are parallel and lapped smooth, and is surrounded by an impact ring against which the mix impinges as it leaves the valve. This is shown in Fig. 4.4. The break-up of fat globules is caused by the following.

After extensive study and research, it had been determined that the primary factor in homogenization is cavitation, and the secondary factor is turbulence. To create these two effects, the mix enters the homogenizing valve assembly from the pump section of the machine at high pressure and low velocity. As the product enters the space between the valve and the seat, which can be as narrow as 0.0015 inch (0.038 mm), the velocity increases dramatically. There is a corresponding decrease in the vapour pressure of the liquid, and vapour bubbles form in the liquid. As the product flows through the valve/valve-seat area, the velocity decreases and pressure regains, resulting in the implosion of the bubbles. The phenomenon, the formation and implosion of bubbles, is referred to as cavitation. The intense energy release and turbulence associated with cavitation causes disruption of the particles. The homogenization process occurs over the extremely small distance of 0.0005 inch (0.00128 mm) with a corresponding elapsed time of less than 0.005 sec.

Fig. 4.3 Gaulin two-stage homogenizer

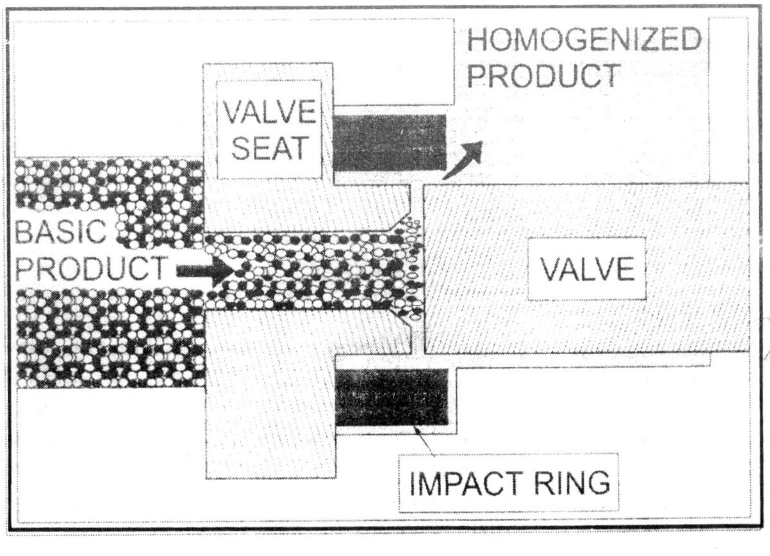

(Fig. 4.4 Basic working principle of a homogenizer

Physical Effects of Homogenization

Homogenization causes reduction in the size of the fat globules to about 1/10 of the normal size which increases the total surface area of the globules about 10 times. On homogenization, protein are adsorbed on the outer surfaces of newly formed membranes and this greatly increases the hydrated surface area. This accounts for increased viscosity and the increased smoothness of texture of homogenized mixes. Homogenization produce effects which differ considerably with the varying composition, acidity, temperature, pressure, etc. The substances in their true and colloidal solution tend to be concentrated on the fat globule surfaces. Varying conditions will have different effects on the films forming at these surfaces. There is a tendency for fat globules to form in groups as the mix passes away from the homogenizing valve. This is particularly true of cold or acid mixes or mixes containing butter and frozen cream. This clumping of the fat globules, if marked, causes excessive viscosity. For this reason, most of the homogenizers are equipped with a second valve which breaks up the clumps, in other words the mix passes through one valve (called the first stage), under a high pressure (above 100 kg/cm2) where clumping may occur, and then through another valve (called the second stage) under a low pressure (35-50 kg/cm^2 is sufficient where the clumps are broken up, and then the mix passes out of the homogenizer towards the cooler.

Homogenizing Temperature

The mix is homogenized at temperature from 63°C to 76°C because at low temperature (50-55°C) homogenization increases the formation of clumps of fat globules, increases the viscosity, and increases the freezing time in batch freezers. When high pasteurizing temperatures are employed in the batch system, the mix may be cooled to 65°C for homogenization to reduce the intensity of the cooked flavour, especially when homogenization is not likely to be completed within 30 min. If homogenization precedes pasteurization, the minimum temperature recommended for homogenization is 60°C in order to inactivate lipase enzyme, thereby ensuring lipolysis will not take place as protective membrance is stripped from the fat globules during homogenization.

Pressure for Homogenization

The pressure for homogenization depends upon the composition of the mix, desired viscosity, stability of the mix, temperature used and construction of the homogenizer. Various worker have recommended different homogenizing pressures for homogenization, depending on the type homogenizing value used. "LW' valves are commonly used in single stage homogenizers while "flat" valves are used in double stage homogenisers. Tabl[illegible]ves approximate pressures for single and double stage [illegible]on.

On homogenization, there is a tremendous increase in surface area of the fat globules. There is not enough membrane material to form membranes round all the new fat globules. The formation of new membranes takes some time, during which many of the fat globules are unprotected. Therefore, mix having a higher fat content should be homogenized at a lower pressure, because the distance between globules in a high fat mix (if homogenized using the same pressure) will be very small and recoalescence of the fat globules will tend to occur. Lower pressures are also used when mixes contain butter, plastic cream, etc., as the only source for fat or mixes having concentrated products as the only source of MSNF.

The effect of pressure and temperature of homogenizationis given in 4.5. The unhomogenized mix has large and small fat globules. It can be observed that clumping occurs when either low temperature or excessively high pressure is employed; however, pronounced clumping takes place at lower temperature. Small single fat globules are obtained when mix is homogenized at 200 kg/gm^2 at 75^{0}C.

Table 4.2 Approximate Homogenization Pressures for Mixes of Different Fat Contents

Fat	Single Stage	Double Stage	
%	(kg/cm^2)	First Valve (kg/cm^2)	Second Valve (kg/cm^2)
8	210	210	50
10	180	180	45
12	130	130	35
14	105	105	35
16	85	85	35

Factors which favour high viscosity and the clumping of the fat globules are:

(i) Low temperature of the mix when homogenized

(ii) Low stability of the mix due to high acidity or improper salt balance;

(iii) Excessively high pressures especially with a single valve, and

(iv) A high ratio of fat content of the MSNF content. In order to reduce the viscosity produced by homogenization, lower pressures should be used, especially when homogenizing mixes of low stability.

Excessive viscosity of the ice cream mix, as it flows through a cooler, indicates that there is too much clumping or clustering and the homogenizing pressure should be lowered, or the second stage readjusted. Use of proper pressure and temperature results in less clumping of fat globules,and consequently, a lower viscosity and shorter freezing time in a batch freezer.

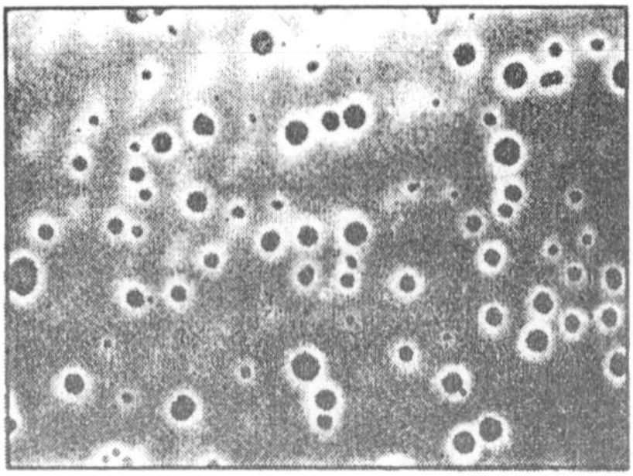

1. Unhomogenized

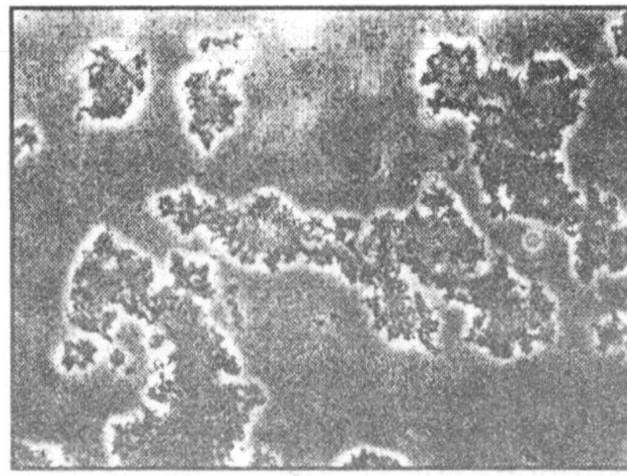

2. Temperature 40^0C; homogenized at 200 kg/cm^2

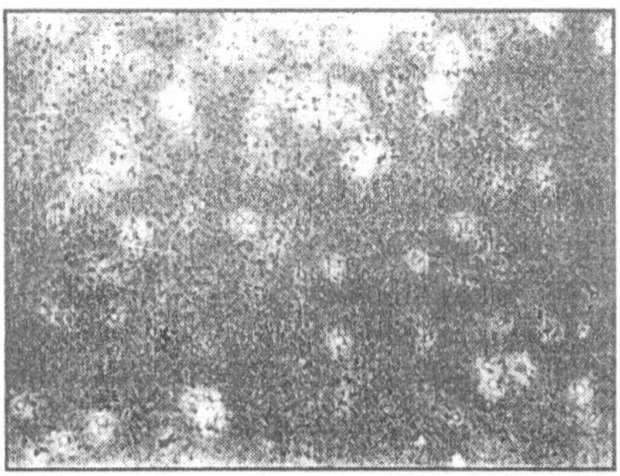

3. Temperature 75^0C; homogenized at 100 kg/cm^2

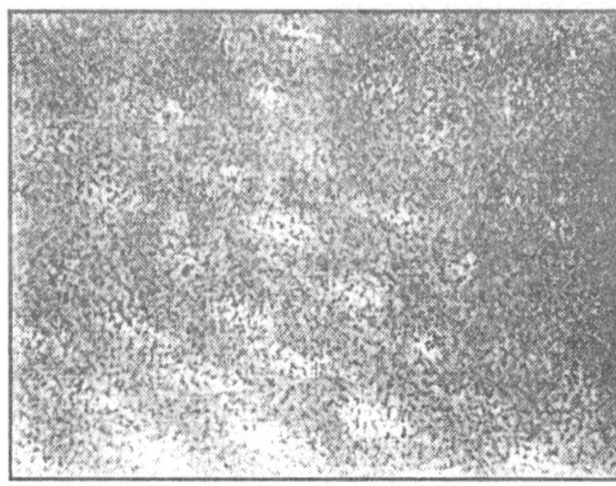

4. Temperature 75^0C; homogenized at 200 kg/cm^2

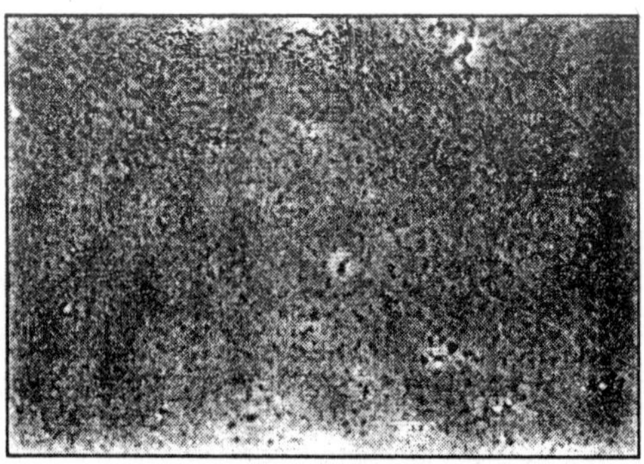

5. Temperature 75^0C; homogenized at 300 kg/cm^2

Fig. 4.5 The effect of different pressure and temperature of homogenization on fat globules

Improper or defective homogenization can be detected by examining a sample of the mix with a microscope. An experienced operator can measure the size of the fat globule and detect clumping.

Care of the Homogenizer

Homogenizer is one equipment which is subjected to a lot of wear and tear. It, therefore, demands special care from the standpoint of mechanical efficiency and sanitation.

The homogenizing valve is the heart of the machine. The care of the homogenizing valve varies with the type of valve. It should always be kept smooth and precautions taken to guard against accidental marring of its surface. The grooves that develop as a result of use, produced by the abrasion of the liquid should be resurfaced so that the valve seats perfectly. Some homogenizers have a daily replaceable unit, thus eliminating the necessity for resurfacing the homogenizing valve.

Suction and discharge valves must be kept in good condition, otherwise there will be wide fluctuations in pressure and, as a result, part of the mix might pass through the machine at low pressure. The suction and discharge valves must open easily so that the plungers can draw in full charge at each stroke without loss of capacity, and they must close tightly on the pressure stroke so that there is no leakage. Many of the new homogenizers have a light spring on the discharge valves to make them close more quickly.

Care must be exercised to prevent air leaks in the suction line of the homogenizer, since it causes irregular pressure resulting in poor homogenization, foaming and increased strain on the pump.

For cleaning, the machine should be dismantled, preferably after each use, parts scrubbed with mild cleaning solution, rinsed in water and laid out on suitable rack so that they remain dry until machine is again used.

Cooling the Mix

Mix should be cooled immediately after homogenization to 0-5^{0}C and held in storage tanks until used. Slow cooling of the mix from 30-40^{0}C down to 5^{0}C imparts increased viscosity to the mix and also results in ice cream that does not melt smoothly. Also temperatures below 5^{0}C retard the growth of bacteria. Cooling of mixes to 0-2^{0}C increase the capacity of freezers.

The mix is normally cooled by the internal tubular cooler of plate cooler. But if the mix is too viscous to be cooled effectively by the internal tubular cooler or plate cooler, coolers of the surface or cabinet types are used. The surface cooler should be so constructed that the moisture condensation forming on the ends of the tubes cannot flow into the mix or drop into the lower trough. The cabinet cooler, which is essentially a battery of small surface coolers, works very satisfactorily with ice cream mix.

Ageing the Mix

Ageing of the mix is beneficial for the ice cream. The changes which occur during ageing are:

(i) The fat is solidified; increased adsorption of the emulsifier on the fat globules;

(ii) Stabilizers, especially gelatin swell and combine with water and

(iii) Increased adsorption and hydration of the milk proteins. In the presence of the emulsifier protein displacement from the fat globules also occurs (on cooling the emulsifier becomes more surface active and displace protein from the interface), though this is a slower process. The combined effect of all these changes is an increase in viscosity during ageing.

Ease of whipping, smoothness in body and texture, resistance to melting are improved by ageing. Studies have shown that under average commercial conditions 3-4 hr of ageing is essential for continuous freezers. For the batch-type freezers, which have limited whipping mechanisms, a longer ageing period is necessary. Also for high fat mixes, which have been homogenized at very low pressures, 24hr or ageing produces good results.

The ageing temperature should not exceed 5^0 C. At temperatures lower than 5^0 C the bacterial count will not increase during ageing.

When the mix has been properly aged, it is ready for the freezing process which generally follows immediately. Holding the mix for more than about five days likely to cause at least some deterioration in both flavour and quality.

Making the Mix in a Vaccum Pan

A vaccum pan is sometimes used in making extremely large quantities of ice cream mixes, and is also used in making condensed and powdered ice cream mix.

Several different procedures are possible, the most commonly used method is given below :

(i) Figure the mix, as indicated in Chapter 6.

(ii) Mix all the ingredients and pasteurize. Pasteurization also serves the purpose of forewarming the pan operation .

(iii) Concentrate it in the pan.

(iv) Drop the concentrated mix from the pan and weigh.

(v) Homogenize the mix.

(vi) Cool the mix.

(vii) Test and standardize the mix.

Hening suggested another procedure for making the mix in the pan. His studies showed that less fat clumping occurs, if the mix in homogenized before it is condensed and before the sugar the stabilizer are added. Though the procedure is more tedious, it leads to a higher whipping ability and somewhat bettertexture. The procedure is as follows;

(i) Figure the mix.

(ii) Mix only the dairy products called for the computed mix and forewarm them.

(iii) Homogenixe this mixture.

(iv) Condence the mixture of dairy products to the desired point.

(v) Drop the concentrated dairy products from the pan, weigh, and draw a sample for fat and total solids analyses.

(VI) In a batch mixer, add the sugar and stabilizer, and complete the pasteurization.

(vii) Cool the mixer.

(viii) Standardize on the basis of the fat and solids test taken or on the basis of weight alone under step 5.

Forewarming

The mixture need not be heated to a temperature that is adequate for pasteurization, but needs to be at a temperature that is adequate for homogenizing and for the pan operation. The pasteurization of the dairy products might be done at this stage, but in view of the fact that sugar and stabilizer must be added later, it is advisable to pasteurize then. A forewarming temperature of 710^{0}C is desirable. This can conveniently be attained by means of a tubular heater.

Homogenize this mixture in the usual manner.

Concentration the Dairy Products

The point at which the mixture of dairy products is to be concentrated is determined by a specific gravity test. The mixture should be over-condensed slightly to permit standardization.

Weighing Concentrated Dairy Products

After concentration the mixture should be weighed. The mix is standardized on the basis of weight alone, by adding enough water (assuming the mix has been over-condensed slightly) so that the combined weight of the entire mix will be up to the weight for which the mix was calculated.

A more accurate method is to take a sample for fat and total solids test of the concentrated dairy products. These tests can be conducted, while the procedure is carried to the following steps, and on the basis of the test the mix be standardized before it is cooled.

Adding Sugar and Stabilizer, and Pasteurizing

After the mixture has been dropped from the pan and weighed, sugar and stabilizer are added in batch mixer, and the entire mix is pasteurized. If the forewarming was adequate for pasteurization, then no further heating is required at this step. However, the temperature and agitation must be maintained long enough to dissolve the sugar and stabilizer. Some stabilizers do not dissolve readily and it becomes necessary to dissolve the stabilizer, in 6 to 8 times its weight of water before adding it to the mix. The water used in soaking and dissolving the stabilizer should be taken into consideration in the standardization of the mix.

Cooling, Standardizing and Ageing

After sugar and stabilizer have been dissolved and the pasteurization completed, the mix is cooled in the usual manner. If the standardization is to be done on the basis of the fat and solids test mentioned, it is done either immediately preceding or following the cooling. The mix is then aged, and is ready for freezing.

Chapter 5

Ice Cream Freezing

In the making of ice cream we are concerned with the freezing of the mix. The freezing produces not only ice crystals, but also other crystals under certain conditions. It is essential, therefore, to know some general facts about freezing and crystallization.

The Freezing Point of Solutions

The freezing point of pure water is 0°C. If we dissolve anything in the water, the solution formed will require a lower temperature to freeze; the more concentrated the solution is, the more the freezing point will be depressed.

If we compare the effect of various substances on the freezing point of water, we find that their depressing varies. Solutions of the same concentration do not freeze at the same temperature. There is very definite relationship that holds for substances that do not dissociate or associate; this relationship is expressed by the formula:

$$D = K \frac{G}{M}$$

in which D is the depression of the freezing point in degrees centigrade, K is a constant charateristic for each solvent, G represents the weight of the dissolved substances in 1000 g of the solvent, and M is the molecular weight of the dissolved substance. For water the value of K is 1.86. Therefore, the formula in cases where water is the solvent, is

$$D = 1.86 \frac{G}{M}$$

Since the fraction G/M rrepresents the number of moles of the dissolved substance in 1000 g of the solvent, it follows that the freezing point depression is not dependent upon the nature of the dissolved substance, but is dependent upon the number of moles of the dissolved substance. According to the laws of chemistry, mole of various substances (the molecular weight in grams= 1mole) have equal number of molecules. Thus, solutions that contain the same number of molecules in a given amount of solvent, will have the same freezing point.

The above does not hold true for electrolytes because the electrolytes dissociate, and on dissociation, each molecule yields two or more ions. For example,

NaCl on dissociating (NaCl $\rightleftharpoons$ Na + Cl) yields two ions; Na_2SO_4 on dissociation ($Na_2SO_4 \rightleftharpoons$ 2Na+ SO_4) yields three ions.

The effect of electrolytes on the freezing point is greater than expected on the basis of the above rule. In the case of common salt, NaCl, the effect approaches twice than expected: the more dilute the solution, the more nearly it approaches this limit, because the dissociation becomes more complete as the dilution is increased. Ions affect the freezing point in the same manner as molecules, therefore, we must restate the above rule as follows:

Solutions, that contain the same number of partilces (ions and molecules) in a given amount of the solvent, will have the same freezing point. They will also have the same boiling point, and the same osmotic pressure.

The Freezing Point of Ice Cream Mixes

The freezing point of ice cream mixes varies appreciably with the composition. The mix constituents, which affect the freezing point directly, are sugar, milk sugar (lactose), milk salts, and any other substance that is added and that is in true solution. The mix constituents which affect the freezing point indirectly, are the fat content and the protein content or any other constituent not in true solution. When these constituents are increased, there is less water in the mix, and the resulting higher water concentration of the truly soluble substance causes the freezing point to be lowered. Leighton(1927) developea a method for the calculation of the freezing point of ice cream which has been found to be reasonably accurate. It is based on the percentage of lactose in MSNF, the percentage of sucrose and milk salts. Leighton assumes that 54.5 per cent of the serum solids is lactose, and that the mixtures of sucrose and lactose follow the freezing point curve of sucrose.

The methods of calculating the freezing point of an ice cream mix makes use of the sum of the freezing point depression values for the sugars and the calculated values for the salts. For the sugars, lactose and sucrose, the following equation is utilized to determine the parts of disaccharide sugar (expressed as sucrose equlvalent) to 100 parts of water in the mix.

$$\frac{(MSNF \times 0.545) + s \times 100}{W} = \text{parts of sucrose equivalent /100 parts of water.}$$

Percentage of milk solids not fat (MSNF) x 0.545 is the amount of lactose in the MSNF.

S is the percentage of sucrose in the mix, W is the percentage of water in the mix. The lowering of the freezing point due to the sugar (sucrose equivalent) is obtained by interpolation from data tables.

The freezing point due to the milk salts is calculated from the equation

$$\frac{W}{MSNF \times 2.37} = \text{Freezing point depression due to milk salts}$$ 2.37 is a

constant based on the apparent molecular weight of the salts.

The lowering of freezing point due to the sucrose equivalent plus the lowering caused by the milk salts gives the freezing point of the mix.

Example: The freezing point of a mix having 12% fat, 11% MSNF, 15% sugar, and 0.3% stabilizer can be calculated as follows:

(1) $\dfrac{[(11 \times 0.545) + 15] \times 100}{61.7}$ = 34.03 parts of sucrose per 100 parts of water will lower the freezing point by 2.09°C.

(2) $\dfrac{11 \times 2.37}{61.7}$ = 0.42°C is the lowering of freezing point due to salts.

Total lowering = 2.09 + 0.42°C

= 2.51°C

The freezing point is - 2.51°C

The above calculation involves assumptions, and, therefore, may not give accurate results, if we deviate from these assumptions. For instance, if the mix is made from dairy products that have soured slightly, the lowering effect due to the serum solids will be greater than the above; this is also true for neutralization.

Beside the substances discussed above, glucose (corn sugar), invert sugar, honey, fruits and extracts should also be considered. A given weight of glucose depresses the freezing point almost twice as much as the same weight of sucrose. This can be predicted on the basis of the fact that solutions containing the same number of particles in a given amount of solvent have the same freezing point. Since the molecular weight of glucose is 180.1, and that of sucrose is 342.17, it follows that when we take equal weight of the two, we will have 342.17 / 180.1 or 1.9 times as many glucose molecules as we have of sucrose molecules. Therefore, the freezing point depression due to a given amount of glucose should be approximately 1.9 times as get as caused by same weight of sucrose. Thus, when glucose is used as a sweetening agent, the lowering effect due to glucose may be calculated as follows:

$$\frac{\text{Per cent glucose} \times 100}{\text{Per cent water in the mix}} = \text{parts of glucose per 100 parts of water}$$

The effects of the solids in invert sugar and honey are the same as that of glucose. Invert sugar, the hydrolysis product of sucrose, consists of equal parts of glucose and fructose. Honey solids contain mainly invert sugar. Corn syrup (liquid or dried) contains dextrins, maltose and dextrose, in proportions that vary according to the stage to which hydrolysis of corn starch was carried. The average molecular weight of this mixture of the hydrolysed products is somewhat higher than the moleicular weight of sucrose. Therefore, corn syrup solids depress the freezing point less than sucrose.

Fruits contain sugar-fructose, glucose and sucrose, fruit acids and some salts. Besides, fruit preparation contain large amounts of added sugar. The sugar that is used in the fruit preparations is glucose (corn sugar) or sucrose (cane or beet sugar). In the preparation of fruit ice cream, the addition of fruit preparations made with glucose cause appreciable lowering of the freezing of the freezing point. When sucrose is used in the fruit preparations, a similar low freezing point is found on account of the fact that the fruit acids cause extensive hydrolysis of sucrose into invert sugar, especially in preparations made by heating. Where this low freezing point is troublesome, fruit preparation made with glucose or preparation in which sucrose has been extensively hydrolysed, should be avoided.

Heat Units Involved in Freezing

In order to compute the heat units that must be added or removed in heating or cooling a product, it is necessary to know its specific heat which varies with temperature. The heat capacity of water (specific heat) varies comparatively little with temperature. In the case of other compounds, particularly organic compounds (and in the presence of water), the specific heat increases appreciably with temperature. This holds good in the case of serum solids in skim milk. The average specific heat of serum solids for the temperature range 0-60°C is 0.4628, assuming that the serum solids content of skim milk is 9%, and the fat content is ignored. Studies have revealed that specific heat and latent heat of fusion of milk fat are 0.50 and 19.5 calories per g respectively. For sugars and stabilizers of ice cream mixes, the value of carbohydrates, viz., 0.300 (°C) + .0015 per degree C above 0°C is used. Thus, the average specific heat of sugar and stabilizer is calcutated as follows:

$$0.300 + \frac{.0015 \times 60}{2} = 0.345 \text{ (average specific heat between } 0^0\text{-}60^0\text{C)}$$

On this basis, an ice cream mix containing 12% fat, 11% serum solids, 15% sugar, 0.3% stabilizer, and 61.7% water would have the following specific heat from 0°C to 60°C.

To heat (or cool) 100g of such ice cream mix would require.

12.0 x 0.500 x 60	=	360.00 calories, sensible heat for the fat
	=	12.0 x 19.5
	=	234.0 calories, latent heat of fusion for the fat.
11.0 x 0.4628 x 60	=	305.4 calories, sensible heat for the serum solids.
15.3 x 0.345 x 60	=	316.71 calories, sensible heat for sugar and stabilizer.
61.7 x 1.00 x 60	=	3702.00 calories, sensible heat for water.

Total calories = 4918.11 calories.

Sensible heat of 100 g of water = 100 x 1.00 x 60 = 6000 calories.

Specific heat of the mix (for the range 0°-60°C)

$$= \frac{4918.11}{60 \times 100} = 0.8196$$

Refrigeration Requirements for Ice Cream Freezing

The actual heat extracted in freezing ice cream is dependent upon the composition of the mix and the temperature to which it is frozen. The extraction of heat takes place in three different steps:

(i) the extraction of the sensible heat of the liquid;

(ii) the extraction of the latent heat of the wate frozen; and

(iii) extraction of the sensible heat of the semi-frozen slush. The exact calculation of the amount of heat extracted is difficult to estimate, but a reasonably close value can be obtained.

Problem: Find the kilo calories of heat extracted from 1 kg of mix of the composition 10% fat, 11% serum solids, 14% sugar and 0.4% stabilizer, if the mix is at 4.44°C is frozen to a temperature of -5°C.

Solution: H (Total heat) = (Sensible heat of the liquid + latent heat of fusion of the water frozen as ice) + sensible heat of the semi-frozen mixture below the initial freezing point of the mix.

It is assumed that the specific heat of the mix is 0.82; the specific heat of the frozen ice cream is 0.65 and the latent heat of fusion of water is 80 kilo calories.

From the freezing curve for ice cream mix (Fig. 5.1) it is seen that 48% of the water is frozen as ice at -5°C and the mix begins to freeze at -2.4°C. Then:

Temperature of mix	=	4.44°C
Freezing point of mix	=	-2.4°C
Percentage of water in mix	=	64.6
Percentage of water frozen at -5°C	=	48.0
Sensible heat of mix	=	4.44 -(-2.4) 0.82 = 5.61
Latent heat of fusion	=	80 (0.48 x 0.646) = 24.8
Sensible heat of slush	=	(5.0-2.4) 0.65 = 1.69

Total kcal absorbed per kg of ice cream = 32.1 kcal. During the actual freezing of ice cream in a freezer, an additional amount of refrigeration must be added to overcome the heat of friction due to the dasher and other losses.

The freezing process is divided into two parts.

(i) the mix, with an appropriate amount of colour and flavour, generally added at the freezer, is quickly frozen while being agitated to incorporate air in such a way as to produce and control fromation of ice crystals to give smoothness in body and texture, satisfactory overrun and palat ability in the finished ice cream, and

(ii) when ice cream is partially frozen to a certain consistency, it is drawn from the freezer into packages and quickly transferred to hardening tunnels or cold storage room where the freezing and hardening process is completed without agitation.

Freezing is characterised by short production runs, necessitated by frequent changes in flavours and container size. Freezers may be classified as follows:

1. Batch freezers
   - (a) Salt and ice type (obsolete)
   - (b) Brine freezers (obsolete)
   - (c) Direct expansion (ammonia or freon refrigerant)

   - (i) Vertical—used mainly is some counter freezers
   - (ii) Horizontal—mostly replaced by continuous freezers
   - (iii) Single—tube freezers
   - (iv) Triple—tube freezers
   - (v) Four—tube freezers.
2. Continuous freezers-Horizontal, direct expansion; used by commercial plants.
3. Soft serve freezers-Batch and automatic continuous freezers of the direct expansion type.

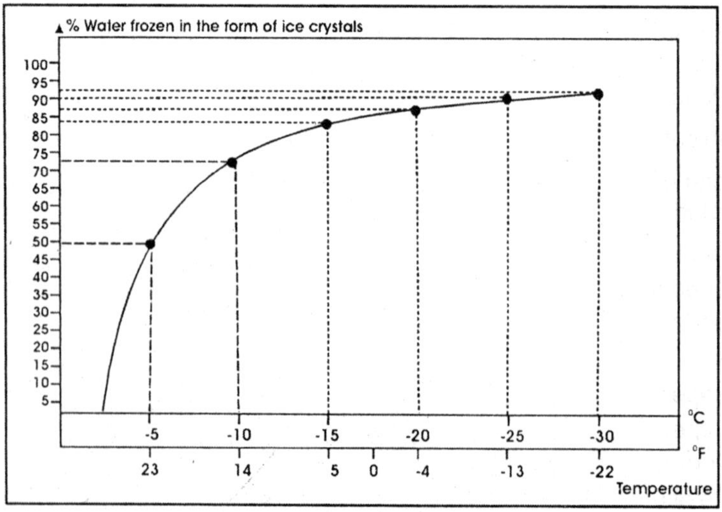

Fig 5.1 Freezing curve for ice cream mix

Importance of the Freezer

Fast freezing ensures the production of small ice crystal. Therefore, fast freezing is essential for a smooth product because ice crystals that are formed quickly, are smaller than those formed slowly. Hence, it becomes necessary to freeze and draw from the freezer in as short a time as possible. This is achieved in a continuous freezer in a few seconds, while batch freezers take 6-10 min. Also, since freezing continues after the ice cream is placed in the hardening rooms, the ice crystals formed during the hardening period are larger because they form more slowly than in the freezer. Thus, it is desirable to freeze the ice cream as stiff as possible, and yet have it liquid enough to draw out of the freezer.

Table 5.1 shows the freezing time and temperature as affected by the type of freezer used.

Table 5.1 Freezing Times and Drawing Temperatures

Kind of Freezer	Freezing Time to 90% Overrun (Approx.)	Drawing Temperature (°C)
Batch freezer	7 min	- 3.3 to -4.4°C
Continuous freezer	24 sec	- 5.5 to-6° C
Low temperature Continuous freezer	26-36 sec	- 8 to -9° C
Soft serve freezer	3 min	- 6.6 to -8° C
Counter freezer	10 min	- 3.3° C

The are two factors which influence the freezing time:

(1) Mechanical, and

(2) Character of the mix. The mechanical factor which influence the freezing time include:

   (a) type and make of freezers;
   (b) speed of the dasher;
   (c) condition of the freezer wall and blades;
   (d) velocity of the refrigerant passing around the freezing chamber;
   (e) temperature of the refrigerant;
   (f) temperature at which the ice cream is drawn from the freezer;
   (g) overrun desired, and
   (h) rate of unloading the freezer.

Character of the mix is influenced by

(a) composition of the mix,
(b) acidity of ingredients;
(c) freezing point of the mix;
(d) kind of ingredients, particularly those having fat;
(e) methods of processing the mix, and
(f) kind and amount of flavouring materials added.

CHANGES DURING THE FREEZING PROCESS

The function of the freezing process is to freeze a portion of the water of mix, and to incorporate air into the mix. This involves lowering of the temperature of mix from ageing temperature to the freezing point, freezing a portion of the water of the mix, incorporating air into the mix and cooling the ice cream from the temperature it is drawn from the freezer to the hardening room temperature. When the mix is put into the freezer its temperature drops very rapidly, while the sensible heat is being removed and before any ice crystal are formed. This process should take less than 1-2 min. At the same time, the rapid agitation reduces the viscosity by partly destroying the gel-like structure and by breaking up the fat globule clusters. The gel-like structure and by breaking up the fat globule clusters. The gel-like structure may partially reform during the hardening process in the hardening room. Besides, the rapid agitation incorporates air quickly into the mix.

When the freezing point is reached, the liquid water changes to ice crystals which appear in the mix. The ice crystals are practically pure water in a solid form, and, thus, the sugar and other solutes become more concentrated in the remaining liquid water. Increasing the concentration of these solutes causes the freezing point of the liquid portion to the lightly lower so that the temperature (also called sensible heat) must be lowered before more ice crystals are formed. However, the heat that must be removed to change liquid water into ice crystals is not measured by the thermometer, and is called the latent heat of fusion. At this stage, the temperature of the mix does not change noticeably while ice crystals are being formed. This actually happens when pure wate is frozen, but in freezing ice cream the freezing point is continuously being lowered by the formation of ice cream. The temperature continues to drop at a slower rate than during the first minute or two while approaching the initial freezing point. While the temperature drops, more ice crystals are formed, increasing the concentration of sugar and other solutes in the remaining liquid water, until the concentration is so great that freezing will not occur. Thus, the entire water is not frozen even after long periods in the hardening room. The approximate percentage of water frozen in the ice cream mix at various temperature is given in Table 5.2.

The first phase of the freezing process accounts for the freezing of 33-67% of the water depending on the drawing temperature. When the mix is in the freezer and ice crystals are forming, more air is incorporated into the mix, and ingredients like acid, fruit juices, fruits, or nuts can be added without any danger of coagulating the mix. Besides, at this time the refrigerant can be shut off from the batch freezers. Agitation in hand or home freezers is usually stopped when the product has reached a certain consistency or stiffness. This point depends upon the amount of water converted into ice crystal, and the amount of air incorporated into the mix. In continuous freezers, when this point is reached, the ice cream is drawn out of the freezers into packages and placed in the hardening room. At this stage, the ice cream contains the desired amount of air, but not the desired amount of ice crystals. The results of the freezing process can be explained by examining the internal structure of the frozen product.

Table 5.2 Approximate percentage of water Frozen in the ice cream Mix at various Temperatures.

Temp. (°C)	Water frozen (%)	Temp. (°C)	Water frozen (%)
-4.0	35	-6.5	58
-4.5	42	-8.5	68
-5.5	48	-12.5	78
-5.5	52	-20.0	87
-6.0	55	-25.9	90

STRUCTURE OF ICE CREAM

Many of the properties of ice cream, such as dryness or wetness of extrusion, resistance to shrinkage, melt-down characteristics and texture, can be explained in terms of the fine structure of the product. Ice cream is a complex formulation consisting of a foam which contains gas (air) dispersed as small air cells in a partially frozen continuous phase. The partially frozen continous phase consists of fat in emulsion, milk proteins and stabilizers in colloidal solution, sugar and salts in true solution and embedded ice crystals. Such a material consisting of air, liquid and solid is called three-phase system. The microstructure of ice cream is illustrated in Fig. 5.2 (Plate 1). The texture of ice cream is to a large determined by the ice-crystal size, the amount and the state of dispersion of fat, the overrun and air cell size and the temperature of the product.

Air Cells

The diameter of air cells varies within a wide range, from 10 to 100 microns. The fineness of dispersion of the air cells dependes on the whipping properties of ice cream mixes; higher the whipping ability, greater the fineness of dispersion of air cells. The whipping properties are affected by product variables such as fat, MSNF, emulsifier and stabilizer.

While MSNF, emulsifier and stabilizer facilitate air incorporation and the production of finely divided foam, fat exerts an inhibiting effect on the whipping ability. This is attributed to breakdown of fat emulsion on freezing and the spread of liquid fat at the air/mix interface which displaces protein and acts as a foam depressant. Moreover, the appearance of coalesced fat in frozen ice cream limits the thinness to which the lamellae between air cells can be whipped.

Ice Crystals

The ice crystal vary from 20 to 60 microns. In ice cream, the amount of water as ice is about 48% at the extrusion temperature (-5° C), about 95% at the hardening temperature of -30° C. Large ice crystals tend to cause greater, destabilization of the fat emulsion (King, 1950). When the amount of MSNF is increased, the freezing point of the mix is lowered, and consequently the amount of water present as ice at a given temperature also decreases. This results in increase in the distances between smaller and larger ice crystals and also larger intercrystal distances. Furthermore, stabilizer and emulsifier produce smaller ice crystals.

Fat Globules, Clumping and Coalescence

A fine emulsion of fat in the mix is obtained by homogenization. The fineness of the dispersion of the fat. emulsion in ice cream mixes depends on MSNF and the mineral salt balance and on the homogenization conditions (number of stages, pressure and temperature). The level of MSNF normally used is sufficient of emulsify the fat present in the mix. Citrates and phosphates increase the negative charge, thereby decreasing clumping while calcium salts increase the positive charge and, thus, cause or increase clumping. A partial "churing out" of the fat is desirable and this is accomplished by the addition of an emulsifier. A two-stage homogenization gives less clumping of fat than a single stage homogenization. The fat/mix and air/mix interfaces are intimately involved in fat destabilization.

The Fat/Mix Interface

Studies by Buchheim under the electron microscope have revealed that fat globules in ice cream have a liquid core surrounded by an outer shell of crystalline fat which is affected by the rate of cooling. Ageing of ice cream mixes is important because if allows time for crystallization of fat and emulsifier, adsorption of proteins at the fat/mix interface and hydration of the stabilizer. Fromherz has suggested that an emulsifier film is formed round the fat globules and that the globular proteins (undenatured protein) can be adsorbed from solution of lipid monolayers to from a hexagonal close-packed arrangement.

When the ice cream mix is aerated and frozen, the protein membranes sorrounding many of the globules rupture during freezing. Fat destabilization is influenced by the amount of fat, emulsifier and stabilizer, the milk protein stability as affected by pretreatment, the mineral salt balance in the mix, freezing time (batch freezers), and extrusion temperature and throughput (continuous freezer). At freezer temperature, the fat globules should exist in a partially solidified state, containing liquid and crystalline fractions in an optimum ratio. If clumping is to occur, a certain amount of the liquid fat is necessay, and this is squeezed out during the mechanical treatment in the freezer, at low temperature. The air cells are stabilized by a chain of fat globules cemented together by viscous liquid fat. Partial fat destabilization gives poor whipping properties, dryness of extrusion, slow melt-down and resistance to shrinkage.

The Air/Mix Interface

Studies by electron microscopy have shown that many fat globules appear at the air/mix interface in ice cream. The studies suggest that a layer of fatty substances is probably complexed with a layer of denatured protein at this interface. When the ice cream mix is aerated and frozen, the mechanical forces operating at low temperature partially or completely rupture the fat globule membranes around many of the emulsion globules. These hydrophobic oil coated globules are repelled to the air/mix interface. If the liquid fat is very sticky, chains of fat globules will tend to form around the air cells, as observed by Arbuckle and Alsafar and Wood. Such an oil layer acts as a foam depressant, and the affected air cells collapse causing coalescence of the stripped oil globules. Surface active substances such as milk proteins, certain emulsifiers and stabilizer improve the whipping properties and diminish the size of air cell and air cell walls, while fat and other emulsifiers worsen the whipping properties. A dynamic situation exists with regard to the action of an emulsifier. The overrun obtained will depend on the acitivity of the emulsifier at the air/mix interface, relative to its action at the fat/mix interface, inhibiting aeration. As mentioned earlier, addition of emulsifier facilitates partial fat destabilization. The liberation of free fat causes collapsing of some of the air cells. The remaining air cells are stabilized by chains of fat globules cemented together by viscous, liquid fat. This strengthens the lamellae between air cells and explains why partial fat destabilization inhibits shrinkage in ice cream.

Milk Protein Particles

The casein particles in milk have been studied by electron microscopy. The micelles are approximately spherical in shape and range from 40 to 400 nm in diameter. On homogenization, the mean diameter of the casein micelles decrease from 100 to 60 nm, due to the adsorption of casein at the fat/mix interface. Heat treatment salt balance, pH and the time-temperature treatment. Heat treatment also causes denaturation of the why proteins (Webb et al 1978). Proteins become more hydrated at low temperatures, but the degree of affinity of protein for water can be increased through chemical changes in the protein molecules as a result of heat treatment. Arbuckle has shown that the use of high heat treated SMP in ice cream gives more viscous mix with a drier extrusion, better resistance to heat shock and storage and improved melting quality.

The Ice/Mix Interface

Studies by electron microsopy by Berger et al have shown that the ice crystals are pitted with little depressions, which are thought to be due to air expelled by freezing, since water alone gives a similar effect. Calculations show that there are apporximately 10 times more fat globules than are needed to cover both the air/mix and ice/mix interface.

The Continuous Phase

During freezing and hardening, water is withdrawn as ice, and the soluble substances such as lactose, sucrose, etc., become more concentrated. Work of Berger and White has confirmed that sucrose and lactose are predominantly present in a non-crystalline form. However, occasionally few sucrose micro crystals, approximately 0.1 micron in size are observed. Sandiness in ice cream is caused by the lactose crystals greater than 25 microns in size.

Agglomeration of fat during freezing is beneficial, particularly in the case of the continuous freezer. But agglomeration should not be carried too far as to cause churning of the fat as visible butter granules leading to the eventual collapsing of air cells. In practice, most ice cream manufacturers aim at controlled fat destabilization in the freezer. Extruded products like ice cream sandwiches and ice cream in fancy shapes have much higher amount of destabilized fat than normal non-extruded products where a high degree of dryness is not necessary.

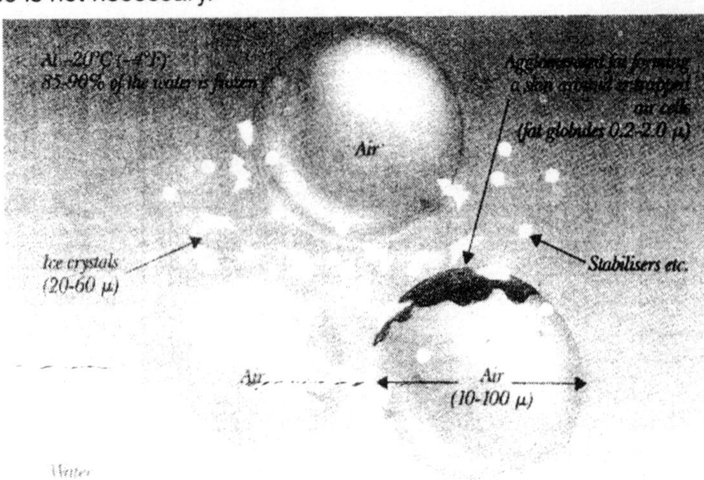

Fig. 5.2 Microstructure of ice cream

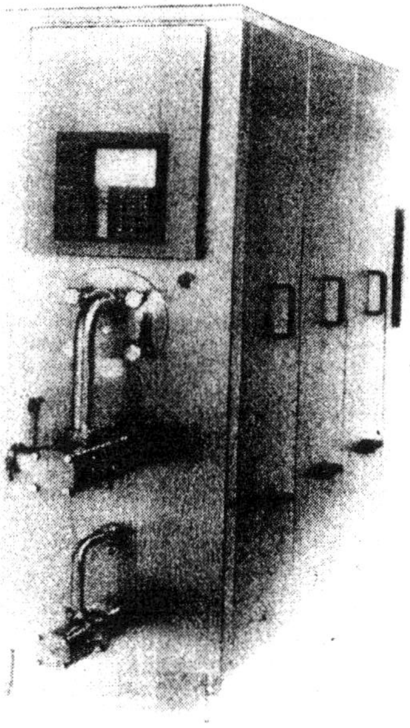

Fig. 5.3 A continuous freezer with automatic control of stop/start, viscosity and overrun

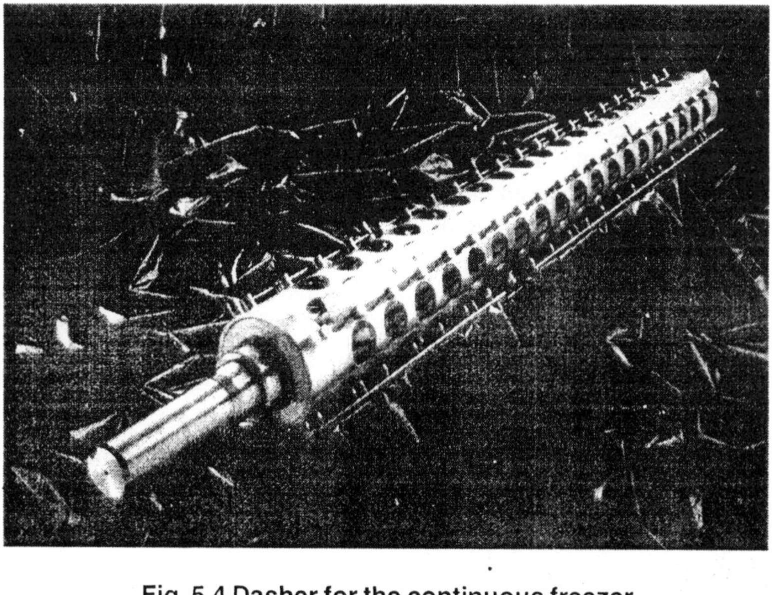

Fig. 5.4 Dasher for the continuous freezer

ICE CREAM FREEZER OPERATION

Principle of the Continuous Freezer

The continuous freezer employs the same fundamental principles of operation as the batch freezer in that the mix is cooled to a plastic state and mixed with a given percentage of air. One major difference, however, is that the machines freeze the ice cream under pressure. This has the advantage of improving the heat transfer; also making possible the proper incorporation of air, even when freezing to low temperatures of -5.5 to -6°C or even down to -9°C with some design. Thus, continuous freezers produce very stiff ice cream at the desired overrun which can be above 100 per cent. Continuous freezers are also equipped with pumps which positively control the percentage of air the mix and which supply the pressure necessary to force the stiff ice cream into containers. An example of currently used continuous freezer is shown in Fig 5.3 (Plate 2) and its dasher in Fig. 5.4 (Plate 3).

Some important advantages of the continuous freezer are:

(i) Less stabilizer is needed because a larger amount of the ice crystal can be formed in the freezer instead of the hardening room where slow freezing gives larger crystals.

(ii) A shorter ageing period is possible because air can be incorporated into mix having lower viscosity.

(iii) Incorporation of air is less dependent upon the character of the mix.

(iv) Ice cream with smoother texture is obtained because the ice crystals are much smaller and more uniformly small, and fewer larger ice crystals are formed in the hardening room.

(v) Since rapid freezing favours small lactose crystal, tendency towards sandiness is greatly reduced.

(vi) There is less variation in volume between packages, especially when small packages are filled.

(vii) Less flavouring material is needed because the smaller ice crystals melt more rapidly in the mouth, and make the flavour slightly more pronounced.

(viii) Continuous freezing facilitates preparation of specialities ice cream having centre moulds, special shapes, variegated ice cream, etc.

(ix) There is less opportunity for contamination when filling packages and specialities.

(x) The volume of ice cream frozen per man-hour of labour is increased, especially when filling packages of the one litre or four-litre size.

Some disadvantages of continuous freezers are given below:

(i) The parts of the machine fit with small clearances and this demands great care and caution while handling.

(ii) Operator and mechanics must have special experience and skill in order to avoid possible damage to the equipment and operation difficulties.

(iii) It is somewhat easy to obtain excessive overrun.

(iv) There is a greater tendency for ice cream to shrink in volume after hardening.

(v) Initial cost of the equipment is high.

Refrigeration System

The refrigeration system for batch and continuous freezers is given below.

Batch Freezer

The freezing cylinder of the batch freezer is made of a liner, usually of nickel silver or stainless, pressed inside a steel or copper tube which forms the inside wall of the cooling jacket. This jacket, if the machine is for brine cooling is constructed of copper with narrow passageways, to make the brine travel a long distance around the cylinder so that it will have a high velocity and provide good heat transfer. The outside is insulated with cork and covered with an air tight metal housing.

If the machine is to be cooled by direct expansion of a refrigerant such as ammonia, the outer jacket is usually built of heavy steel, properly insulated, and with suitable connections. A connection has to be made at the bottom for liquid ammonia inlet and for oil draining, and a connection at the top carries off the vapour from the refrigerant. Many of the modern direct expansion freezers use the flooded principle on account of its greater efficiency and ease of control. This necessitates the so-called ammonia control with liquid accumulator.

In one system, the cold liquid ammonia is dropped from the accumulator into the freezer jacket by opening a valve when the freezing is to start; when the freezing is finished and it is desired to whip, then the valve is closed, and the gas forming in the jacket collects at the top of the ammonia space and blows the liquid refrigerant out at the bottom and up into the accumulator, thus stopping the freezing, as the liquid is no longer in contract with the freezing stops very quickly after the closing of the valve. The valve must be gas tight when closed, otherwise their freezer will not empty itself of ammonia when the valve is closed, and the freezer will continue to freeze, causing poor whipping and lack of overrun.

Continuous Freezer

The refrigeration system of a typical continuous freezer is given in Fig. 5.5. It is based on the principle of "full flooded evaporator." This means that the liquid ammonia level in the system is kept at a higher level than the freezing cylinder. The fact that the liquid level is higher than the level of the freezing cylinder ensures a brisk circulation in the system. The circulation effect comes come from the fact that the specific gravity of ammonia in the upward pipe of the freezing cylinder (gas and liquid) is much lower than the specific gravity of the ammonia (pure liquid) in the downward leg of the system. A float which controls the level of ammonia by opening and closing the liquid supply valve is a standard soleniod valve. Due to the flash gas created during the expansion of the liquid valve, the liquid separator is always kept empty during productiốn, since the flash gas will push down the liquid through the bottom outlet of the liquid separator. The valve connected to the evacuation line remain closed.

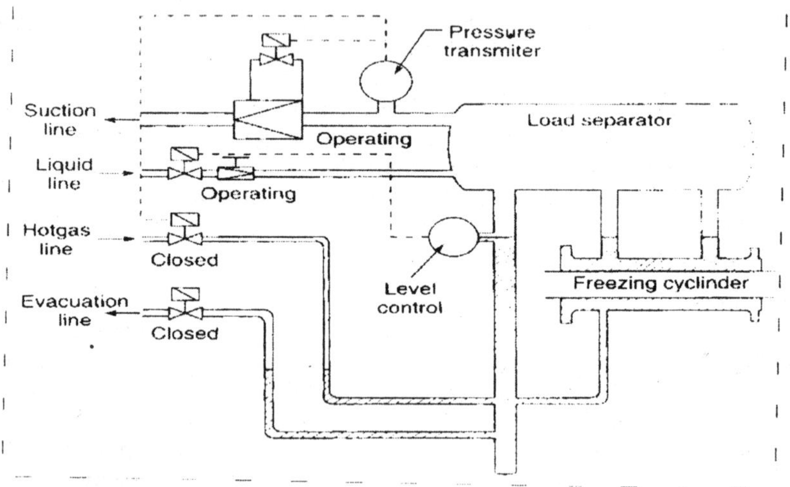

Fig. 5.5 Diagram of the refrigeration system of a continuous freezer

For instant stopping of the machine, the liquid supply is cut off and valve connected to the evacuation line is opened. As a result, the receiving tank is by passed and the ammonia vapour, which builds up in the freezing cylinder, forces the liquid ammonia out of the cylinder, thus ensuring that the freezing is immediately terminated.

The proper operation of a continuous ice cream freezer depends largely on the proper installation of the refrigeration system. Provisionmust be made for direct connection to the suction lines. It is also essential to remove oil from the system. A special hot gas line is also provided to quickly clean the freezer jacked of oil and ammonia. The operator can also use this line for bringing hot gas to the machine for defrosting of the freezing cylinder.

The operation of the continuous freezer demands care and management on the part of the operator. Following are the chief requisites:

(i) Keep the ammonia jacket clean and free from water, oil and non-volatile ammonia fractions. Check oil trap oil, water, etc. Drain as needed.

(ii) Keep the scraper blades sharp and straight.

(iii) Keep the mix pumps in proper working condition. Check pump motor for proper lubrication, and tightness of pulley belts.

(iv) Make sure that there is plentiful supply of ammonia at the freezer as it ensures proper freezing.

(v) Provide a steady suction pressure at all times, a little lower than that at which the freezer must operate to give ice cream of the proper temperature. Any rise in the suction pressure will soon make itself evident by the softness of the ice cream on being discharged.

The capacity of freezer is reduced due to the following reason:

(i) The scraper blades are not maintained in a proper condition. The blades must be handled with extreme care in oder to avoid scratches and burrs. Blades in poor condition can adversely affect the texture of the ice cream and cause insufficient overrun. Besides they will also cause a reduction of the capacity of the freezer as it will not renew surface films of ice cream efficiently inside the cylinder.

(ii) The oil is not removed completely from the freezer.

(iii) There is very little ammonia in the space around the freezing cylinder as the float valve is not working satisfactorily.

Automatic Ingredient Feeder

The automatic ingredient feeder (Fig. 5.6) is designed for injecting fruit or

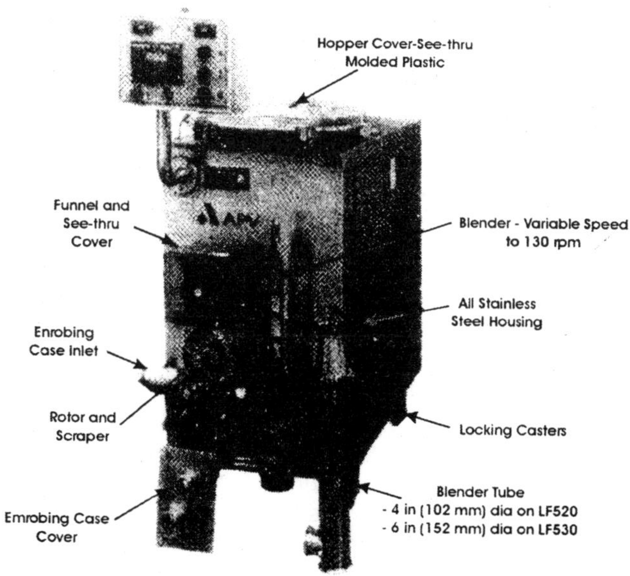

Fig. 5.6 Automatic ingredient feeder

nuts continuously into the finished ice cream by weight rather than volume. The unit is designed to accept an input signal from an ice cream freezer so that it can change ingredient feed rates (auger speed gets adjusted) as the freezer speed changes. A low level gives a signal that it is time for filling. This reduces the amount of operator attention required, and helps prevent product from passing through without the ingredient being added. The alarm signal can also be used automatic refilling from a supply source.

The Batch Freezer

The batch freezer is mostly used in small plants and in large for specials, sherbets and ices. The dasher is an important part of every batch freezer. It fits into the freezing chamber and can be easily removed for cleaning. The dasher consists of two parts, the scraper blades and the beater to perform the following functions:

(i) aids in the transmission of refrigeration by keeping the mix in continuous contact with freezer walls;

(ii) scrapes the freezer walls free from ice crystals;

(iii) beats in air, and

(iv) pushes the mix continuously forward which is essential in unloading the freezer. It is important to have the dasher in proper alignment with the sharp blades.

The temperature of the refrigerant varies from -23 to -29^0 C in order to obtain a rapid formation of ice crystals. This rapid formation results in small ice crystals and a smoother ice cream. The freezing should be slow enough to permit the whipping of air since this influences the body and texture of the ice cream. The most desirable refrigerant temperature to use depends upon:

(i) the freezing point of the mix which is dependent upon the amount of sugar, MSNF and the kind of flavouring material used;

(ii) the sharpness of scraper blades,

(iii) the amount of refrigerant available, and

(iv) the efficiency of the freezer, i.e., the rate of heat transfer of the walls.

In the freezer having direct expansion system, the freezing chamber is surrounded by liquid ammonia or other refrigerant. Ammonia is the most common refrigerant. It is cheaper than the other refrigerants as it enables to save power and equipment, and increases refrigeration capacity.

Freezing Procedure for Batch Freezers

The first step in the freezing procedure is to prepare the freezer. Its parts should be inspected to be sure they are clean and dry, and then assembled in accordance with the manufacturer's instructions. The operator's hands should be clean, and care taken to avoid contact of the freezer with human hands. When the freezer is assembled, the machine is sanitized by running hot water or cold solution of a chemical sanitizing agent through the machine. This also serves the purpose of testing leaks and faulty operating condition. While sanitizing, the dasher should not be turned more than a few revolutions, thus avoiding excessive wear. If hot water is used, it must be at least 85^{0}C to obtain the desired sanitizing effect. This should be followed by a cold water rinse to cool the freezer. When a chemical sanitizing agent is used, complete draining is essential.

After the freezer has been properly prepared, the measured amount of mix, flavouring and colour are added. It is always desirable to have the temperature of the mix below 5^{0}C when it goes into the freezer. The total volume of the mix, flavour and colour should be about half the total capacity of the freezing chamber.

The flavouring and colouring materials must be added so as to be uniformly distributed, but the actual moment or order of adding them can be varied. Special precautions should be observed while adding nuts, acid fruits, etc., and these should be added only after some ice crystal have formed. Acid fruits will coagulate the mix if they are added before the ice crystals are formed. Cookies, nuts and candies are less likely to dissolve if added late, and fruits will remain in larger pieces. Such materials, therefore, should be added as late as possible and still given enough time to have them uniformly distributed. It is best to determine the exact time for each machine, since some machines are more efficient in carrying the nuts back into the freezer. When using a continuous freezer, the solid materials (nuts, fruits, etc.) must be added as the ice cream is being discharged from the freezing chamber, and all the liquid material including fruits juices must be added to mix before it passes into the freezing chamber.

After the mix is put into the freezer, the dasher is started and the refrigerant turned on to the freezing chamber. To avoid rapid and wearing of the scraper blades, the dasher must never be operated when there is no mix in the freezer. The refrigerant must never be turned on unless the dasher is in motion because a small amount of water can freeze and cause the dasher to adhere firmly to the wall of the freezer and this can cause the dasher to be bent or twisted when attempting to start the machine.

It is important to know the correct time to shut off the refrigerant. At this time, only a small part of the water in the mix is frozen giving it a certain lustre and consistency which the operator must learn to recognize. If the refrigerant is shut off too soon it will result in

(i) longer time to obtain overrun;

(ii) low overrun as the softer condition will repel overrun, and

(iii) a soft ice cream having a tendency for coarse texture, since the ice crystals formed slowly in the hardening room will be larger.

When the refrigerant is not shut off immediately, the mix will be hard resulting in

(i) difficulty in obtaining overrun;

(ii) stiff ice cream which repels overrun, and

(iii) a smooth rice cream provided it does not become soft while obtaining overrun.

After the refrigerant is shut off, the machine continues to operate, incorporating air and freezing more of the mix until the product attains both desired overrun and the desired consistency. Then the product is drawn from the freezer. Since air is incorporated during the freezing process and by the whipping action of the dasher, the operator must adjust the refrigerant to allow the right amount of time for whipping. The time will vary with the composition of the mix, the design of the freezer, the rate of cooling or freezing, and the temperature, consistency, etc., in freezer. While there is some loss of air it can be said that up to a certain point air is being continually whipped into the ice cream mix. However, after that point is reached, it loses air faster than it gains it, if the whipping is carried on incessantly. Therefore, the operator must adjust the refrigerant so that the ice cream can be drawn the moment he has obtained the desired overrun and consistency. When the ice cream is drawn from the freezer, it should have a ribbon-like consistency and stiff enough to hold its shape, and yet soft enough to "settle" or lose its shape within a minute or two.

Filling the Containers

The container or packaged into which the ice cream is drawn should be cooled sufficiently to prevent the melting of the ice cream. When such melting around the edges occur, ice cream will be frozen again later in the hardening room and the ice crystal formed will be large, giving a coarse and icy condition at the edge of package. This melting will cause loss of overrun. If the ice cream is too stiff when drawn, air pocket may form leaving the container partly filled.

The freezer should be emptied as rapidly as possible to minimize the variations in overrun in the packages. The overrun can vary from 70 to 100%. The extent of variation depends on the length of time required for filling each container. While the ice cream is being drawn from the freezer, it gradually becomes softer and should not be "drained" out when it gets too soft. The small amount left in the freezer should be taken into the next batch, which can follow immediately without stopping the dasher. However, if the next batch is of a different flavour or colour, i.e., one which will not cover up or blend with the previous batch, it is necessary to take out the dasher and clean the freezer. This is especially true of nut and fruit ice cream, pieces of nuts and fruit cannot be removed from the dasher without taking the freezer apart, but, if left in the freezer, they will appear in the next batch of ice cream.

HOW TO OBTAIN AND CONTROL OVERRUN

Overrun is defined as the volume of ice cream obtained in excess of the volume of the mix. It is usually expressed as "per cent overrun". Mathematically, it is expressed as-

$$\% \text{ Overrun} = \frac{\text{Volume ice cream - Volume of mix}}{\text{Volume of mix.}} \times 100$$

This formula is useful in computing the average overrun of a day's freezing, or the average overrun obtained in freezing a number of freezer batches. Where the amount to air is to be measured while the product is still in the freezer, it is best done on the basis of comparative weights of the mix and the ice cream rather than on the basis of volumes. Since the weight per unit volume is inversely proportional to the amount of air incorporated, the formula becoms-

$$\% \text{ Overrun} = \frac{\text{Wt. of mix - Wt. of same volume of ice cream}}{\text{Wt. of same volume of ice cream}} \times 100$$

The overrun is important because of the following reasons:

(i) Its direct relation to yield and profit.

(ii) Its effects on body, texture, and palatability.

If the ice cream is frozen with no air or only limited amount of air, it would be excessively cold in the mouth, heavy and soggy in body, coarse in texture and unpalatable. If the amount of air incorporated is too low, the product will be heavy and soggy in body. But the amount is excessive, the product will be frothy and snowy in the texture.

The amount of air which should be incorporated depends upon the composition of the mix and the processing method employed. Generally, an overrun of two to three times the percentage of total solids content of 40% justifies an overrun as high as 100%.

Following factors are considered for determining the amount of overrun:

(i) Total solids content of the ice cream. Higher total solids permit the use of a higher overrun.

(ii) Legal regulations in the market area.

(iii) Selling price of the ice cream.

(iv) Fruit and nut ice cream require a lower overrun than plain ice cream in order to obtain an equally desirable body and texture.

(v) Type of package; so called "bulk" packages which are sold for dipping usually contain 90 to 100% overrun, while packages of the carry home type (not dipped before reaching the consumer) are most satisfactory, if they contain 70-80% overrun. Dipping refers to the transfer of ice cream from bulk package into a new container. Thus, the volume of ice cream after dipping is less than the volume before dipping. This decrease in volume is due to air being expelled from the ice cream with a corresponding loss in overrun. Thus, bulk packages have higher overrun to compensate for the loss due to dipping.

The ability to obtain overrun in the freezer depends partly on the concentration and type of ingredients in the mix and on the freezing itself. Sharpness of the scraper blades, speed of the dasher, volume of refrigerant passing over the freezing chamber and temperature of the refrigerant are important to produce rapid freezing and favour overrun. The stiffness of the product at the time refrigerant is shut off and the fullness of the freezer are two of the most important factors and, perhaps, the two most likely to fluctuate under careless operation.

On the basis of detailed studies on overrun, England (1968) concluded following:

The factors which depress overrun include fat content, MSNF content, corn syrup (solids) content, fruits, cocoa and chocolate, excessive calcium salts, increased amount of stabilizer, poor homogenization, amount of mix in the batch freezer, insufficient refrigeration, dull freezer blades, mix too warm and freezing the mix too stiff. For continuous freezers, low overrun is due to the slow freezer speed, slow pump speed, worn out pumps or pumps which need adjustment and fruit feeder operation.

The factors which increase overrun are; whey solids, egg yolks, solids caseinate, emulsifiers, certain stabilizers and salts and pasteurization of mix at a higher temperature. Factors for continuous freezers include air leaks in the mix intake line, erratic spring in the air intake valve, height of the flavour taken, volume of mix in the flavour tank, distance of the flavour tank from the freezer and worn out second stage air pump.

The overrun should be maintained as constant as possible. A variation of 10% in overrun represents a sizeable difference in profit to the manufacturer. The overrun range for different products is shown in Table 5.3.

Table 5.3 Percentage Overrun for Different Products

Product	Overrun (%)
Ice cream (packaged)	70-80
Ice cream (bulk)	90-100
Sherbet	35-45
Ice	25-35
Soft ice cream	40-60
Ice milk	80-100
Milk shake	50-80

CALCULATING PERCENTAGE OF OVERRUN

There are two fundamental methods of calculating percentage overrun; one is by volume and the other weight.

(i) Calculation by volume:

$$\frac{\text{Volume of ice cream - volume of mix}}{\text{Volume of mix}} \times 100$$

= Per cent overrun

When 100 gallons of mix are frozen into 190 gallons of ice cream, then

$$\frac{\text{190 gallon ice cream - 100 gallon mix}}{\text{100 gallon mix}} \times 100$$

= 90% overrun.

Assume the mix weighs 4.9 kg per gallon, then 100 gallon mix will weigh 490 kg, and 190 gallon of ice cream will also weigh 490 kg. What should be the overrun? Calculation by weight:

$$\frac{\text{Wt. per unit vol. of mix - Wt. per unit vol. of ice cream}}{\text{Wt. per unit volume of ice cream}} \times 100$$

= per cent overrun

Wt. per unit volume of ice cream = $\frac{490}{190}$= 2.58 kg.

Using the gallon as the volume and 4.9 kg and 2.58 kg as the respective weights then,

$$\frac{4.9 - 2.58}{2.58} \times 100 = 90\% \text{ overrun}$$

Practical control of overrun demands frequent weighing of filled packages like cups, carry-home packets and bulk packages. Thus, it becomes necessary to determine the weight of ice cream and cup at desired overrun.

For example, for a desired overrun of 90% with the net weight of a cup of mix at 125 g and the empty cup weight at 3 g, then-

$$\left[\frac{\text{Net wt. of cup of mix}}{\text{100 + Overrun desired}} \times 100\right] + \text{Wt. of empty cup}$$

= Wt. of ice cream and cup at desired overrun.

Thus-

$$= \frac{125}{100 + 90} \times 100 + 3g$$

$$= \frac{125}{190} \times 100 + 3g$$

= 68.78 g of ice cream and cup at 80% overrun.

Calculation of Overrun on Fruit Ice Cream

Exaple: If 15 litres of pineapple are added to 100 litres of the mix and 200 litres of ice cream are produced, what is the overrun on the fruit ice cream?

1. Ignoring the fruit in the mix

$$\frac{200-100}{100} \times 100 = 100\% \text{ overrun}$$

2. Considering the fruit as a part of the mix, there are 115 litres of the flavoured mix.

$$\frac{200-115}{115} \times 100 = 73.9\% \text{ apparent overrun}$$

3. Actual overrun on the mix

$$\frac{200-(100+15)}{100} \times 100 = 85\%$$

considering no overrun on the fruit.

Example: It is desired to add 20 litres of strawberries to each 100 litres of the mix. To what overrun should the ice cream be frozen so that 80% overrun is obtained on the mix?

The per cent apparent overrun should be calculated as follows:

$$\frac{\text{Vol. of mix}}{\text{Vol. of mix + Vol. of fruit}} \times \text{actual mix overrun desired}$$

= apparent overrun

$$= \frac{100}{100+20} \times 80\% \text{ desired mix overrun}$$

= 66.6% apparent overrun

At 66.6% apparent overrun, each litre of the flavoured mix yields 1.66 litres of fruits ice cream.

120 litre flavoured mix x 1.66 = 199.9 fruit ice cream.

Proof: 100 litre mix x 80% overrun 180 litre ice cream.

180 litre ice cream + 20 litre fruit = 200 litre fruit ice cream.

Modifications when Calculating Percentage Overrun by Volume

1. Usefull for plain ice cream:

$$\frac{\text{Vol. of ice cream - Vol. of mix}}{\text{Vol. of mix}} \times 100 = \% \text{ overrun}$$

For example : When 50 litres of mix are frozen to make 95 litres of ice cream, then

$$\frac{95 - 50}{50} \times 100 = 90\% \text{ overrun}$$

2. For evaluating "plant overrun" for cost studies.

$$\frac{\text{Vol. of ice cream - (Vol. of mix + Vol. of flavour)}}{\text{Vol. of mix + Vol. of flavour}} \times 100 = \% \text{ overrun}$$

For example: When 80 litres of unflavoured mix is coloured and flavoured with 20 litres of mango pulp and frozen tc 190 litres of ice cream, then

$$= \frac{190 - (80 + 20)}{80 + 20} \times 100 = \frac{90}{100} \times 100$$

$$= 90\% \text{ overrun}$$

3. Useful in determinig the overrun on the plain mix used in making ice cream-

$$\frac{\text{Vol. of ice cream - (Vol. of mix + Vol. of flavour)}}{\text{Vol. of mix}} \times 100$$

$$= \% \text{ overrun}$$

For example: When 85 litres of unflavoured (plain) mix is coloured and flavoured with 15 litres of banana pulp and frozen to 190 litres of ice cream, then

$$\frac{190 - (85 + 15)}{85} \times 100$$

$$= \frac{90}{85} \times 100 = 105.9\% \text{ overrun}$$

Modifications when Calculating Percentage Overrun by Weight

1. For plain ice cream-

$$\frac{\text{Wt. of 1 litre of mix - Wt. of 1 litre ice cream}}{\text{Wt. of 1 litre ice cream}} \times 100 = \% \text{ overrun}$$

2. Wt. of 1 litre of flavoured mix

$$\frac{\text{(plain mix + colour and flavour) - Wt. of 1 litre ice cream}}{\text{Wt. of 1 litre ice cream}} \times 100 = \% \text{ overrun}$$

For example, when the flavoured and coloured mix weighing 1.1 kg per litre is frozen into ice cream, weighing 0.6 kg per litre, then-

$$\frac{1.1 - 0.6}{0.6} \times 100 = 83.3\% \text{ overrun.}$$

3. The overrun on the plain mix used in making ice cream is calculated as follows:

$$\frac{\text{Wt. / litre flavoured mix-Wt./ litre ice cream}}{\text{Wt./litre ice cream}} \times \frac{\text{Vol. plain mix + Vol. flavour}}{\text{Vol. plain mix}} \times 100$$

$$= \%\text{ overrun}$$

Example: 85 litres of plain mix is flavoured and coloured with 15 litres of strawberry pulp to give a flavoured mix weighing 1.09 kg per litre. When this is frozen into ice cream weighing 0.60 kg litre, then-

$$\frac{1.09 - 0.60}{0.60} \times \frac{85 + 15}{85} \times 100 = 96.1\% \text{ overrun}$$

Calculating the Desired Overrun for Bulky Flavour Ice Cream

The overrun at which to draw ice cream has been discussed earlier. The discussion has emphasized the importance of the right amount of incorporated air in proportion to the amount of plain mix and the solids in the mix. When the most desirable overrun has been established for plain ice cream can be calculated.

Bulky flavour ice cream having high overrun, weak and fluffy body and texture characteristics: This can be overcome by having a sufficiently low overrun to obtain the same ratio of incorporated air to plain mix, as is obtained in plain ice cream. The desired overrun is calculated as follows:

$$\%\text{ overrun for bulky ice cream}$$

$$= \frac{\%\text{ overrun used for plain ice cream} \times \text{litres of plain mix} \times 100}{\text{litres of flavoured mix}}$$

Example: Calculate the overrun for a bulky flavour ice cream having 3 litres of colouring and flavouring material and 17 litres of the, plain mix, if 95% is the desired overrun for plain vanilla ice cream.

Solution: 17 litres + 3 litres = 20 litres of flavoured mix.

Substituting values in the formula—

$$0.95 \times \frac{17}{20} \times 100 = 80.7\% \text{ overrun}$$

Weight Per Package of Plain Ice Cream

Frequently it is necessary to know the correct weight of a package of ice cream when the ice cream contains the desired amount of overrun. This is obtained by adding the weight of the empty package to the calculated weight of ice cream per package. The formula assumed a 1 litre package by any other size of package may be substituted.

$$\frac{\text{Wt. of 1 litre of mix}}{1.0 + \text{desired \% overrun}} = \text{Wt. of ice cream per litre}$$

Example: The mix weighs 1.1 kg per litre and the desired overrun is 90%. Calculate the weight of a 1 litre package which weighs 0.03 kg when empty.

Using the above formula, we get-

$$\frac{1.1}{1.0 + 0.90} = \frac{1.1}{1.9} = 0.58 \text{ kg ice cream per litre}$$

Gross weight of the full package

$$= 0.58 + 0.03 \text{ kg} = 0.61 \text{kg}$$

Weight Per Package of Bulky Flavour Ice Cream

When making bulky flavour ice cream, such as fruit and nut, it is desirable to have a lower overrun to ensure the same proportion of air to plain mix as is used in the vanilla or plain ice cream. The desired weight of bulk-flavour ice cream is calculated as follows:

$$\frac{\text{Wt. of 1 litre of flavoured mix}}{\text{x Vol. of plain mix}}$$

$$1.0 + (\text{\% desired overrun}) \quad \text{x Vol. of flavoured mix}$$

$$= \text{wt. per litre of ice cream}$$

Example: the overrun used on plain ice cream is 90%. Butterscotch ice cream is to be made using 2.5 litres (4.5 kg) of colouring and flavouring material to every 17.5 litres of plain mix (1.1 kg per litre). What should be the weight of a 1 litre package of the finished butterscotch ice cream if the empty package weighs 0.03 kg?

First find the weight of 1 litre of the flavoured mix:

2.5 litres flavoured mix = 4.5 kg

17.5 litres of plain mix = 19.25 kg

Thus, 20 litres of the flavoured mix = 4.5 + 19.25 kg = 23.75 kg

Therefore, wt of 1 litre of the flavoured mix $= \frac{23.75}{20}$ kg = 1.187 kg

$$\frac{\text{Vol. of plain mix}}{\text{Vol. of flavoured mix}} = \frac{17.5 \text{ litres}}{20 \text{ litres}}$$

Using the above formula and substituting:

$$\frac{1.187}{1.0 + (0.90) \times \dfrac{(17.5)}{20}}$$

$$= \frac{1.187}{1.7875} = 0.664 \text{ kg.}$$

= wt of 1 litre of ice cream

The wt. of empty 1 litre package	= 0.03 kg
finished ice cream	= 0.664 kg
Total wt of package	= ͜.694 kg

CLEANING THE FREEZER

The cleaning and sterilization of freezers pose certain special problems not encountered in other item of equipment, and as far as possible the instructions furnished by the manufacturer with each freezing machine should be followed. For details on cleaning and sanitation of freezers, refer to Chapter 15, "Hygiene and Sanitation".

FRUIT ICE CREAM

The ice cream trade in one of the chief markets for fresh, frozen and canned fruits. Also available are fruit flavours which are

(i) extracts prepared from the fruit;

(ii) artificial compounds; and

(iii) true extract, fortified artificially.

Although these flavours are used to supplement the fruits in cases where it is necessary to avoid excessive amounts of fruit, they are quite inferior to the flavour obtained from the fruit itself and do not supply the desired fruit pulp.

Since fruit ice cream contains a higher percentage of sugar than plain ice cream it should be drawn from the freezer at about 0.6°C colder. A drawing of -5°C (23°F) for the batch freezer or -6.6 (20°F) for the continuous freezer is satisfactory under most conditions.

Fresh Fruit

Fresh fruit ice cream have a special sales appeal. The fruit should be washed and hulled or peeled and then mixed sugar in the ratio of 2-7 kg fruit to 1 kg sugar, and held for about 12-24 hr before using. During this ageing period a large part of the juice and flavour of the fruit will combine with the sugar, by osmotic action, to form a fruit syrup. This syrup will impart to the ice cream the full flavour of the fruit much more effectively than would the fresh fruit used immediately. Seedy fruits such as raspberries should be pureed so that about 3/4 of the seeds are removed. Peaches should be sliced, strawberries need not be mashed or sliced, as it does not enhance their flavouring ability.

Fresh fruit and fresh frozen fruit are the most desirable flavouring materials. The aged fruit-sugar mixture used at the rate of 15-20% produces good results with many fruits. Fruits can be used whole, crushed, sliced, diced, pureed (coarse, medium or fine) or used as juice. A coarse texture results when whole or large slices of fruits are used. A greater amount of fruit is often required to obtain the desired flavour when a puree is used. From the standpoint of fruit distribution, appearance and desired flavour and texture characteristics, diced fruit or coarse pureed fruit is preferred. A combination of fruit puree and sliced fruit is highly desirable.

Fresh or frozen packs are preferable for fruits such as strawberries whose destinctive flavour is easily impaired by heating. Fruits like pineapple or cherries, whose flavours are relatively stable or improved by heating, are usually preserved by heat, that is canned. Peaches are canned or frozen. Usually raspberries are used in the frozen form though they withstand heating much better than strawberries.

The amount of fruit required to impart the desired flavour varies with the characteristic intensity of the flavour. This amount varies from 10-25% of the weight of the finished product. When fruits are expensive, less fruit is often used, and enough true fruit extract added to produce a flavour approximately the same as the natural fruit flavour. A little artificial colour is added to give the delicate tints associated with these fruits.

Fruit Concentrates and Essences

Concentrated fruits juice and essences are also used in ice cream and related products. The most desirable flavour is influenced by the composition of ice cream mix, the sugar-acid ratio and the amount of flavouring material. Fruit concentrates and essences have been found to be valuable products in improving fruit ice cream and sherbet flavours, either when used to supplement the use of fruit or when used as the sole source of flavour.

Candied and Glaced Fruits

Candied or glaced fruits such as cherries, pineapple and such candied fruit peels as the orange, lemon and grapefruits are very good flavouring materials. They are used chiefly in rich types of ice cream like mousses, aufaits and puddings. They may also be used as decorative material for fancy moulded ice cream, sherbets and ices.

Dried Fruits

Dried fruits like almond, pistachio, walnut, cashewnut, apricots, figs, dates and raisins make delicious ice creams. Dates, figs and raisins have long been used in frozen puddings.

Freeze Dried Fruits

Lazer studied the use of freeze dried strawberries, peaches and bananas. an acceptable flavour was obtained only with the strawberries. However, in all the cases the fruit remained leathery, and soaking in water or 25% sugar solution failed to eradicate the defect.

Procedure and Recipes

strawberry Ice Cream

The quality of strawberry ice cream is influenced by the variety of the fruit and maturity. Berries picked, when fully ripe, give a superior flavour over berries which are picked for shipment. Morever, cold packed berries are superior to canned berries. Also berries frozen with sugar at -29°C give best flavoured and best textured ice cream. The following procedure can be adopted.

The berries should be sliced. A ratio of berries to sugar of 2 to 1 or the use of a 75% sugar solution (2.5 kg of berries to 1.6 kg of syrup) gives good results. It is desirable to freeze the fruit quickly to -13°C and to hold it at -18°C or below to retain the maximum flavour. Before using the berries they should be thawed at a temperature not exceeding 4°C and soaked in their syrup for 12-24 hr to soften them. If strawberries are not soaked in their syrup, the fruits particles in ice cream are likely to be icy, and hence, the product will not have good consumer acceptance. The use of 20% of fruits give a highly desirable flavour and plenty of visible fruit. Arbuckle states that there are two schools of thought with regard to the appearance of strawberry ice cream, One group believes that the berries should be completely broken up so that only the seeds show. The other group believes that the berries should appear in large portions. He believes that both groups can be satisfied and suggests that one-half of the berries be pulped and added to the flavour vat and the remainder be added through the fruit feeder.

Peach Ice Cream

Yellow-fleshed peaches give a greater concentration than white, and since the fruit is firmer in texture, large shreds of the yellow peaches are evident in the ice cream. Peaches do not yield sufficient flavour, and it becomes necessary to add a flavouring extract. The following procedure is recommended by Hening and Dahlberg.

Fresh and repened peaches of a standard variety with a fairly pronounced flavour should be dipped in boiling water, skinned,and ground or very finely sliced. The pulp should be mixed with sugar in the ratio of 5 to 1, and immediately frozen to -18°C or below and held at this temperature. A day before using, the frozen peaches should be held at 4°C to thaw. The colour and peaches should be added to the ice cream mix in the freezer. About 25% of the peaches give a recognizable peach flavour. Peaches do not increase the moisture and sugar content of the ice cream as much as strawberries.

The intensity of the peach flavour is increased by adopting the following:

About 20-30% of the fresh ripe peaches are skinned like an apple, and after grinding the skins finely and adding 20% sugar them for 4 min below the boiling point. The cooked skins with pulp are frozen and used to increase the intensity of the peach flavour by replacing 5-10% of the peaches in the ice cream. The skins must be fine enough to avoid detection in the ice cream.

Addition of one per cent of apricot increase the intensity of the flavour noticeably.

Pineapple Ice Cream

Generally the fruit preserved by heat or canned product is used. About 15% of the fruit gives desirable flavour and texture to ice cream. In order to avoid icy fruit particles in ice cream, the fruit pieces should be dipped in diluted sugar syrup (approx. 35% cane sugar syrup) for 2 hr before use. Use for frozen pineapple in place of the canned product has been shown to give equally satisfactory result.

Other Fruit Ice Cream

Hening and Dahlberg found that a 20-25% quantity produced an excellent flavoured ice cream. The whole berry, which had been packed in 80% cane sugar syrup and stored at -18°C, was mixed into the ice cream after it was drawn from the freezer. It was observed that raspberry ice cream stored at -10°C for six months was of poorer flavour and texture than the same lot stored at -18°C for the same length of time. Mack and Fellers reported that less fruits was necessary to make a desirable flavoured ice cream of raspberries than any other fruit flavour. They used 10-15% of raspberry puree from which 75% of the seeds had been removed. This gave a product having a superior flavour, but somewhat seedy in texture. After reducing the puree to 10% and combining it with a commercial extract, a product of equally good flavour and better texture was produced.

Hening and Dahlberg produced apricot ice cream using a ration of 4 kg of fruit to 1 kg of sugar. The pulp was preheated to 82-88°C and held for 5 min before freezing. When the fruit was mixed into the ice cream after it was drawn from the freezer, the flavour was satisfactory, and the colour and texture acceptable.

Red currant fruit can be used at the rate of 10-15%. The result should be dipped in sugar syrup (approx. 35% cane sugar syrup) for 2 hr before use in order to avoid icy fruit particles in the finished produced. Both fresh and canned red currant can be used.

Litchi can be used in the fresh or frozen form. However, canned litchi is also available in the market. The outer skin of litchi should be peeled, seeds removed, and the fruit broken into small pieces and dipped in 70% cane sugar syrup for 3 to 4 hr before use. Litchi can also be pulped and soaked in sugar syrup in the ratio 4 : 1 to enhance flavour. Addition of 10 to 15% of the fruit gives a product with desirable flavour and body and texture characterisitcs.

Nuts

Nutmeats and nut extracts are extensively used as flavouring in ice cream. Almond, cashew nuts, pistachio, walnuts and raisins are among the most popular. Nutmeats should be sound and clean, and free from rancid flavours. They should be stored in tight containers in a cool place until used. Great care should be taken to ensure that no foreign material such as pieces of wood, pieces of shell and nails from containers gain entry into the mix.

Since nut meats are often high in bacterial count and constitute potential source of pathogenic bacteria, they are subjected to special heat treatment before incorporating them in the mix. The different bactericidal treatment are given below:

(i) The nuts should be soaked for 15 sec in boiling sugar solution (50 per cent concentration) containing one per cent salt and then dried for 2 to 3 min in an oven at 250°C. Instead of sugar solution, the nuts can be dipped in hot butter at 97°C, and then dried in an oven.

(ii) Nuts having 12 to 21 per cent moisture content can be heated in an oven at 72°C for 30 min maintaining the relative humidity of 70%. For nuts of lower moisture content the temperature shall have to be raised to about 84°C.

(iii) The nuts may also be roasted gently in an oven at 70-80°C, either dry or using a little butter.

VARIEGATED ICE CREAM

This type of ice cream becoming increasingly popular and offer unlimited possibilities for flavour combinations. It is prepared by adding approximately 10-15% of a prepared base into the ice cream. Some popular flavours are mango, respberry, strawberry, chocolate. Ripple machines are available which make possible precise control of the amount of ripple desired in package ranging from half litre to 4 litres.

A base can be prepared for fruit flavour syrup by using 55 sugar, 0.6 kg stabilizer (usually pectin in combination with sodium alginate is used as it gives very desirable results) and sufficient water to make 100 kg of base syrup. The fruit syrup is prepared by using 1/3 fruit puree and 2/3 base syrup. The addition of 0.3 to 0.4 kg of citric acid per 100 kg of syrup can be used for fruit flavours.

Chapter 6

Ice Cream Mix Calculations

The dairy products to be used in making the mix of the desired composition are selected on the basis of quality, availability and price. The proportions of these dairy products are computed to have the specified composition.

For preparing ice cream mixes, we ordinarily need the following dairy products:

(i) Cream or other dairy product with a fat content higher than desired in the mix;

(ii) Plain condensed milk, skimmed milk powder or other dairy product with a serum solids content higher than desired in the mix, and

(iii) Milk or skim milk.

For computing the mix, the proportion in which the dairy products are added are calculated so that the desired percentages of fat and serum solids, and the desired total weight are obtained. Various methods of computation - algebraic, graphical and arithmetical are used for this purpose.

In figuring ice cream mixes, at various stages in the calculation, some method is required for figuring the proportions in which two products must be mixed to produce a mixture of the desired intermediate test. For this purpose, the Person Square Method is used.

Pearson Square Method

The Pearson Square Method is used when it is required to mix two substance to make a mixture of a definite test. The two substances to be mixed must be chosen so that one has a higher and the other a lower test than desired in the mixture.

Problem 1: Let us assume that we have 50% cream which we want to standardize down to 25% by adding skim milk. We know that we must mix the 50% cream and the skim milk in equal by weight, because the desired test is halfway between the 0% and 50% of the two substances. In other words, when.

(high testing product) - (desired test) = (desired test) - (low testing substance), we know that we must mix the two in equal parts.

Problem 2: Suppose we wish to reduce the 50% cream down by means of 10%, we know that we need more of the 10% than was required in the case of skim milk. In other words, the closer the low testing substance is to the desired, test the more of the low testing substance will be needed for standardizing. Mathematically, it can be states as follows:. The amounts in which the two substances must be mixed to produce a mixture of a desired intermediate test are inversely proportional to

(i) the difference between the test of the high testing substances and the desired test, and

(ii) the difference between the desired test and the test of the low testing substance.

In the Pearson Square Method, we write the desired test in the centre of a square, and on the left hand corner of the square the two test representing the two substances to be mixed, thus:

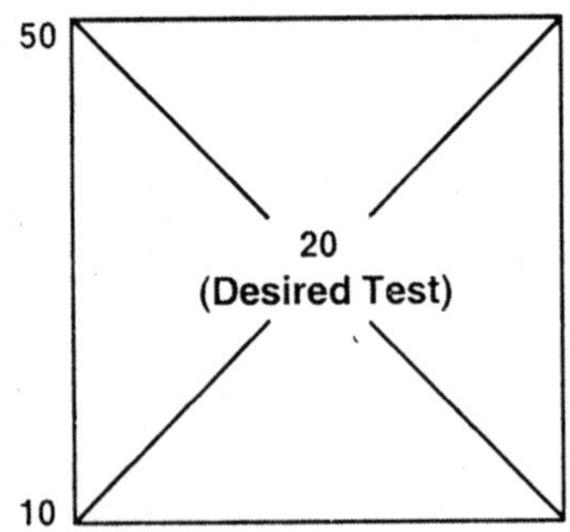

Now by subtracting diagonally across the square, in each cease subtracting the smaller figure from the larger, we get the following result:

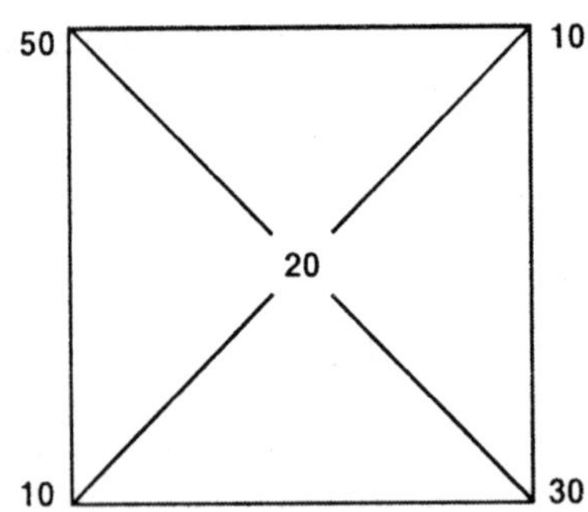

Thus, 10 parts of 50% cream must be mixed with 30 parts of 10% cream to produce a mixture testing 20%.

It can be noted that the difference between the high test and the desired test by this means is placed opposite the low testing substance across the page. Similarly, the difference between the desired test and the low test is placed opposite the high testing substance across the page. In other words, substracting diagonally across the square is merely a convenient method of inverting the figures to comply with the fact that the proportions are the inverse of the differences between the tests of the two substances respectively and the desired test.

Thus, from the above illustration it is clear that in order to get a 20% mixture, we must mix in the proportions of 10 kg of 50% cream to 30% of 10% cream.

The proportions can be used in two different ways:

(i) to figure for a definite weight of the finished mixture, or

(ii) to figure how much of one substance must be taken to standardize the definite weight of the other substance.

For clarity, these two calculations are illustrated separately. Let us assume that we wish to make a definite amount of 20% cream, e.g. 500 kg. Thus, we know that the proportions must be— 10 kg of 50% cream and 30 kg of 10% cream giving us 40 kg of 20% cream.

Since 500 kg is 500/40 or 12.5 times as many as the above, we must take the following:

10 x 12.5 = 125 kg of 50% cream, and 30 x 12.5 = 375 kg of 10% cream, giving us 500 kg of 20% cream.

To illustrate the latter, let us assume that we have a definite amount of 50% cream e.g., 200 kg and we want to standardize it down to 20% cream by means of 10% cream. From the square we know that for every 10 kg of 50% cream, we need 30 kg of 10% cream. Since we have 200 kg of 50% cream, which is 200/10 or 20 times as much, we need 30 x 20 = 600 kg of 10% cream to mix with the 200 kg or 50% cream giving us 800 kg of 20% cream.

Thus, while standardizing by the Pearson Square Method, always decide first which of the two above cases you have in your problem.

A Simple Mix

In this case, the amount of milk and cream required is calculated to obtain a certain fat content. The serum solids content is not taken into consideration. While such ice cream mixes are not used commercially at present, the method of calculation is given here so that it may serve as an introduction to the more difficult calculations.

In this calculation and in all the following calculations the figures are given on the basis of a 100 kg mix. This makes the figuring easier and from the 100 kg mix any desired weight can be figured out.

Problem 3: Figure a 100 kg mix to contain 15% sugar, 0.3% stabilizer and 12% fat. Use 40% cream and 7% milk.

Step-1: Tabulate the mix in the following form filling in all the information available. The question marks call attention to the figures to supplied by the calculations.

Table 6.1 Available Ingredients for Problem 3

Weight		Ingredients	Fat	Serum Solids	Total Solids
	15.0	Sugar	0.0	0.0	15.0
15.3					
	0.3	Stabilizer	0.0	0.0	0.3
	?	40% Cream	?	?	?
84.7					
	?	7% Milk	?	?	?
100		Total	12.0	?	?

From the above tabulation it is clear that in 100 kg of mix we need 15 kg of sugar and 0.3 kg of stabilizer. Further, milk and cream must add upto 84.7 kg in order to make a total of 100 kg with the sugar and stabilizer. The exact amount of milk and cream must still be measured.

Step-2: Calculate the amount of fat necessary in the mixture of milk and cream so that it furnishes the required amount of fat.

From the above step it is seen that 84.7 kg of milk and cream mixture must furnish 12 kg of fat. The percentage fat in the mixture must be

$$\frac{12}{84.7} \times 100 = 14.2\% \text{ (Figured to the nearest tenth decimal)}$$

Step-3: Apply the Pearson Square Method to figure the amounts of milk and cream required to make the mixture of the required weight and test.

This means that 25.8 kg of 7% milk, mixed with 7.2 kg of 40% cream will make a mixture testing 14.2%. The weight would be 25.8 + 7.2 = 33.0 kg.

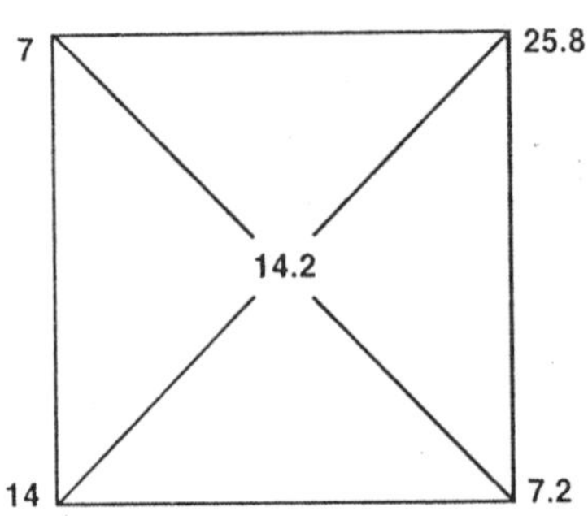

In order to make 84.7 kg, we need to take 84.7/33 times as much of each.

$$\text{Thus, kg of 7\% milk} = 25.8 \times \frac{84.7}{33} = 66.2 \text{ kg}$$

$$\text{and kg of 40\% cream} = 7.2 \times \frac{84.7}{33} = 18.5 \text{ kg}$$

Step-4: Tabulate the finished mix and figure the fat, serum solids and total solids in the mix.

Table 6.2 Completed Proof Sheet for Problem 3

Weight	Ingredients	Fat	Serum Solids	Total Solids
15.0	Sugar	0.0	0.0	15.0
0.3	Stabilizer	0.0	0.0	0.3
18.5	40% Cream *	7.40	1.07	8.47
66.2	7% Milk	4.60	5.96	10.56
100.00	Total	12.00	7.03	34.33

* Serum solids content of 40% cream figured on the assumption that the cream has been separated from milk testing 7% fat and 9% MSNF.

The serum solids content of 40% cream is $\frac{(100 - 40)x9}{(100 - 7)} = 60 \frac{9}{93} x = 5.81\%$

**Serum solids of 7% milk is 9%.

In the above example, it can be noted that the serum solids content of the mix is low, in this case only 7.03%. A better product can be made by increasing the serum solids content. This is accomplished by using an additional ingredient, a condensed milk product or skimmed milk powder. These dairy ingredients should be mixed in the right proportions to obtain both a definite fat and serum solids content. This involve a complex calculation. Such mixes are referred to as "complex mixes" and these are described below:

Complex Mixes

Complex mixes involve problems of the following types:

(i) A mix in which only one of the three dairy products contains fat.

(ii) A mix in which two or all three of the dairy products contains fat.

(iii) A mix in which two or all three of the dairy products contain fat, and one of them contains sugar.

(iv) A mix in which different lots of cream of different tests are to be used.

(v) A mix that is to be made up in a vacuum pan.

1. Where Fat is Furnished by Only One Ingredient

In this case, fat is furnished by one of the three dairy products. Hence, the calculations are quite simple; only a slight modification of the method for figuring a simple mix is necessary.

Problem 4: Figure a 100 kg mix to contain 15% sugar, 0.3% stabilizer, 12% fat and 10% serum solids. Use 40% cream, skim milk, and condensed skim milk containing 35% total solids.

Step-1: Tabulate the mix in the following skeleton form by filling in the information already available.

Table 6.3 Available Ingredients for Problem 4

Weight	Ingredients	Fat	Serum Solids	Total Solids
15.0	Sugar	0.0	0.0	15.0
0.3	Stabilizer	0.0	0.0	0.3
30.0	40% cream	12.0	1.74	13.74
?	Skim milk	0.0	?	?
?	Condensed skim milk	0.0	?	?
100.0	Total	12.0	?	?

In this tabulation, note the following

(i) The amount of sugar and stabilizer is listed on a 100 kg basis.

(ii) Since we must have 12 kg of fat, and since all the fat is to be derived from the 40% cream, the amount of 40% cream can be calculated directly.

$$\frac{12}{40} \times 100 = 30 \text{ kg } 40\% \text{ cream.}$$

(iii) This amount of cream contains 30 x 0.058 = 1.74 kg serum solids. The total amount of serum solids required is 10 kg. Therefore, the remainder 10-1.74 kg = 8.26 kg must be supplied by the skim milk and condensed skim milk.

(iv) The sugar, stabilizer and cream total to 45.3 kg, therefore, the skim milk and condensed skim milk together must weigh.

$$100 - 45.3 = 54.7 \text{ kg}$$

Step-2: Figure the percentage of serum solids necessary in the mixture of skim milk and condensed skim milk so that it may furnish the required balance of serum solids.

$$\frac{8.26}{54.7} \times 100 = 15.1\% \text{ (to nearest tenth)}$$

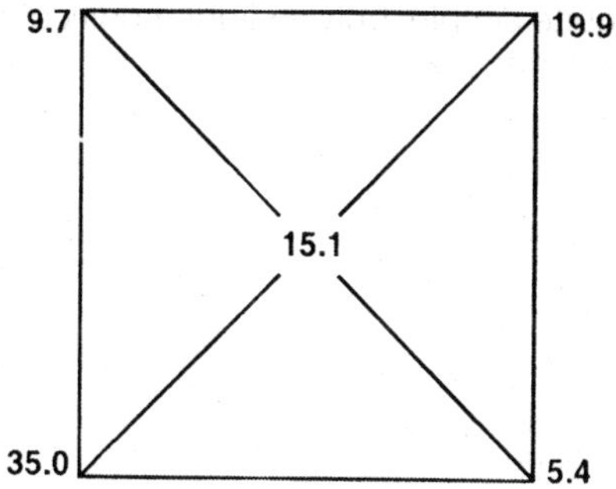

Step-3: Figure the amounts of skim milk and condensed skim milk to make the required weight of mixture of the above test.

19.9 kg of skim milk mixed with 5.4 kg of condensed skim milk will produce 25.3 kg of mixture testing 15.1% serum solids. In order to get 54.7 kg of this mixture we must take

$$\frac{19.9 \times 54.7}{25.3} = 43.0 \text{ kg skim milk}$$

$$\frac{5.4 \times 54.7}{25.3} = 11.7 \text{ kg condensed skim milk}$$

Step-4: Tabulate the mix and figure the percentage of fat, serum solids and total solids.

Table 6.4 completed Proof Sheet for Problem 4

Weight	Ingredients	Fat	Serum Solids	Total Solids
15.0	Sugar	0.0	0.0	15.0
0.3	Stabilizer	0.0	0.0	0.30
30.0	40% cream	12.0	1.74	13.74
43.0	Skim milk*	0.0	4.17	4.17
11.7	Condensed skim milk	0.0	4.09	4.09
100	Total	12.0	10.00	37.30

*Skim milk was assumed to contain 9.7% SNF after separating it from the whole milk testing 7% fat and 9% SNF. For calculations it has been assumed not to contain any fat.

2. A mix in Which Two or All the Three Dairy Products Contain Fat

When more than one of the dairy products to be used in ice cream mix contain fat, the calculations are more complicated. Although several methods of figuring mixes have been proposed, the serum point method has been found to be more comprehensible and is presented here.

Problem 5: Figure a 100 kg mix to contain 15% sugar, 0.3% stabilizer, 12% fat and 11% serum solids. Use 40% cream, 7% whole milk, and plain condensed milk testing 9% fat and 22% serum solids(31% total solids).

Step-1: Tabulate the mix in the following skeleton form, indicating all the information already available.

Table 6.5 Available Ingredients for Problem 5

Weight	Ingredients	Fat	Serum Solids	Total Solids
13.0	Sugar	0.0	0.0	15.0
0.3	Stabilizer	0.0	0.0	0.3
?	40%	?	?	?
?	7% milk	?	?	23.0
?	Cond. milk	?	?	?
100.0	Total	12.0	11.0	38.3

Step-2: Figure the amount of condensed milk to be used.

This is done using the following steps:

(i) Figure what the serum solids content of the mix would be, if only the dairy products of normal serum solids content were used.

(ii) Figure how much of the above would be short of the desired serum solids content.

(iii) Figure how much of the serum solids content of the condensed milk is in excess of normal.

(iv) Using the result under (iii), figure how much of the condensed milk will be required to make the serum solids indicated under (ii).

Calculations and Explanation

Here the term "normal serum" means the natural milk serum unchanged by concentration or dilution, the serum as found in skim milk, whole milk and cream. A normal serum is skim milk; if we take the fat out of the milk or cream, the serum remaining is skim milk. If we take the fat, sugar, stabilizer and egg solids (if used) out of the ice cream mix, the reminder is the serum. If no concentrated dairy product is used in the mix, this serum may be called a normal serum.

In the calculations, we should know the serum solids content of a normal serum (skim milk). The serum solids content of skim milk varies with the fat test of the milk from which it was obtained. The figure that we use for the serum solids content of the skim milk should, therefore, be based on the average fat content of the milk.

In all the calculations in this chapter, a serum solid content of 9.7% has been assumed for skim milk. This figure is based on the average conditions as found by experience in the pooled buffalo milk in Western India.

The calculations are made as follows : 100—(%fat+% sugar+%stalislizer+%etc.) = % of serum in the mix.

In this problem:

100 — (12 + 15 + 0.3) = 72.7% serum in the mix.

In other words, in 100 kg of mix there are 72.7 kg of serum.

(i) If this amount of serum were of normal concentration, it would contain;

72.7 x 0.097 = 7.05 kg of serum solids.

Therefore, if the mix were made from dairy products of normal serum slids content, it would contain 7.05% serum solids.

(ii) To figure how much the above would be short of the desired serum solids (in this case 11%) —

11.0 — 7.05 = 3.95% serum solids short of required %

* Ingredients or constituents added to the mix not containing milk solids, eg. fresh, eggs, cocoa, egg yolk solids, etc.

(iii) To figure the excess of serum solids normal in the condensed milk, proceed as follows:

100 - (% fat + % sugar, if sweetened condensed) = % serum in the condensed milk.

100 — 9.0 = 91% serum in the condensed milk.

If this amount of serum were of normal concentration, the serum solids content of the product would be-

91 x .097 = 8.8%

But since the serum solid content of the condensed milk is 22%, the excess of serum solids above normal is—

22 — 8.8 = 13.2%

(iv) From the shortage of serum solids in the mix (if it were made without condensed milk (in this problem 3.95%) and the excess of serum solids above normal in the condensed milk, compute the amount of condensed milk required —

$$\frac{3.95}{13.2} \times 100 = 29.9 \text{ kg of condensed milk (to the nearest tenth)}$$

Step-3: Enter this amount of condensed milk in the tabulated mix, and figure the amount of milk and cream that must be used to furnish the required additional weight and the required amount of additional fat and serum solids.

Table 6.6

Weight		Ingredients	Fat	Serum Solids	Total Solids
45.5	15.0	Sugar	0.0	0.0	15.0
	0.3	Stabilizer	0.0	0.0	0.3
	29.9	Condensed milk	2.69	6.58	9.27
54.8	?	40% cream	9.31	?	?
	?	7% milk	?	?	?
100.0	Total		12.00	11.0	38.3

From this tabulation it is apparent that after the calculated amount of condensed milk had been added, there remains 54.5 kg weight and 9.28 kg of fat, to be supplied. If these requirements are now furnished by the products of normal serum solids content, then the serum solids content will take care of itself. To furnish 9.31 kg of fat in 54.4 kg, the required product testing-

$$\frac{9.31}{54.8} \times 100 = 17.0\% \text{ fat (figured to the nearest tenth, actually 16.99\%)}$$

To furnish the equivalent of 54.8 kg of 17% cream, the amount 40% cream and 7% milk required, are figured as follows:

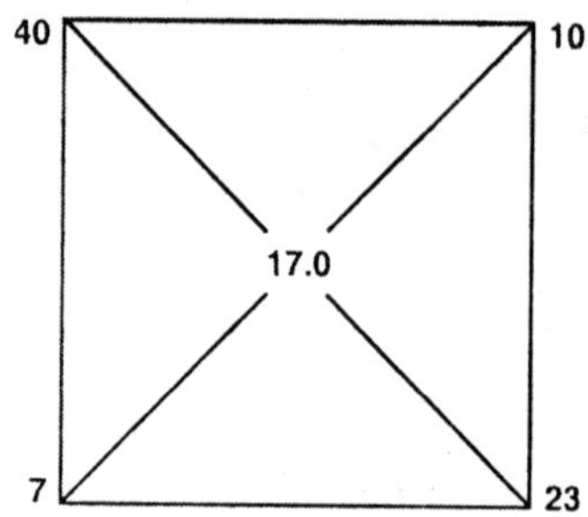

Thus, 10 kg of 40% cream mixed with 23 kg of 17% milk will make 33 kg of mixture of the required test. To get 54.8 kg take —

$$10 \times \frac{54.8}{33} = 16.6 \text{ kg or 40\% cream (to the nearest tenth)}$$

$$23 \times \frac{54.8}{33} = 38.2 \text{ kg or 7\% milk (to the nearest tenth)}$$

Step-4: Enter the above computed amounts of milk and cream in the tabulated mix, and figure the total fat, serum solids and total solids content.

Table 6.7 Completed Proof sheet for Problem 5

Weight	Ingredients	Fat	Serum Solids	Total Solids
15.0	Sugar	0.0	0.0	15.0
0.3	Stabilizer	0.0	0.0	0.3
29.9	Condensed milk	2.69	6.58	9.27
16.6	40% cream	6.64	0.96	7.60
38.2	7% milk	2.67	3.44	6.11
100.0	Total	12.00	10.98	38.28

3. A Mix in which One of the Dairy Products Contains Sugar

In figuring a mix in which sweetened condensed milk is to be used as one of the ingredients, the same principle is used as in the preceding problem. The only difference is that the amount of condensed milk is figured before the amount of sugar to be added can be computed. A sample calculation is given below:

Problem 6 : Figure a mix to contain 15% sugar, 0.3% stabilizer, 12% fat and 11% serum soilds Use 40% cream, 7% milk and sweetened condensed milk containing 9% fat, 22% serum solids and 42.0% sugar.

Step-1 : Tabulate the mix in the following skelton form :

Table 6.8 Available Ingredients for Problem 6

Weight	Ingredients	Fat	Serum Solids	Total Solids
?	Sugar	0.0	0.0	?
0.3	Stabilizer	0.0	0.0	0.3
?	Sweetened Condensed milk	?	?	?
?	40% cream	?	?	?
?	7% milk	?	?	?
100.0	Total	12.0	11.0	38.3

Step-2: Figure the amount of sweetened condensed milk to be used. The logic and procedure of this calculation is the same as under Step 2 of the preceding problem.

(i) The serum solids content of mix, if only dairy product of normal serum solids content were used, would be 100 - (% fat + % sugar + % stabilizer)

= % serum in the mix.

100 - (12 + 15 + 0.3) = 72.7% serum in the mix

72.7 x 0.097 = 7.05 kg of serum solids.

(ii) The shortage of serum solids would be:

$$11 - 7.05 = 3.95\%$$

(iii) The excess of serum solids above normal in the sweetened condensed milk is figured as follows:

100 - (% Fat + % Sugar) = % serum in the sweetened condensed milk

100 - (9 +42) = 49% serum in the sweetened condensed milk.

If this amount of serum were of normal concentration, it would contain

$$49 \times 0.097 = 4.75\% \text{ serum solids.}$$

The sweetened condensed milk contains 22% serum solids; therefore, it contains 22 - 4.75 = 17.25% serum solids in excess of the normal.

(iv) From the results under (ii) and (iii) the amount of sweetened condensed milk required is,

$$\frac{3.95}{17.25} \times 100 = 22.9 \text{ kg of sweetened condensed milk.}$$

Step-3: Enter this amount of sweetened condensed milk in the tabulated mix, and figure the amount of sugar, fat and serum solids contributed by it. Then figure the amout of additional sugar to be added. After this, the additional weight and fat required is figured, and the amount of milk and cream to be used are calculated.

Table 6.9

Weight	Ingredients	Sugar	Fat	Serum Solids	Total Solids
5.4*	Sugar	5.4	0.0	0.0	5.4
0.3	Stabilizer	-	0.0	0.0	0.3
22.9	Sw. cond. milk	9.6	2.06	5.04	?
?	40% cream		?	?	?
?	7% milk		?	?	?
100.0	Total	15.0	12.0	11.0	38.3

*22.9 x 0.42 = 9.6 kg sugar is obtained from sweetened condensed milk. Therefore, 15 - 9.6 = 5.4 kg sugar must be added as such.

After the sugar has been supplied, other ingredients need to be added and in this weight there must be 9.94 kg fat. This additional weight must be supplied by the dairy product of normal serum solids content. Therefore, the additional weight must be of cream and milk and its test must be —

$$\frac{9.94}{71.4} \times 100 = 13.9\% \text{ fat (to the nearest tenth)}$$

The amounts of 40% cream and 7% milk that are equivalent to the above are figured.

Thus, 6.9 kg of 40% cream mixed 26.1 kg of 7% milk will produce 33.0 kg of mixture testing 13.9% fat. The amounts to be used to make 71.4 kg of this mixture are

$$6.9 \times \frac{71.4}{33} = 14.9 \text{ kg } 40\% \text{ cream}$$

$$26.1 \times \frac{71.4}{33} = 56.5 \text{ kg } 7\% \text{ milk}$$

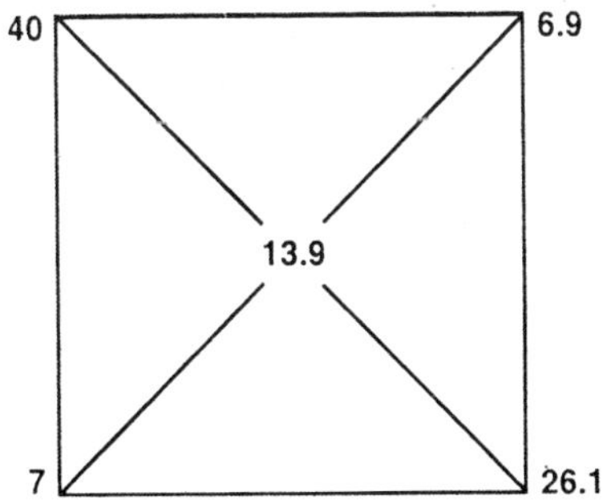

Step-4: Enter the above figures in the tabulated mix and figure the amounts of sugar, fat, serum solids and total solids.

Table 6.10 Completed Proof Sheet for Problem 6

Weight	Ingredients	Sugar	Fat	Serum Solids	Total Solids
5.4	Sugar	5.4	0.0	0.0	5.4
0.3	Stabilizer	0.0	0.0	0.0	0.3
22.9	Sw. cond. milk	9.6	2.06	5.04	16.7
14.9	40% Cream	0.0	5.96	0.865	6.82
56.5	7% Milk	0.0	3.95	5.085	9.03
100.0	Total calculated	15.0	11.97	10.990	38.25
100.0	Total desired	15.0	12.0	11.0	38.3

4. A Mix in Which Several Different Lots of Cream are to be Used

At times, a plant may receive cream from different sources, thus there may be different lots of cream of different tests. Usually, it is not advisable to mix these creams to make one larger lot, on account of differences in age and keeping quality. Thus, different lots should be used separately, using the oldest stock first.

Problem 7: Figure a 5,000 kg mix to test 15% sugar, 12% fat, 11% serum solids and 0.3% stabilizer. Use 7% milk and plain condensed milk testing 9% fat and 22% serum solids, and then as much of the following lots of cream as may be needed, and in the order given —

Lot 1 ..... 400 kg of 38% cream

Lot 2 ..... 500 kg of 35% cream

Lot 3 ..... 700 kg of 40% cream

Assume all the lots of cream have a serum solids content of 5.81%.

Step-1: Figure the mix on a 100 kg basis by methods already given up to the point where you have determined the required weight and test of the milk and cream mixture. Then figure proper multiple of the determined amounts to give the weight of mix called for—

The mix has already figured in Step 4, Page 105 and the amounts found were:

15.0 kg	Sugar
0.3 kg	Stabilizer
29.9 kg	Condensed milk
54.8 kg of 17.0%	Cream (16.6 kg of 40% cream and
38.2 kg of 7%	milk equal 54.8 kg of 17.0% cream)

For a 5,000 kg of mix, we need—

15 x 50 =	750 kg of sugar,
0.3 x 50 =	15 kg of stabilizer
29.9 x 50 =	1495 kg of condensed milk
54.8 x 50 =	2740 kg of 17.0% cream

Step-2: List the amounts, tests and kg of fat contained in each lot of cream. By inspection, comparing the kg of fat needed, with the kg of fat in the lots of cream determine which lots will be needed in full. Figure the balance of the weight of milk and cream by the Pearson Square Method. The fat required in the total milk and cream is

2740 x 17.0 = 465.8 kg

The fat contained in the respective lots cream is —

Lot 1 — 400 x 0.38 = 152.0 kg of fat

Lot 2 — 500 x 0.35 = 175.0 kg of fat

Lot 3 — 700 x 0.40 = 280.0 kg of fat

By inspection, it is obvious that only the first two lots of cream will be needed in full leaving a balance of weight and fat to be furnished by the milk and part of Lot 3.

Total weight of fat required = 600 kg

Fat already available from condensed milk =

$\frac{1495 \times 9}{100}$ kg = 134.55 kg.

Fat to be obtained milk and cream is

600 - 134.55 kg = 465.45 kg

Weight of milk and cream required = 2740 kg

Weight of cream Lots 1 and 2 = 900 kg

Therefore, weight of milk and cream required

= 2740 - 900 = 1840 kg.

Weight of fat from lot 1 and 2

= 152 + 175 kg = 327 kg.

Kg of fat to be obtained from milk and cream

= 465.45 - 327 kg = 138.45 kg

Therefore the fat content of the balance mixture

$\frac{138.45}{= 1840} \times 100 = 7.51\%$ fat.

The amounts of milk and cream required and figured as follows:

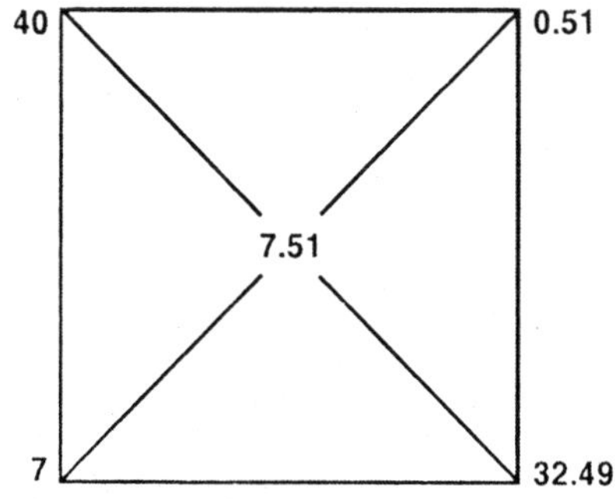

Thus 0.51 kg of 40% cream mixed with 32.49 kg of 7% milk will produce 33.0 kg of mixture testing 7.51% fat. To produce 1840 kg of such a mixture we must take

$$\frac{0.51 \times 1840}{33} = 28.42 \text{ kg of 40\% cream.}$$

and $$\frac{32.49 \times 1840}{33} = 1811.58 \text{ kg of milk}$$

Step-3: All the ingredients should be listed and the amounts of fat and serum solids contained in the ingredients checked against the total required.

Table 6.11 Completed Proof Sheet for Problem 7

Weight	Ingredients	Fat	Serum Solids	Total Solids
750.0	Sugar	0.0	0.0	750.0
15.0	Stabilizer	0.0	0.0	15.0
1495.0	Condensed Milk	134.55	328.90	463.45
400.0	38% Cream	152.0	23.24	175.24
500.0	35% Cream	175.0	29.05	204.05
28.42	40% Cream	11.37	1.64	13.02
1811.58	7% Milk	126.81	163.04	289.85
5,000.00	Total Calculated	599.73	545.87	1910.61
5,000.00	Total required	600.00	550.00	1,915.00

Chapter 7

Packaging of Ice Cream

PACKAGING

When ice cream is drawn from the freezer, it is usually collected in containers which give it the desired shape and size for convenient handling during the hardening and marketing processes. Ice cream can be filled into cups, cones or family pack containers on the ice cream filling machine (Fig. 7.1) Cups, cones or containers are taken down from a magazine, and placed into seats on a conveyor belt. These are taken one by one from a stack and placed in the lamellae of the conveyor, whereupon they are filled and lidded. Decoration with a number of different viscous or solid ingredients its possible. Various stations for filling, decoration are placed overhanging the conveyor, allowing easy control and cleaning.

Waxed paper cups are largely used for ice cream packaging which are usually of 50 ml and 100 ml size. Some of the important requirements are given below:

Paper

The paper used for the manufacture of cups and lids should be good quality material made from virgin chemical wood pulp. It should be capable of being waxed.

Substance of Paper

The substance of paper used for cups and lids should conform to IS: 1776 - 1989.

Stiffness

The board should be stiff and not easily delaminate, and after being properly creased should fold through 180^0 without cracking (IS: 1776-1989).

Ink

The ink and other additives used for printing of the cups and lids should be commercially free from toxic metals, such as lead and chromium and free from residual odour. The ink should be suitable for food packaging, and should be fast to light and wax. In order to prevent ink set-off, a coating of an edible starch can be applied to the surface of a printed board by spraying.

Wax

The wax for coating the board should be extra refined paraffin wax and made to comply with the requirements given in IS : 4654-1993.

Ahesive

The adhesive used to manufacture cups should be resistant to deep freeze condition of -35°C, and should to non-toxic.

Fig 7.1 Ice cream filling machine. Ice cream can be filled into cups, cones of family pack containers on this machine.

Wax Content

The Cup and lid should be evenly coated with wax on both sides as far as possible. The total wax content of the board should be 30 g/m^2 minimum.

Odour and Taint

The composition of the board and paper, ink coating material and adhesives should not give rise to any deleterious effect on the flavour, odour or appearance of the product packed. For detecting odour and taint the method given in IS : 4006-1985 should be adopted.

Toxicity

The composition of the board, ink, coating material should be such as not to introduce any substance into the product packed, injurious to health, or which might otherwise lead to infringement of the Prevention of Food Adulteration Act, 1954.

Resistance to Deep Freezing

The printed waxed cups should withstand deep freeze conditions of 35°C for a period of 30 days.

Leak proofness

The waxed cups should be leak proof. There should be no cracks on the outer curling of the cups, and the base curling should be uniform. Glue spots should be absent where the cups are seamed.

To test the leakproofness of cups the sample cups should be filled with water and checked after 5 min for any leakage.

The cups should be packed in either polyethylene bags, or in suitable protective wrapper and then packed in protective containers. The cups and lids should be transported under hygienic conditions.

A wide variety of cartons is used in the packing of ice cream. Most of the ice cream manufacturers, however pack in 500 ml and 1000 ml waxed cartons, and these are termed family and party packets, respectively. Some of the important recommendations are given below.

The shape of the cartons should conform to tongue and slitlock end style (see Fig. 7.2)

Paper Board

The paper board used for the cartons should be of a good quality material, of solid white or duplex-type made from virgin chemical wood pulp and should be capable of being waxed.

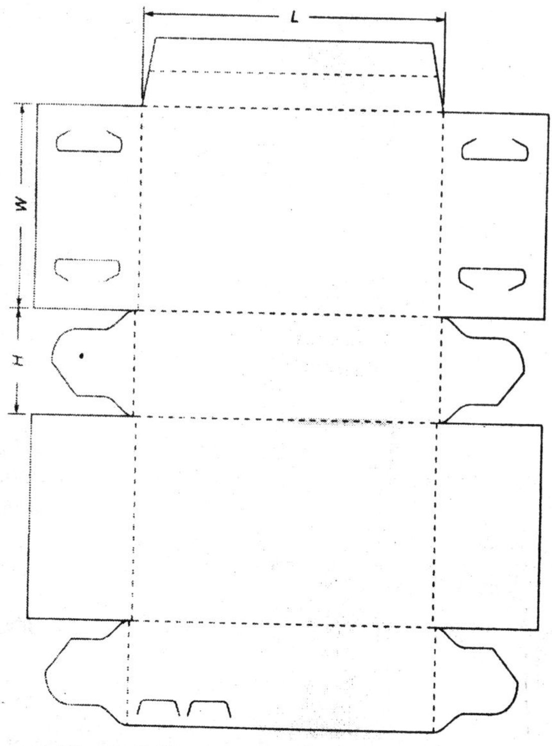

Fig. 7.2 Waxed carton for ice Cream

Thickness

The thickness of the unwaxed board should not be less then 0.30±0.02 mm.

Wax Content

The minimum wax content of the waxed board should be 5g/m^2 on each side. The total wax content of the board should be 10g/m^2.

Stiffness

The stiffness of the waxed board should comply with the requirements give in IS : 1776-1989.

Ink

The ink used for printing the cartons should be commercially free from toxic metals like lead and chromium. It should be suitable for food packaging and should be fast to light and wax. It should not have any residual odour. In order to prevent ink set-off, a coating of an edible starch should be applied to the printed board by spraying.

Wax Quality

The wax for coating the board should be extra refined paraffin wax and conform to IS : 4654-1993.

Varnish and Lacquer

The materil used should have no toxic effect.

Adhesive

The adhesive used to form and seal the carton should withstand a temperature of - 35°C and should be non-toxic.

Odour and Taint

The composition of the board, ink, coating materials and adhesive should be such as not to have any deleterious effect on the flavour, odour and appearance of the product packed (IS : 4006 (Part 2) -1985).

The waxed board carton should withstand deep freeze conditions (-35°C) for a period of 30 days.

The composition of the board, ink, coating materials and adhesive should be such as not to introduce into the product packed, any substance which is injurious to health or which might otherwise lead to an infringement of the PEA Act, 1954.

Dimensions

The recommended inner dimensions of the cartons are given in Table 7.1

Table 7.1 Inner Dimensions of the Cartons

	300 ml Carton	500 ml Carton	100 ml Carton
Length L, mm	113	152	152
Width, W, mm	75	97	97
Height H, mm	38	38	76

A tolerance of ± 1 mm is allowed for these dimensions.

In order to produce a suitable forming of the carton, the prefolding should be such that the glue seams are square and glue spots are absent.

The Cartons should be supplied in collapsed form, and ready to use after erection. These should be packed in suitable protective transit containers.

Ice Cream of different flavours is also packed in biscuit cones wrapped in aluminium foil laminates. The BIS recommendations (IS : 8970-1991) for aluminium laminates are given below.

The aluminium foil is laminted to paper with adhesive. The application of adhesive should be continuous or of even intermittent pattern so that the laminates do not open out while being used.

Adhesive

The adhesive used should be based on substances such as starch, dextrin, sodium silicate, casein, rubber, vinyl, polyethylene or wax. The choice of the adhesive should be governed by the end-use. For ice cream, starch, polyurethane or sodium silicate may be used as adhesive. During prolonged stroage at low temperature, starch and sodium silicate tend to develop brittleness which may result in delamination. Polyurethane has better adhesive properties under similar conditions and is widely used nowadays.

Aluminium Foil

The aluminium foil used should be plain or printed, soft or hard annealed, 0.006 mm to 0.15 mm thick. The surface of aluminium should be smooth so as to permit satisfactory adhesion to the paper.

Paper

The paper used for lamination should be uniform, evenly finished and generally free from specks, holes and other blemishes, should comply with the requirements as laid down in IS : 1060 (Part-I)-1966 (Methods of sampling and test for paper and allied product) and IS : 1060 (Part-II)-1960 (Methods of sampling and test for paper and allied product).

The laminate should not import any objectionable odour or taint. The laminate should comply with the requirements given in Table 7.2.

Ice cream candies and ice candies are usually packed in glassine wrappers. After packaging in glassine wrappers, the candies may be packed in unwaxed cartons. The unwaxed cartons should be made from paper board of solid white or duplex type made from virgin chemical wood pulp. Candies can also be packed only in waxed cartons made from paperboard.

Table 7.2 Requirements for Paper-Aluminium Foil Laminate

Characteristic	Requirement
Arsenic content, ppm, Max.	2
Total Copper, ppm, Max	30
Water Soluble copper, ppm, Max	10
Total iron, ppm, Max	70
Water soluble iron, ppm, Max	15
Lead, ppm, Max	20

The exterior packing used for cups and candies are corrugated fibreboard boxes. BIS (IS : 2771, Part-I, 1990) has prescribed requirements for corrugated fibreboard boxes for general packaging purposes for the maximum mass of the contents up to 75 kg.

Corrugated fibreboards are made from board consisting of one or more sheets of fluted paper stuck to flat sheets of paper or board or between several liners, usually kraft. The flat sheet is called liner. The fluted sheet is called the fluting medium.

The type of corrugations known as flutes are given in Table 7.3

Table 7.3 Types of Corrugations

Flute	No. of corrugations per 30 cm	Height of corrugation (mm)
A (Board)	32 to 38	4.2 to 4.6
B (Narrow)	50 to 56	2.2 to 2.8
C (Medium)	36 to 43	3.5 to 3.7
E (Micro)	90 to 96	1.2 to 1.6

The corrugated fibreboard is classified on the basis of number of paper sheets forming the board, the caliper of the board and the number of flutes per metre of the board.

Following are the various classes of corrugated fibre board boxes (CFB) :

(i) Single faced CFB (2 ply)

(ii) Single walled CFB (3 ply)

(iii) Double walled CFB (5 ply)

(iv) Triple walled CFB (7 ply)

These are shown in Fig. 7.3.

A CFB box has the following components :

Liner

Fluting medium or corrugation

Adhesive

Manufacturer's joint

Liners are generally made kraft paper, which may be virgin, semi-virgin or recylced. Virgin Kraft has better strength than semi virgin or recycled. The strength also depends on the method of pulping, grammage, moisture content, etc. Chemical pulping gives strongest paper. Higher the bursting strength, puncture resistance and grammage, better is the strength.

Moisture content should be between 8-10%. Fibre orientation in one direction should be minimum.

(a) Single-wall corrugated fibre board

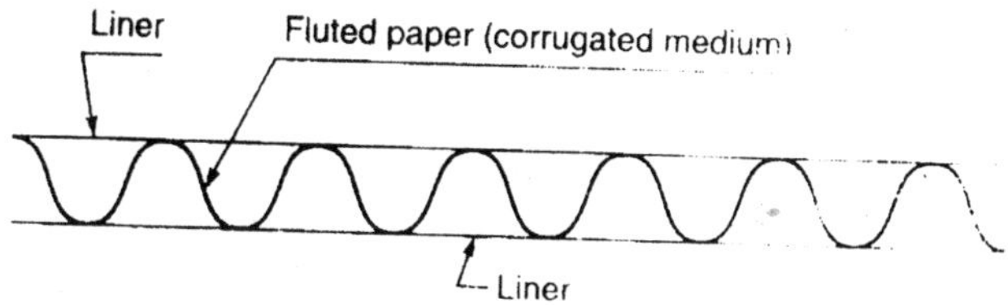

(b) Double-wall corrugated fibre board

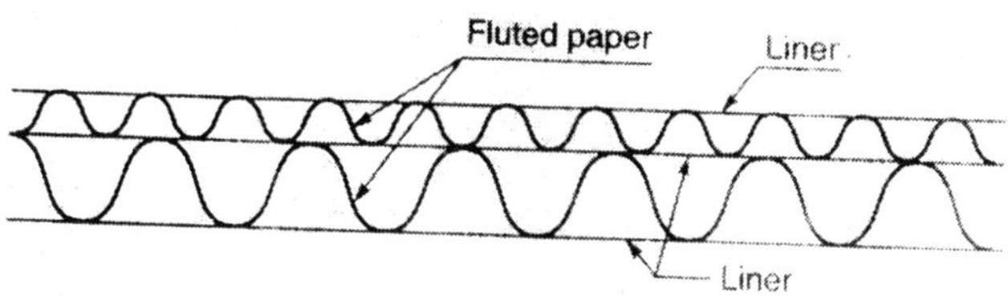

(c) Triple-wall corrugated fibre board

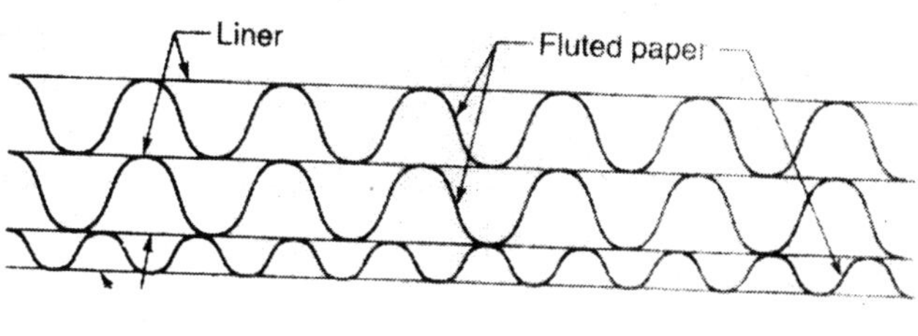

Fig 7.3 Showing flute and liner of a corrugated fibre board

Flutes or Corrugations

The flutes are generally made of semi-chemical kraft paper. Generally lower grammages are used for fluting medium. The flutes resemble a sine or cosine curve and these impart strength and cushioning properties to CFB boxes.

Different types of flutes are employed in different combinations to form a uniform or combined corrugated fibre board.

For example a three ply board with E flute is termed as "E-fluted-3 ply CFB Board" and a 7-ply board with combination of A, B, C, will be termed as 'A/B/C & 7-ply CFB'.

During the formation of flutes, the kraft paper loses around 5% of its strength.

Following factors should be taken into consideration while deciding the type of flute to be used :

(i) The load of the contents

(ii) Stack height

(iii) Nature of items packed

(iv) Cushioning required.

The flutes should run vertically to the liner to give better stacking strength to the boxes.

Adhesives

Any suitable adhesive, capable of firmly adhering the various piles together should be used. Sodium slicate or any other highly alakaline adhesive should not be used.

Manufacture's Joint

The manufacturer's joint may be made either by lap or by butting the edges. The lap joint may either be stapleα or glued. If stapped, it should be checked that—

- Staples are not rusted
- Spacing between two successive staples is even
- Stapling is done at an angle of 45°.
- Stapling is done at the centre of lap width.
- The width of the lap is not less than 30 mm.

The properties of corrugated fibre board boxes that may be considered for the packaging of ice cream are :

(i) Types of flutes
(ii) Grammages of liners and fluters
(iii) Bursting strength
(iv) Cobb value (Water penetration)
(v) Puncture resistance
(vi) Edge crush resistance
(vii) Flat crush resistance
(viii) Type of adhesive
(ix) Solid content of adhesive
(x) Moisture content of board.

A consideration of the above factors depends on the nature of the items to be packed, design of items, weight of items to be packed, handling system, storage conditions, stack height, climatic conditions at the manufacturer's as well as the customer's place, size and style of boxes and whether partitions are used or not.

Type of flutes depends upon the cushioning required. Grammage, moisture content, bursting strength and puncture resistance depend on the weight of items to be packed and the hazards anticipated. Flat crush resistance, edge crush resistance depend upon the stack height desired.

Type, amount and solid content of the adhesive also influence of the board.

Hardening

when ice cream is drawn from the freezer and put into the container to be placed in the hardening room, it has a semi-fluid consistency and not stiff enough to hold its shape. Therefore, the freezing process is continued without agitation until the temperature of the ice cream reaches - 18°C or lower, preferably - 26°C. It is desirable to get quick freezing or quick hardening, since slow hardening favours large ice crystals and coarseness. The time required for hardening has been assumed to be the time necessary for the temperature at the centre of the package to drop to -18°C.

Factors affecting the hardening time

(i) *size and shape of package :* Doubling the size of the package increases the hardening time by about 50%. The shape is important in determining the amount of surface area per litre of ice cream as well as the speed of air-flow around the package. Packages which have good reflecting surfaces and are light coloured are slower to cool.

(ii) *Temperature of Air :* Temperatures above-23°C and colder than-31°C are less desirable from the standpoint of quality of product and economical operation.

(iii) *Air-circulation :* Hardening with forced air circulation system requires about 60% of the time required in still air. The speed of the air blast is also important. Proper stacking of packages facilitates rapid air movement. It is also desirable to harden each package rather than bundles of packages.

(iv) *Temperature of Ice Cream Drawn from the Freezer :* Drawing the ice cream at one degree higher temperature will increase the hardening time by about 10-15%.

(v) *Section of the Hardening Room :* In the still air type of room the ice cream hardens about as quickly near the ceiling as on the floor, while ice cream placed directly on the ammonia coils requires only two-thirds as much time.

(vi) *Composition of the Mix :* There is a tendency for shorter hardening time as the freezing point of the mix rises and as the fat content decreases.

(vii) *Per cent Overrun :* There is a slight tendency for the hardening time to increase as the percentage overrun increases.

For economical operation, the hardening room should be entered through an anteroom which may be large enough to permit storage of some ingredients at about O°C.

Precautions to observe in the operation of hardening room :

(i) Do not place newly frozen ice cream close to packages that are already hardened.

(ii) The packages should be dated and older packages removed first.

(iii) Ice Cream packages should not be placed together until hardened.

(iv) The frost should be removed from ammonia coils frequently. Frost 1/4 in thick or more greatly decreases the efficiency of the coils.

(v) Avoid fluctuations in temperature.

(vi) Do not store non-dairy products, wooden boxes or crates in the hardening room.

(vii) Keep floors, walls, ect., clean. Novelites like cassata decorated with whipped cream acquire off-flavours from odours in the air due to dirty floors, etc.

(viii) Do not keep materials like kerosene oil, etc., as freshly frozen ice cream is likely to acquire off-flavours.

(ix) The hardening room should be provided with an alarm system or telephone for calling for help, and should be installed in such a manner as to attract help from outside when regular workers in the plant are absent.

(x) Keep both an axe and a sledge hammer in a definite place just inside the door. These might be needed for breaking through the door a last resort in case assistance cannot be obtained.

Hardening Tunnels

Manufacturers handling larger volumes perfer to use hardening tunnels (Fig. 7.4) containing an air blast for fast hardening. These offer greatest advantages when hardening the smaller packages which can be hardened in an hour. Ice cream products—cups, cones, containers are loaded on trays either manually or automatically and are transported through the tunnel on an endless conveyors system. The conveyor speed can be adjusted in order to obtain the desired hardening time for the products in the tunnel. Cooling units supply the refrigeration and ensure that cold air at a temperature of -35°C to -40°C is circulated inside the tunnel at high velocity. In order to obtain satisfactory freezing capacity in the tunnel the air coollers and fans (Fig 7.5) are carefully dimensioned to suit the actual space and capacity conditions of the tunnel. When three or more cooling units are employed, defrosting of the individual coolers can take place separately while the tunnel is still in operation. It is also possible to have an automatic defrosting system for the tunnel.

Hardening cabinets are economical for a limited volume of business and are usually operated at a temperature between -23°C to -26°C. When ice cream is frozen in the continuous freezer and subsequently hardened by contact with refrigerated plates, or immersed in - 40°C brine or placed in moving air room, very little difference could be detected in the body and texture scores of the ice cream after storage in a cabinet maintained at -18°C for 24 and 72 hr. The brine and plate hardened samples where judged to be slightly superior to samples air hardened at -29°C. It is evident, therefore, that rapid freezing both in the freezing phase and the hardening phase influence the texture of ice cream.

Very rapid hardening is accomplished by exposure to liquid nitrogen. Ice cream hardened by exposure to liquid nitrogen is decidedly whether in appearance than that which was slowly hardened. This phenomenon is attributed to the formation of much smaller ice crystals than does the conventional hardening method resulting in greater light reflection. Although immersion of packages in liquid nitrogen produces an ice cream with desirable body and texture characteristics immediately after hardening, it also causes pronounced shrinkage in the ice cream after a tow-week storage period. Besides shrinkage, the surface of the ice cream appears dry and craced, becomes, yellow in appearance and is gummy to taste. This indicates a visible breakdown in the structure of the ice cream at the surface.

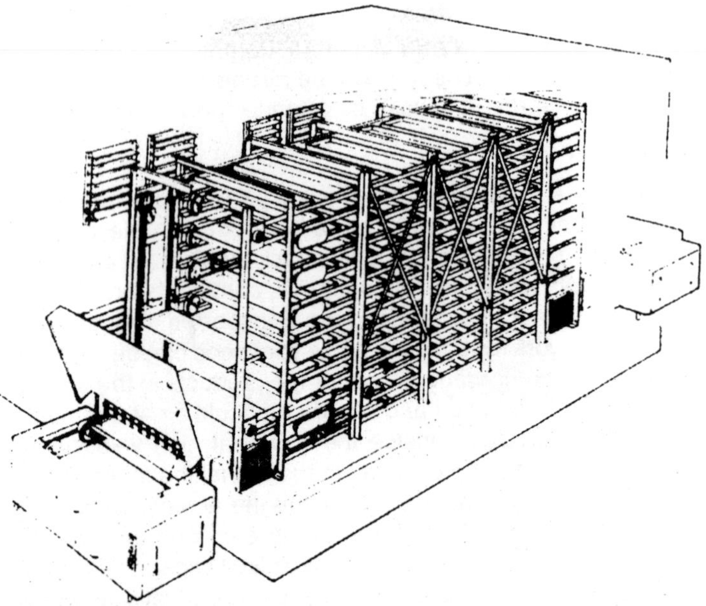

Fig. 7.4 A hardening tunnel. Ice cream products—cups, cones and containers are loaded on trays and transported through the tunnel on an endless conveyor system

Fast hardening System for Ice Cream

The ice cream manufacture adopts the following to harden ice cream quickly.

These are

(i) Improve hardening room design,

(ii) Install fast hardening system for contact or blast hardening, and install fast hardening system with controlled handling in a portion of the hardening room.

Hardening Room

Fast hardening can be accomplished by having

(i) Plenty of refrigeration to maintain temperatures at -30°C or colder;

(ii) Providing sufficient space for a 5 or 6 day inventory, and

(iii) maintaining good air turbulence around the products. Most factories employ ammonia as the refrigerant to maintain a temperature of -30°C or -33°C.

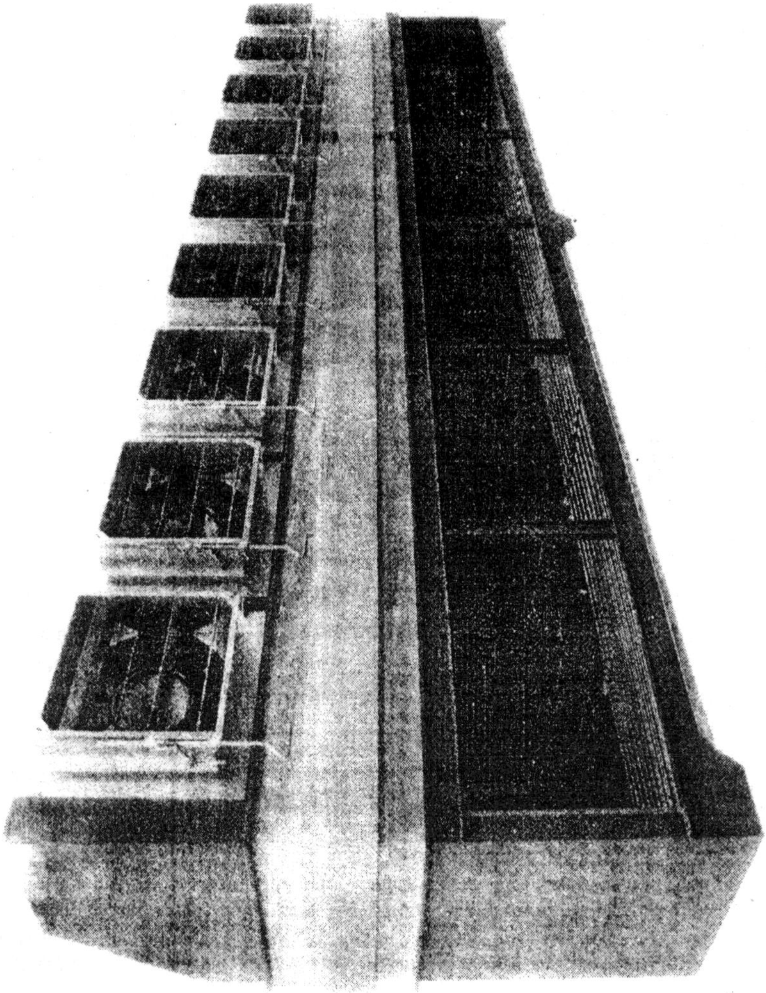

Fig. 7.5 Air coolers and fans of the hardening tunnel

Storage

After the ice cream is hardenced, it can be immediately marketed, or stored for a week or two at the most. Manufacturers should plan on a maximum of five days between freezing and marketing, with an average three day turnover. The time required for hardening varies with the size of the package. As mentioned earlier, the time required for hardening has been assumed to be the time necessary for the temperature at the centre of the package to drop to -18°C. Since the hardened ice cream can be stored satisfactorily at slightly higher temperatures than is required for hardening, it is more eonomical to use special storage rooms. Thus, retailers can use one cabinet for storage in addition to the dispensing cabinets.

In storage rooms, the temperature should be maintained uniformly at a point between -18 to -23°C. The package should be piled very closely to delay changes in the temperature of the ice cream.

Shipping

When the ice cream is marketed, the manufacturer usually ships it to the retailer under refrigeration at the same temperature as is maintained in the retailer's cabinet.

Mechanical refrigeration is most commonly used for the refrigeration of ice cream during shipping. This uses a complete refrigeration system with the expansion coils cooling the van. These vans are similar to storage room and are mainly insulated truck bodies for trucking large volumes and for long hauls as much as 48 hours. Ice cream is loaded directly from the hardening room into refrigerated trucks for shipment to distribution stations near the point of consumption, often many miles from the manufacturing plant. At the distributor's point, the ice cream is loaded into rigid, insulated, but light containers. Usually, thermocole is used as the insulating material. Beside insulation, a limited amount of refrigeration is provided by the use of brine discs. Depending on the size, the container can have two or three brine discs. These brine discs are filled with salt brine and pemanently sealed. To freeze the brine discs properly a temperature of -23°C or lower is advisable. This is accomplished by immersing sealed brine discs in tanks having calcium chloride brine. The calcium chloride has much lower freezing point than common salt brine, and is cooled to low temperature by mechanical refrigeration using ammonia as the refrigerant. The common salt brine should be of such concentration that it will not freeze completely unless the temperature is -21°C or lower. This condition is attained by having 28.87 parts of sodium chloride per 100 parts of solution by weight. The brine discs are placed on the sides of the container, and the container closed with tight fitting, insulated cover. These containers keep the ice cream in good condition for a number of hours. The insulated containers are transported in insulated vans from the distributors point to the retailers.

For direct supply of ice cream to local retailers, most ice cream manufacturers employ autorickshaws. Hardened ice cream is loaded directly into autorickshaws provided with adequate space for brine discs.

For supplying to local distributors, refrigerated vans or insulated vans are used since these are enconomical for trucking large volumes.

Insulated containers having thermocole insulation are becoming obsolete. Nowadays some leading ice cream manufacturers are using plastic boxes provided with insulating material. The box is made of linear low density polyethylene and polyurethane. Polyurethane constitutes the insulating material and is 50 mm in thickness. The box is provided with rubber gaskets and stainless steel clamps for better sealing, and has slots for the brine discs.

Dry ice is used extensively for package deliveries. The ice is sawed into pieces of appropriate size, which are wrapped in paper to delay the rapid evaporation and then placed around the package in an insulated packer, which are thermocole boxes or cardboard boxes insulated with corrugated cardboard. There are several distinct advantages of this type of refrigeration.

(i) Free from moisture and messiness.

(ii) Requires no salt.

(iii) Package is neat in appearance.

(iv) Is very light in weight

(v) Is especially good for specialities sold direct to the consumer where no return trip to pick up packers is required.

The main disadvantages of dry ice are :

(i) Present high cost and limited availability

(ii) Loss during handling and storage, amounting to 10-15% in many cases due to the impracticability of providing sufficient insulation in storage boxes.

(iii) Danger of "burns" to handlers. The very low subliming point makes it easy to freeze fingers without the sensation of cold, causing severe damage. Therefore, care must be taken by those who handle it.

(iv) The ice cream must be unpacked or removed from the dry ice sufficiently long to allow it to soften so as to be easily eaten and that the delicate flavours can be properly appreciated.

(v) The greater opportunity for "heat-shock". When ice cream warms up and then freezes harder again, it receives a "heat-shock". Which can injure the texture. Dry ice freezes the ice cream to lower temperatures than do the usual hardening rooms. The freezing point of dry ice (solid carbon dioxide) is about-78.3^{0}C.

Chapter 8

Frozen Dairy Products and Formulations

There is a significant demand for "soft" ice cream. The term soft ice cream applies largely to those products which are marketed in a soft form, and are consumed immediately after they are drawn from the freezer. Marketing of ice cream in a soft form enables manufacturers to use a wide variety of different formulations.

The principal types of mixes used in the production of soft frozen dairy products are :

(i) the mixes to be frozen and served in a soft form

(ii) mixes to be used in the preparation of milk shakes, and

(iii) Products to be frozen in soft-serve freezers, drawn into package and hardened.

The differences between soft-serve ice cream and regular ice cream include: composition, freezing procedures, stability and whipping properties of the mix, and maintenance of dry, smooth, stiff characteristics of the products as drawn from the freezer. If the fat content is low, i.e., less than 4%, the product tends to be coarse, weak any icy. If the fat content is high (about 12%), the freezing problem that is encountered involves possible fat separation, and also, the product being too rich and less palatable.

The milk solids not fat (MSNF) content of soft frozen products, varies somewhat inversely with the fat content and cab be high as 13% for a low fat formula. Milk solids not fat serves to provide proper firmness of body. In products having a high MSNF content, the lactose may separate during freezing and cause a sandy defect.

High amounts of emulsifiers and stabilizers are added to provide desirable whipping properties, smoothness, firmness and melting resistance.

Products like calcium sulphate can be used at the rate of 0.12% to produce dryness and stiffness in ice cream.

The sugar content of soft frozen products is 13-15% which is slightly lower than or regular ice cream. The amount of corn sugar used to replace cane sugar is limited to about 25% in order to avoid too low a freezing point. However, corn syrup solids, instead of corn, syrup, can be added as they provide firmness and also raise the freezing point slightly (corn syrup solids depress freezing point less than corn syrup and sucrose), thereby enabling the drawing of ice cream at almost the same temperature as normal ice cream.

Soft frozen products are usually drawn from the freezer at -6.5 to -7.5°C. A soft ice cream freezer is very similar to the old style batch freezer of ice cream. It is usually a self-contained machine in which the low pressure refrigeration system is either directly attached, or is adjacent to the freezer. The design of the dasher is such that it gives a good degree of aeration to the mix as it freezes and can operate for a long period of time without undue breaking down of the ice cream mix. Excessive speed of the dasher causes too much of air to be incorporated, and adversely affects the body of ice cream if the dasher ran for extended periods of time. The refrigeration system is so designed that the freezer cylinder is kept at the proper temperature for a soft-serve ice cream for an indefinite period of time. Many of these freezers use Freon as the refrigerant. In this case, they often use a the rmovalve control rather than the flooded system. Care and maintenance of this type of freezer consists mainly of keeping the scraper blades properly sharpened, and ensuring that the refrigeration system is properly adjusted.

The automatic cycling of the ice cream can cause major problems including fat separation, occurrence of sandiness due to lactose crystallization or coarse texture.

The overrun of soft-serve products varies between 40-60% depending on the total solids content. It is possible to achieve high overrun and desired body and texture characteristics on a product with a high solids content.

There is considerable difference of opinion regarding the correct serving temperature for different types of ice cream. The standards generally used are given in Table 9.1

Table 8.1 Serving Temperature for Different Types of Ice Cream

Products	Overrun %	Serving Temp. deg. C
Soft-serve	40-60%	-5.5 to -6.6
Sherbet	30-50%	-6.1 to -7.2
Milk Shake	50-80%	-2.2 to -3.3
Hard Ice Cream	80-100%	-12.8 to -15

Formulae for Soft-serve Products

Soft ice cream is very similar in composition to ice cream which is frozen and hardened. The drawing temperature from the freezer is -6.5 to -7.5°C or some what lower. The sugar content can be 2 or 3% less than for regular ice cream, and the overrun of about 50% in soft serve is lower than for ice cream. The amount of stabilizer-emulsifier used and the proportion of emulsifier to stabilizer is generally greater for soft-serve ice cream. Soft-serve mixes should have a slightly lower MSNF than normal ice cream, as a slightly lower MSNF (MSNF factor 16-16.5) contributes to a higher degree of fat destabilization, thus, ensuring better stand-up and slower melt-down (a

MSNF factor of 17 is recommended for plain, hardened ice cream). Since the soft-serve mix is exposed to a mechanical treatment for a longer period of time in the freezer, this can cause excessive churning of fat, resulting in a grainy texture. This can be avoided by incorporating whey proteins which impart greater stability to fat emulsion, and consequently less fat destabilization and "churning out" effect of the emulsifier. Replacement of 10-15% MSNF with way powder adds to the freshness of soft-serve ice cream and fat destabilization is also brought under control.

The formulae for soft-serve ice cream are given in Table. 8.2

Table 8.2 Formulae for Soft-serve Ice Cream

Constituents		Percent	
Fat	8.0	10.0	12.0
MSNF	10.7	10.4	10.0
Sugar	12.0	12.0	11.0
Corn syrup solids	4.0	4.0	4.0
Stabilizer-emulsifier	0.5	0.4	0.4
Total Solids	35.2	36.8	37.4

Ice Milk

Ice milk accounts for three-fourths of the soft-serve gallonage in the USA. Ice milk can have a fat ranging from 2 to 7% with a minimum of 11% total milk solids. Due to a lower fat content, a higher MSNF content is always used to provide a balanced mix. Some formulae for soft-serve ice milk are given as follows :

Table 8.3 Formulae for Soft-serve Ice Milk

Constituents	Per cent	
Fat	4.0	2.0
MSNF	12.0	12.5
Sugar	12.0	13.0
Corn syrup solids : 42 DE	4.5	4.5
Stabilizer-emulsifier	0.5	0.5
Total Solids	33.0	32.5

Soft-serve Mellorine

These products are quite similar in composition to ice cream. Mellorine-type products are not marketed in India as ice cream. However, these may be sold as frozen desserts. The formulation may be the same as for regular ice cream, except that vegetable fat is substituted for milk fat. The source of fat includes coconut fat, palm kernel oil, hydrogenated palm kernel oil, cotton seed oil, soybean oil, cottonseed-soybean blend, safflower oil, or other oils. The use of coconut oil results in the best product. But hydrogenated palm kernel oil (45% hydrogenation) is widely used as it is cheaper and gives a product almost similar to coconut oil. Additional stabilizer and emulsifier can be used in the formula. In the United States, regulations in some states require not less than 8400 USP units of vitamin A per gallon of 10% fat product since vegetable fat does not contain this vitamin.

Milk Shake

The product has low fat content, relatively high MSNF content and contains a lower sugar content than ice cream. A milk shake should have ice crystals and a good body. The milk shake mix is homogenized at 200 bars and pasteurized at 80-85°C, cooled and frozen to 50 to 80% overrun, on a milk shake machine. A UHT sterilized milk shake mix is manufactured by homogenizing at 200 bars, heating at 142°C for 5-10 sec, cooling and filling aseptically. The formula for milk shake mix is given in Table 8.4.

Formulae for frozen Custard

Custards contain egg yolk solids. In the US, these are required to contain egg yolk solids not less than 1.4% of the weight of the finished custard for pain flavoured products and

Table 8.4 Formula for Milk Shake Mix

Constituents	per cent
Fat	4.0
MSNF	12
Sugar	10
Emulsifier-stabilizer	0.5
Total Solids	26.5

1.12% for bulky flavoured products. The formulae for frozen custard are given in Table 8.5

Table 8.5 Formulae for Frozen Custard

Constituents	per cent	
Fat	5.0	11.0
MSNF	11.0	11.0
Sugar	14.0	14.0
Egg yolk solids	1.4	1.4
Stabilizer	0.5	0.4
Total solids	31.9	36.8

SPECIAL FORMULATIONS

Diabetic and Dietetic Frozen Foods

These are special preparations for persons on restircted diets. Excepting the use of non-caloric sweeteners, diabetic frozen dairy foods are made in the same way as ice cream or ice milk. The butter fat content of diabetic frozen ice cream can vary from 6 to 10%. For diabetic ice milk, the desirable fat content is 2 to 3%, and this should be free from substitute sweeteners. Table 8.6 provides formulae for diabetic products.

When ice cream contains glycerol and sorbitol, artificial sweetener like aspartame cab be added to obtain the desired sweetness. In several countries, fructose is allowed in ice cream for diabetics. Due to the rather high sweetening effect of fructose, it is possible to obtain sufficient sweetness in the ice cream with a relatively small addition of fructose and without adding any artificial sweetener. When using fructose, it is also possible to produce an ice cream with a low fat content. Cocoa powder improves flavour and consistency of ice milk having 3% fat.

Table 8.6 Formulae of Diabetic Ice Cream and Ice Milk

Constituents	Per cent			
Fat	9.0	9.0	3.0	3.0
MSNF	12.0	11.5	12.0	11.5
Glycerol*	4.0	2.0	1.0	-
Sorbitol	3.0	3.0	4.0	5.0
Fructose	-	5.0	5.0	5.0
Cocoa solids	-	-	-	4.0
Stabilizer	0.6	0.6	0.65	0.65
Total Solids	28.6	31.1	25.7	29.2

*If for legislative reasons glycerol is not allowed it can be substituted by sorbitol.

The ingredients are mixed and pasteurized as for ordinary ice cream. The mix is homogenized at 75°C. Homogenization pressures of 195 kg.cm^2 and 235kg/cm^2 are employed for ice cream mix containing 9% and 3% fat respectively.

Low Calorie Ice Milk

Reduction of fat content of frozen desserts below the fat content of ice milk has been of major interest to ice cream producers over the past four to five years. The trend to reduce fat to below 0.5% in frozen desserts started in the USA and has, to some extent, spread all over the Western world. Most ice cream companies have intensified research and development efforts to develop non-fat-frozen formulations which have the body and texture characteristics of normal ice cream. Though non-fat frozen desserts have been available in the market in the USA for approximately five years, there has been insignificant growth in sales. Non-fat frozen desserts account for 2% of the total sales of frozen desserts in the USA. The formula for low calorie ice milk as suggested by Danisco Ingredients (bullein F6a, 1996), Denmark is given in Table 8.7.

The mix is pasteurized at 80-80°C for 20 to 40 sec, homogenized at 80°C and 200 bars, cooled to 4°C, aged for minimum 4 hr and frozen to an overrun of 80-100%, hardened at -30 to 40°C and stored below - 20°C.

Fat and sugar have important functional and organoleptic properties in ice cream. A low calorie product has a low content of dry solids as compared to a standard product.

Table 8.7 Formulae for Low Calorie Ice Milk

	Non fat Normal Sugar	Low fat (1%) Non-sugar
Fat (Vegetable butter fat)	-	1%
MSNF	11.50	11.90
Sugar	12.00	-
Corn syrup 42 DE, 75% TS	9.00	-
Polydextrose (litesse)	-	12.00
Maltodextrin DE 15	4.00	4.50
Cocoa powder, 22/24% fat	-	2.00
Aspartame	-	0.03
Emulsifier / hydrocolloid blend	1.0	1.0
Water and flavouring	62.50	67.57
Total	100.00	100.00
Fat (per cent)	0.0	1.0
MSNF (per cent)	11.0	11.4
Total solids (per cent)	34.75	31.90

Thus, the role of functional ingredients, like stabilizer and emulsifier, assumes greater significance in these products. In non-fat products having normal sugar content, maltodextrin and specially formulated emulsifier-stabilizer blends containing micro crystalline cellulose are added to obtain a creamy sensation and improved melt down properties. These products also contain corn syrup solids to adjust the level of sweetness, to obtain a firmer body on extrusion, and to raise the level of total solids. A considerable reduction in calorie content is achieved by using a bulking agent and an artificial sweetener. In low fat, non-sugar formulation, a bulking agent is added to provide the bulk and functional properties of sugars. The bulking agents available in the market today are lactitol, polydextrose and palatinit, each contributing 2 kcal, and 2 kcal per gram, respectively. Use of polydextrose results in a hard product, since it lowers the freezing point far less than sucrose. Lactitol and palatinit add more sweetness and lower the freezing point more than polydextrose, and give a more natural taste to ice cream. Polydextrose is commonly preferred since it contributes less calories than lactitol and palatint. It may be desirable to use an ingredient like glycerol at 1-2% level to obtain the desired depression in freezing point.

Low calorie products do not have a pleasing flavour, characteristic of normal ice cream. It is, therefore, necessary to add specially developed cream and butter flavourings to produce a richer tasting product.

The special significance of stabilizers and emulsifiers in these products justifies a detailed discussion on this subject. A great amount of work has already been carried out on the selection, testing and optimization of emulsifiers and stabilizers for traditional frozen desserts. Monoglycerides are commonly used in the commercial manufacture of frozen desserts as they yield products having good structure, giving a creamy feeling in the mouth with slow, and uniform melt down.

Emulsifiers are most effective in frozen desserts when they are incorporated on the surface of the fat globules. The fat globules are stabilized primarily by the emulsifier and secondary by the milk proteins.

During ageing of the normal ice cream mix, the fat globules and the emulsfier begin to crystallize, and the surface activity of the monoglycerides increases. These changes cause desorption of the secondary protein membrane from the surface of the fat globules. This change is clearly seen in electron microscopic pictures. Destabilization of the fat globule membrane results in an emulsion which is less stable when the mix is subjected to mechanical treatment in the continuous freezer. This results in a partial churning of fat. The free fat formed will form a film around the air cells. But the effect of any emulsifier in a fat-free or low-fat system is different. Generally, a formulation with a low-fat content requires more emulsifier than formulation with a relatively higher fat content. In a low fat recipe, the size of fat globules is smaller than the recipes with a higher fat content since higher homogenization pressure is employed in low-fat mixes. Thus, despite the low fat level in the recipe, the total area of fat globules will be higher, and a higher amount of emulsifier will be required to obtain the same relative concentration of emulsifier on the surface of the fat globules. Secondly a recipe with less fat contains relatively more protein than fat, which means that desorption of a large amount of protein is necessary in order to destabilize the fat globules. In the case of non-fat formulation, this is not the case and it is only possible to add small amounts of emulsifier before the foam becomes difficult to break. It is a well established fact that emulsifier reduces the surface tension and, therefore, will concentrate at the air serum interface, that is, their stabilizing effect is the same as that of agglomerated fat.

Generally emulsifiers with a high melting point of 60-70°C are used where as the melting point of fat is 30-35^{0}C. In low-fat recipes, the fat will melt quicker in the mouth as compared to a non-fat system which solely consists of fatty acids (from emulsifier) with a high melting point. Thus, in a non-fat system, the dosage of emulsifier should be more precise since a low level will result in a poor air distribution while at a higher level it will be difficult to break the foam in the mouth. Therefore, the effect of several factors should be taken into account while considering the dosage of emulsifiers.

Stabilizers

The hydrocolloid combinations used as stabilizers in non-fat and low-fat frozen dessert formulations differ from those used in formulations containing fat because non-fat and low-fat formulations generally contain less solids, and thus require a higher degree of water binding. Furthermore, hydrocolloids should contribute to creaminess and have fat sparing properties. Microcrystalline cellulose has been widely used to improve creaminess as it imparts the sensation of fat on the tongue. It is not permitted in frozen desserts in some countries. Therefore, low viscosity CMC in combination with other hydrocolloids has been used to obtaint the same effect of creaminess as microcrystalline cellulose.

It is possible to produce a non-fat frozen dessert with good creaminess, body and texture and heat-shock resistance, but melting resistance is reduced significantly irrespective of the combination of emulsifiers and stabilizers used. A reduction of fat to less than 1% often results in a woody or cardboard like taste. Use of appropriate stabilizer and emulsifier is crucial to non-fat frozen desserts. Further research work on stabilizers and emulsifiers is required to produce low fat and non-fat frozen dessert having body and texture characteristics comparable to traditional ice cream.

Semi Freddo

This product is of Italian origin and popular in some areas. It has a high milk fat and total solid content, and a low overrun, 20 to 30%. A higher drawing temperature (preferably -2^{0}C) is employed and a lower amount of emulsifier is added in order to avoid excessive destabilization of fat. The typical formula is given in Table 8.8

Table 8.8 Semi Freddo

Ingredient	per cent
Cream (38% fat)	52.65
Skimmed milk	23.05
Sugar	15.10
Egg yolk with 10% sugar	8.90
Emulsifier-stabilizer blend	0.30
Colouring and flavour	

Total	100.00
Fat (per cent)	20.00
MSNF (per cent)	5.00
Total Solids (per cent)	43.00

Pudding Pop

It is a gelled milk dessert on a stick. The overrun generally varies between 20 to 30%. The formulation is given in Table 8.9

Table 8.9 Formula for Pudding Pop

	Vanilla (per cent)	Chocolate (per cent)
Fat	4	4
MSNF	11	11
Sugar	12.5	14.5
Corn syrup solids (42 DE)	5.5	5.0
Cocoa powder, 22/24% fat	-	2.0
Maltodextrin	1.0	1.0
Emulsifier-stabilizer	2.0	2.0
Total	36.0	39.5

A special polysaccharide / emulsifier-stabilizer system recommended by Danisco Ingredients (bulletin F12a, 1996), Denmark, consists of maltodextrin, mono and diglycerdes of fatty acids, guar gum, locust bean gum and carrageenan. A gelled consistency is obtained due to the synergy between the locust bean gum and carrageenan.

Frozen Yoghurt

Frozen yoghurt is very popular among consumers. It is a highly nutritious food with high levels of protein and calcium. It enhances calcium absorption, is easily digestible and especially suited for lactose intolerant people. The product has refreshing and clean eating characteristics. Presently, concerted efforts are being made to develop new strains of bacteria to produce different flavour and textural characteristics.

Freshly frozen yoghurt with a high yoghurt content (50%) has a relatively low pH and usually an acidic flavour when yoghurt used has a pH of 4.5-4.6. However, it is not necessary to achieve this pH since good flavour may be obtained at a pH of 5.5.3. Another benifit associated with a high pH yoghurt is in the freezing process itself. Frozen yoghurt having high content of yoghurt may be very dry on extrustion; it is also brittle and it may be difficult to achieve a good dispersion of air. At pH levels higher than the isoelectric point of casein, that is pH 4.6, the protein is denatured to a lesser extent. This yields a product similar to conventional ice cream. It is preferable to have low fat content in frozen yoghurt, a fat content of 6-7% gives a heavy and greasy body. Generally, the higher the fat content, the less fresh eating is the product. A low fat content and addition of fruit enhances the flavour of the product. A fat content of 2% gives a balanced product having refreshing taste.

The formula for frozen yoghurt having 2% fat and 3% yoghurt content is given in Table 8.10

Table 8.10 Formula for Frozen Yoghurt

	Ice Cream base (per cent)	Yoghurt Mix (per cent)	Finished Mix
Fat	2	2	2
MSNF	12	10	11.4
Sucrose	17	—	11.9
Dextrose	3.3	—	2.3
Corn syrup solids	4.0	—	2.8
Stabilizer-emulsifier	0.85	—	0.6
Total Solids	39.15	12	31.0

Frozen yoghurt having 30% yoghurt has a pH of 5.2 to 5.3.

The processing procedure is given below :

Ice Cream Base Mix

(i) Mix all the ingredients.
(ii) Pasteurize at 80-85°C for 20-40 sec.
(iii) Homogenize at 80°C using a homogenizing pressure of 220 bars.
(iv) Cool to 5°C

Plain Yoghurt

(i) Mix all the ingredients.
(ii) Homogenize at 75°C, using 150 bars pressure.
(iii) Pasteurize at 95°C for 3-4 min.
(iv) Cool to the fermentation temperature.
(v) Add yoghurt culture and ferment to a pH of 4.2.
(vi) Cool to 5°C.

Frozen Yoghurt

(i) Mix 70 kg base mix and 30 kg plain yoghurt.
(ii) Age the mix for a minimum period of 4 hr.
(iii) Freeze to 80% overrun.
(iv) Harden the mix between -20°C to 25°C within 5 hr.

Dried Ice Cream Mix

Spray-dried ice cream mix can be conveniently reconstituted to meet the demand for ice cream, especially during periods of low milk production in tropical countries. Moreover, it can be baneficially used by a small scale manufacturer as he need not invest in a homogenizer and pasteurizer to prepare ice cream.

The characteristics of dried ice cream mix and consequently, the quality of the reconstituted ice cream are influenced considerably by the stabilizer and emulsifier employed in its manufacture. Spray-dried mix (having 31.04% fat, 25.13% MSNF, 40-59% sucrose, 1.3% pregelatinized potato starch as stabilizer and 0.13% polysorbate-80 as emulsifier) on reconstitution with water in the ratio 1:1.6 parts by weight, yields a product having excellent body and texture, and melt-down characteristics. When packed in laminated polyester polyethyene pouches, the product, the product has a shelf life of 9 months at 30°C.

The influence of the stabilizers, pregelatinzed potato starch and sodium alginate and the emulsifier, polysorbate 80 on the ultra-structure of spray dried ice cream mix was studied by scanning electron microscopy by Bhandari and Balachandran (1984). The combined use of pregelatinized potato starch and polysorbate 80 resulted in perfectly spherical particles with small blobs ranging from 2 to 6 microns in diameter. The formation of small blobs on the particle surfaces was attributed to the formation of stable air cells due to the incorportion of polysorbate 80.

Variations in the spray drying conditions influenced the particle size and bulk density of powder. When ice cream mix having 25% of the total amount of sugar required in the finished product was spray dried using the inlet and outlet air temperature of 160°C and 73°C and atomizer speed of 16,500 rpm, a bulk density of 0.85 g/ml was obtained. The average particle size varied from 26.6 to 27.3 microns. Dry blending of the dried mix with the remaining sugar (100 parts dried mix and 41 parts refined sucrose by weight) substantially increased the bulk density of the finished product to 0.68 g/ml.

Chapter 9

Ice Cream Varieties, Novelties and Specials

By varying the basic mix formula, different varieties of ice cream are manufactured as demanded by consumer buying habits, costs and competition.

Plain Ice Cream

Formula

Constituents	Percentage
Fat	10.0-12.0
MSNF	11.5-11.0
Sugar	15.0-15-0
Stabilizer-Emulsifier	0.3-0.3
Total Solids	36.8-38.3

The percentage of stabilizer and emulsifier added depends on manufacturer's recommendations. In any case, it should not exceed 0.5 per cent, as required under the Prevention of Food Adulteration Act, 1954.

Variations

The amount of flavour needed will vary with the strength of the flavour, compostion of the mix ingredients used and consumer preference. Similarly, the amount of colour added will vary with market demands and consumer preference. Therefore, the dosage recommended will serve as approximate guidelines.

Vanilla

To 100 kg of plain mix add 80-100 ml of vanilla flavour. Yellow colour may or may not be added.

Strawberry

To 100 kg of plain mix add 70-80 ml of strawberry flavour and colour it to pink.

Rose

To 100 kg of plain mix add 60-70 ml of rose white flavour and colour it to pink.

Pistachio

To 100 kg of plain mix add 50-70 ml of pistachio flavour and colour it to green.

Coffee

To 100 kg of plain mix add 1.5-1.7 kg of instant chickory coffee. 100 to 200 ml of 50% burnt sugar colour can also be added.

Caramel

To 100 kg of plain mix add enough caramel flavour or caramel syrup to impart a caramel taste and colour. A caramel syrup can be made by using 5 parts of sugar and 1.5 parts of 40% cream and boiling it until it becomes light brown.

Mint

To 100 kg of plain mix add 0.4 to 0.6 kg of pure mint extract or enough to get a flavour of desired intensity and colour it to light green.

Bisque Ice Cream

To 100 kg of plain mix add 5-10 kg of macaroons or sponge cake to the ice cream through the fruit feeder

CANDY OR CONFECTION ICE CREAM

Variations

Peppermint Stick

To 100 kg of plain mix add 5-6kg of crushed peppermint candy through the fruit feeder.

Butter Crunch

To 100 kg of plain mix add 6-7 kg of ground butter crunch candy through the fruit feeder.

Peanut Brittle

To 100 kg of plain mix add 5-6 kg of crushed peanut brittle through the fruit feeder.

Toffee

To 100 kg of plain mix add 80-100 ml of toffee flavour and add 8 to 10 kg of broken candy through the fruit feeder.

English Toffee

To 100 kg of plain mix add 8-10 kg of crushed English toffee through the fruit feeder.

Mint Chips

To 100 kg of plain mix add 5-6 kg of green and red mint chips through the fruit feeder.

Mithai Ice Cream (Gulabjamun)

To 100 kg of plain mix add small quantities of coconut powder, cardamom powder, flavour and colour. Add 8-10 kg of *Gulabjamun (Gulabjamun* ball broken into 4 pieces) through the fruit feeder.

Mithai Ice Cream (*Rasogulla)*

To 100 kg of plain mix add small quantity of coconut powder, saffron and flavour. Add 10-12 kg *Rasogulla* through the fruit feeder.

Mithai Ice Cream (Gajar Halwa)

To 100 kg of plain mix add 30 kg of *Gajar Halwa* through the fruit feeder. Appropriate flavour and colour can be added to the plain mix. For best results, *Gajar Halwa* should be prepared by cooking shredded carrot in sweetened milk to which a small quantity of cardamom powder has been added.

Chocolate Ice Cream

To 100 kg of plain mix add 12-15 kg of chocolate paste (made from 3.5 parts cocoa, 4.2 parts sugar and 6.3 parts water by weight). Mix the cocoa and sugar together, and add enough water to make a paste. Heat in a steam jacketed kettle. As the syrup thickness, add the water gradually with constant stirring. Heat to 90°C, pour out the syrup and cool. The syrup can be stored for a few days in a cold store at 3 to 5°C.

For layer batches cocoa powder should preferbly be used along with sugar and other dry ingredients.

Variations

Chocolate Malt

To 100 kg of plain mix add 7 kg of chocolate paste, 3 kg of malt extract and caramel colour.

Chocolate Malt and Nuts

To 100 kg of plain mix add 6-8 kg of malt extract and colour it to light brown. Add 10-12 kg of chopped, roasted or fried cashew nuts and chopped chocolate through the fruit feeder.

Chocolate Almond

To 100 kg of plain mix add 12-15 kg of chocolate paste. Add 10-12 kg of broken candy through the fruit feeder.

Chocolate Toffee

To 100 kg of plain mix add 12-15 kg of chocolate paste. Add 10-12 kg of broken candy through the fruit feeder.

Mocha

To 100 kg of plain mix add 10-12 kg of chocolate paste and enough coffee or coffee extract to give a mild coffee flavour.

Chocolate Cool

To 100 kg of plain add 12-15 kg of chocolate paste and 50-60 ml spearmint flavour. Add 10-12 kg of chopped chocolate through the fruit feeder.

FRUIT ICE CREAM

Basic mixes containing 12% fat can be flavoured with fruit preparations. Fruits can be used whole, sliced, crushed, diced, pureed (coarse, medium or fine) or as juice. For fruit ice cream, it is desirable to make a special mix which has 1% to 2 % higher serum solids contend than regular plain ice cream (regular plain ice cream generally has 12% fat, 11% serum solid, 15% sugar, and 0.3% stabilizer-emulsifier) to compensate for the diluting effect of the fruit preparation and to meet the PFA standards. The fruit preparations are added at the rate of 15 to 20% or more depending on the kind of fruit and intensity of flavour desired. A fruit to sugar ratio 2 : 1 or 3 : 1 is the best for frozen fruit.

Variations

Banana

To 100 kg of plain mix, add 8-10 kg of banana pulp. Add a small quantity of banana flavour and colour it to light yellow. A small amount of citric acid or lemon juice can be added to the fruit to prevent discolouration and to enhance the flavour.

Addition of a small quantity of 67% sugar syrup to the pulp also enhances the flavour.

Pineapple

To 100 kg of plain add 40-50 ml of pineapple flavour and colour it to light yellow. Add 20 kg of crushed pineapple or pineapple tit bits through the fruit feeder. Prior to the addition, pineapple tit bits should be diced to enable uniform incorporation of fruit and dipped in 35% sugar syrup for 2 hr to prevent "icy" fruit particles in the finished product.

Apple

To 10 kg of plain mix and flavour add 20 kg of sliced frozen apples through the fruit feeder.

Orange

To 100 kg of plain mix add 10-12 kg of orange juice (fresh or canned or equivalent of frozen orange concentrate) and 2-3 kg of lemon juice. Add 3 to 4 kg sugar to the juice. To avoid curdling, the juice should be added when the mix is partially frozen in the batch freezer. Colour it to light orange, and if required, add orange essence to strengthen the flavour.

Orange Pineapple

To 100 kg of plain mix add a small quantity of orange oil and colour it to light orange. Add 10-12 kg of crushed pineapple or diced pineapple tit bits through the fruit feeder. For best results, pineapple pieces should be dipped in warm 35% sugar syrup (50-60°C) for 20-30 min to soften the fruit as also to prevent "icy" fruit particles in ice cream.

Lemon

To 100 kg of plain mix add 10-12 kg of lemon juice (or the equivalent of lemon concentrate) and 2-3 kg of orange juice. Add 3-4 kg of sugar to the juice. To avoid curdling, the juice should be added when the mix is partially frozen in the batch freezer. Colour it to lemon yellow and if required, add lemon essence to strengthen the lemon flavour.

Peach

To 100 kg of plain mix add 20 kg of peach pulp. By replacing 1/3 of the peach pulp with apricot pulp, the intensity of flavour is increased noticeably. Add essence and colour it to light yellow.

Red Currant

To 100 kg of plain mix add flavour and red colour. Add 10-15 kg of red cherries through the fruit feeder. Before adding the fruit, the seed should be removed, the fruit sliced and dipped in 35% sugar syrup for 2 hr to prevent "icy" fruit particles in ice cream.

Fig

To 100 kg of plain mix add light tan colour and add 12-15 kg of figs through the fruit feeder. Prior to the addition, figs should be sliced and thoroughly washed in hot water. A small quantity of sugar syrup can be added to figs to enchance the intensity of flavour.

A good fig-nut ice cream is made by using 6-7 kg chopped figs and the same quantity of chopped dates.

Grape

To 100 kg of plain mix add 10-12 kg of black grape pulp and 2 to 3 kg of sugar syrup (70° brix). Colour it to light blue and add essence.

Custard Apple

To 100 kg of plain mix add 20-25 kg of custard apple pulp. A small quantity of 67% sugar syrup may be added to the pulp to enhance the flavour.

Date

To 100 kg of plain mix add light ten colour and essence. Add 12-15 kg of chopped dates through the fruit feeder.

Sapota

To 100 kg of plain mix add 15-20 kg of sapota (*Achras sapota L*). About half of the sapota can be added in the form of pulp, and the remaining half chopped into pieces and added through the fruit feeder for best results.

Sapota is highly susceptible to fungal infection, especially moulds. Ice cream to which sapota is added can develop mould growth on the surface after one month of storage. Therefore, care should be taken to ensure that the fruit is free from fungal growth. Bruised and damaged fruit should not be used. As a safeguard, sapota should be dipped for 10 min in an antifungal agent at low concentrations (Bakar F and Karim MNB, 1994), and chopped into small pieces after removing its outer skin.

Mango

To 100 kg of plain mix add 25 kg of mango pulp; a combination of Totapuri and Alphonso mango pulp (2:1 parts by weight) yields good results. Colour it to yellow and add essence.

Strawberry

To 100 kg of plain mix add 25 kg of strawberries, fresh or freshly frozen. For frozen berries, a fruit to sugar ratio of 2 : 1 is preferred. Colour it to strawberry pink using red colour.

Blueberry

To 100 kg of plain mix add 25 kg of blueberry puree.

Respberry

To 100 kg of plain mix add 10-12 kg of red raspberry or black respberry pulp and add essence. Raspberry pulp with 1: 1 fruit sugar ratio preferred.

NUT ICE CREAM

A basic mix having 10%-12% fat can be flavoured with 3-10% of nut preparations.

Variations

Butterscotch

To 100 kg of plain mix add essence and colour it to light tan. 12-15 kg of candied cashew (*Kaju Chikky)* and small amount of walnuts and salted butter are added through the fruit feeder.

Pistachio

To 100 kg of plain mix add flavour and colour it to light green. Add 3-4 kg of chopped pistachio nuts through the fruit feeder.

Another very popular variety having pistachio nuts is Saffron Pistachio (*Kesar Pista*).

To the plain mix are added saffron flavour and saffron / saffron extract.

Almond Walnut

To 100 kg of plain mix add flavour and 3-4 kg of chopped almonds, and 3-4 kg of walnut halves through the fruit feeder.

Almond Toffee

To 100 kg of plain mix add almond flavour and caramel colour. Add 5-6 kg of chopped almonds and broken toffee pieces (milk toffee gives better crunchiness) through the fruit feeder.

Peanut

To 100 kg of plain mix add flavour and colour. Add 5-7 kg of crushed peanuts through the fruit feeder.

Burnt Almond

To 100 kg of plain mix add almond flavour and some burnt sugar or caramel colour. Add 5-6 kg of burnt or roasted almonds through the fruit feeder.

Caramel Nut

To 100 kg of plain mix add caramel flavour and some burnt sugar colour. Add 3-4 kg of crushed nuts through the fruit feeder.

Fruit and Nut

To 100 kg of plain mix add orange flavour and colour it to light egg yellow. Add 6-8 kg of pineapple pieces and 6-8 kg of cashew nuts through the fruit feeder. Pineapple pieces should be dipped in 35% sugar syrup for 2 hr before adding them through the fruit feeder.

Blackcurrant

To 100 kg of plain mix, add flavour and colour. Add blackcurrant through the fruit feeder.

Prior to the addition, blackcurrant should be washed thoroughly in water to remove dirt and dust particles adhering to the fruit. Blackcurrant colour is prepared by blending Tartrazine, Amaranth and Indigo colours in suitable proportions.

Coconut Pineapple

To 100 kg of plain mix, add 12-15 kg of coconut powder and a small amount of refined coconut oil. Add 10-15 kg of crushed pineapple pieces through the fruit feeder. For best results, diced pineapple pieces should be added to enable uniform incorporation of fruit into the ice cream. Prior to addition, pineapple pieces should be dipped in 35% sugar syrup for 2 hr to prevent "icy" fruit particles in the finished product.

Tutti-Frutti

To 100 kg of plain mix, add flavour and colour it to light pink. Add 12-15 kg of mixture of several fruits—red cherries, raisins, pineapple, candied papaya pieces and nuts through the fruit feeder.

Banana Nut

To 100 kg of mix, add banana flavour, 8-10 kg of banana pulp, 6-8 kg of seedless raisins and chopped nuts. Colour it to light egg yellow :

The raisins should be soft when added to the ice cream. If the preserved raisins are not in this condition they can be soaked in water for some time and water drained before adding to the ice cream.

Rum and Raisin

To 100 kg of plain mix, add rum flavour and yellow colour. Add 12-15 kg of seedless raisins through the fruit feeder. The raisins should be soft when added to the ice cream.

VARIEGATED OR RIPPLED ICE CREAM

The base syrup used in making the fruit syrup and the base fruit syrup used in the variegated ice cream are as follows :

Base Syrup

Sugar	44kg
Glucose syrup (42 DE) (75⁰ brix)	33 kg
Water	22.4 kg
Stabilizer	0.6 kg
	100.0 kg

Base Fruit Syrup

Base Syrup	69 kg
Citric Acid solution	1 kg
Fruit Pulp	30 kg
	100.0 kg

The base fruit syrup pH (3.5-3.6) is added to the vanilla ice cream at the rate of 15% of the weight of ice cream for most fruit flavours. The most common flavours are mango, strawberry and grape. Chocolate ripple is also a popular variety. A chocolate base can be prepared by using 6% cocoa, 55% sugar, 38.6% water, and 0.4% sodium alginate as stabilizer. The stabilizer is mixed with a portion of the sugar and stirred into water at 80°C. The cocoa is mixed with the remaining sugar and added to the stabilizer-water mixture. The mixture is then heated to 88°C for about 20 min, and cooled to 4-5 °C.

Many types of pumps, fillers, etc., are available for making variegated ice cream. As the plain vanilla ice cream is drawn from the freezer, specially prepared syrups, such as mango, chocolate etc., are added by means of a special nozzle. Thus, a stream of soft ice cream and a stream of the specially prepared syrup enter the package in the desired ratio and are slightly stirred to give a marbled effect.

SOUFFLE

The product is made from sherbet mixes, except that whole eggs are added and the mix frozen to a high overrun to give a fluffy product. For 100 kg of base sherbet mix (consisting of sugar, stabilizer, milk solids and water), add 10-12 kg whole eggs and 24-26 kg of fruit pulp.

LACTO

This product is a milk sherbet made from butter milk, cultured sour milk or fermented milk. For grape lacto, use 100 kg of cultured sour milk, 33 kg of sugar, 42 eggs, 2.5 litre lemon juice, and 3.4 litre grape juice.

Sugar is dissolved in the milk and fruit juices, and beaten egg yolks are added. Egg whites are whipped separately and added to the mix in the freezer. Other flavours can be made by using raspberry or orange juice instead of grape juice.

QUICK SUNDAE

It is made by adding a portion of ice cream to a fruit sauce and topping it with fruits and nuts. Some examples are :

(i) Ice cream having pineapple fruit and a fruit sauce having pulp as one of the ingredients; the topping consists of cashew nuts and glazed cherry.

(ii) Ice cream having chocolate ripple and a fruit sauce having flavour of a citrus fruit like orange; the topping consists of cashew nuts and glazed cherry.

The product packed in "dome shaped" transparent plastic cups has attractive appearance and appeal. Usually the sauce and nuts constitute 5-7% and 8-10%, respectively, of the total weight of the finished product. Many ice cream-sauce combinations in different flavours and colours can be made to meet customer's requirements and satisfy regional preferences. The product having fruit ice cream and a sour fruit sauce has been marketed successfully by some leading ice cream manufacturers in India.

SORBET AND ICE CREAM

There are two components in the product; the first component is ice cream, the second component is sorbet. Both the components have the same flavour. The sorbet and the ice cream mix are frozen simultaneously. The whole fruit pieces are added through the ingredient feeder into the ice cream.

The remarkable feature of these products is the low content of calories, about 30 to 50% lower than the conventional ice cream having 12% fat.

Sorbet and ice cream constitute 43-45% of the total weight of the finished product, respectively. The fruit content may vary from 10-14%. The flavoured ice cream mix may contain 33-35% total solids, and 8-9% fat and the flvoured sorbet mix may contain 27-29% total solids.

Manufacturing Procedure

Ice Cream Mix

The ingredients cream, milk, skim milk powder, sugar and stabilizer-emulsifier are blended, homogenized and pasteurized in the usual manner and cooled to 2-4°C. The flavouring compounds and colour are added and the mix aged for minimum 4 hr.

Sorbet

The ingredients sugar, corn syrup, emulsifier-stabilizer and water are blended, homogenized at 120 bars pressure at 70°C, pasteurizied at 80-85°C for 20-40 sec and cooled to 2-4°C. The flavouring compounds; citric acid and colour are added and the mix aged if necessary.

Freezing

Ice cream and sorbet mix are frozen in two paralled freezers to an overrun of 90-100% and 45-55%, respectively and extruded at -6°C. The finished products are blended in a continuous, mechanical way immediately before filling into rectangular cups with an equal "twirl and marble" effect.

Assuming that the finished product has 10% fruit pieces, and the net weight per litre of the finished product is 700 g, the finished product will have the following composition :

Sorbet	—	315 g
Ice cream	—	315 g
Fruit pieces	—	70 g
Total	—	700 g

FANCY MOULDED ICE CREAM

Small manufacturers have been making fancy ice cream and novelties since the early period of the ice cream industry to gain better profit. The larger manufacturer, however, has been slow in pushing this class of ice cream perhaps, due to the high cost of the skilled labour involved. However, recent advances in equipment for making, filling and decorating have enabled mass production at lower costs. In the West, especially some ice cream plants have been meeting the demand for these products.

Ice cream belonging to this class differs from plain bulk ice cream principally in the form in which it is marketed. It may have a slight difference in the formula, but the main difference is in the manner of colouring, and in the size and form of the package. Difference in formula consists usually of a little more stabilizer and emulsifier or a little more milk solids in order to obtain a firmer body.

In the US, the most common item or form is the decorated slice which is easy to serve. However, most of the ice cream is moulded in the form of animals, flowers, statues, fruits or other objects. The fancy moulded ice creams are generally made for special occasions—parties, banquets and the like. A special design or colour scheme requires great imagination and artistic ingenuity, and a customer is willing to pay a special price for these products.

Harmony in colour and flavour is of great importance in bulk as well as in fancy ice cream. The colour must suggest the flavour, and should be in harmony with it. For example, a mango ice cream is yellowish because that is the colour imparted to ice cream by the natural mango fruit. Fruits often do not impart sufficient colour to the mix, so it is customary to add enough colouring to obtain the natural colour of the fruit. The colour, however, should not be too deep for that suggests artificiality and cheapness. Light and dainty tints are the most pleasing to the eye. Therefore, colour should be used sparingly.

DECORATION

In the past, much of the decoration of fancy ice cream was done by hand and by using various forms and screens. The general practice these days is to use a cone-shaped bag as a decorating tool. This is made of parchment paper, and on its tip is inserted a metal point or a number of nozzles through which the cream is extruded and laid down on the cake surface. These points or nozzles come in various shapes such as leaf, rose, star, ribbon, etc. The cone-shaped bag is made by rolling the paper into a cone, cutting the tip of the cone accordingly to allow the nozzle point to be inserted from the inside. The top flap of the cone is left to be turned down over the top after the bag has been filled. The bag is filled with the decorating media, whipped cream, and grasped with the right hand. Using the left hand as a rest for the right wrist, the bag is squeezed enough to extrude the cream at the same time when the nozzle is moved forward over the cake to lay down the desired design. The decorating skill is acquired with practice and artistic sense. However, perfection is achieved through vigorous practice.

Mashed potatoes are an excellent substitute for whipped cream in obtaining this needed practice. After achieving proficiency in handling a one-colour job, a two-colour job can be attempted. By carefully filling one side of the parchment bag with one colour and the other side with a second colour of the whipped cream, a two-colour effect can be produced as the cream is squeezed through the nozzle. The decorator can make up several bags, one for each of the colours, or for the various shapes of nozzles one intends to use for different designs. Whipped cream having 45% fat is generally used.

It is aged for at least 48 hours, chilled to 4°C, then whipped to smooth consistency (not so thick that it becomes grainy or buttery, nor so thin that it runs off the cake) for decorating. To make it more palatable, 5% of sugar and a little vanilla or other flavouring can be added. This cream can be tinted in any desired colour with flavour to harmonize with the rest of the ice cream, and the designs in which it can be shaped are limited only by artistic ingenuity and skill of the decorator.

Frostings can be used for special purposes. The surface of the mould is covered with a thin smooth coating made of sugar, cream, colouring and stabilizer to give a fairly heavy batter. The batter should not be whipped, however, and the cake or the other mould is quickly dipped in the batter, or the batter poured over it, and the excess allowed to drain off. Butter frosting prepared by mixing butter, sugar, colour and flavour is also effectively used.

OTHER SPECIAL PRODUCTS

Fancy Extruded Ice Cream

Ice cream in different shapes and sizes (Fig 10.1, Plate 4) captivates the young, particularly children. The demand for these products is steady and certain. In order to produce ice cream of the desired shape by extrusion, it must be frozen to a certain stiffness so that it retains its form between the time it is extruded until it enters a hardening tunnel. The desired stiffness is achieved by using higher amounts of emulsifier and a low drawing temperature.

The equipment for extrusion and freezing is shown in Fig. 10.2 (Plate 5). It has flexibility and design to make multiflavoured slices and sticks, cones, decorated ice cream, logs, ice cream balls, boats, Tartufo, coated slices and miniatures. The ice cream from continuous freezer (-5.5 to 6.5°C) is extruded through stainless steel nozzles to form any shape or flavour combination. Complex extrusions utilizing more than one flavour or colour can be produced from multiflavour extrusion nozzles supplied by more than one continuous freezer barrel. By placing different extrusion devices inside each other, faces with eyes, nose and mouth, and other intricate designs can be formed.

Ice cream can be extruded both vertically and horizontally. A heated single-wire cutter produces slices which are accurately positioned on conveyor plates. Sandwiches in various shapes can be formed from two sets of wafer dispensers, one set depositing a wafer upside down just ahead of the extruder, and the other depositing a wafer on top of the slice. Stick insertion is accomplished with a dual sticker which is air-driven (Fig 10.3.3 (Plate 6)). For all products, the conveyor passes into a hardening tunnel which is not only specially-designed but also efficient and has a temperature of -43 to -45°C. Here it follows a serpentine path so that the product is rapidly frozen in

9-20 min, depending upon the product size and shape. The product emerges "rock hard" from the freezing tunnel and is ready for further processing like chocolate enrobing, prior to the final packaging (Fig 9.4 (Plate 7). An air-actuated vibrator or tapper ensures the release of the product from the conveyor plate at the proper moment.

Plate 4

Fig 9.1 *Extruded products*

Plate 5

Fig 9.2 *Extrusion equipment (Glacier 600) for the production of frozen confections*

Plate 6

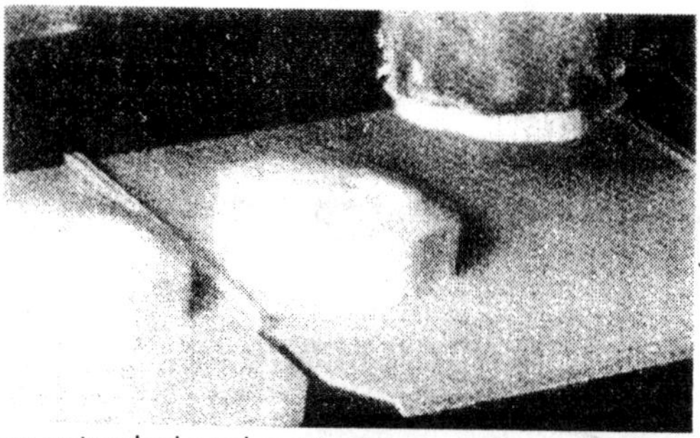

Slices are extruded and cut two per plate—all automatically.

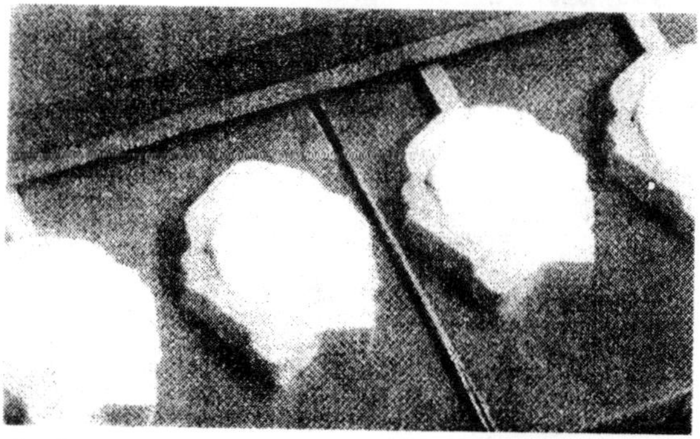

Precise stick placement every time. (Dual sticker inserts stick in every other slice. Product second from left is advancing to sticker position)

Picking up slices from freezer plates. Frozen product enroute for automatic processing and wrapping.

Fig 9.3 ***Showing extrusion and cutting of ice cream into slices, stick placement and removal of ice cream from freezer plates in Glacier 600.***

Plate 7

Tapper (underneath) releases frozen slices from the plate. Hold-down device keeps slices in proper position for rake-off.

Organized rake-off. Dual lanes shown here removing frozen slices from Glacier 600-E product plates prior to enrobing.

Coated slices emerging from side cooling chamber of Glacier 600-E.

Fig. 9.4 ***Showing release of frozen slices from the plate orgainzed rake-off prior to enrobing and coated slices emerging from side cooling chamber of Glacier 600-E***

Fancy Centres with Continuous Freezer

The continuous freezer is fitted with special discharge outlets to produce many combinations, including fancy centres for different type of packages. These can be produced with both speed and economy. Split flavour nozzles produce designs of different flavours of ice cream or ice cream and sherbet. It is possible to have many square designs with such a nozzle.

Ice Cream Cakes and Pies

These products can be made with freezer attachments designed for filling the cake or the pie plate. The cake plate is usually inserted into a cardboard package to support the form of cake during handling and delivery.

Ice cream pies can be modified by using fruit-flavoured gelatin, instead of the filling of preserved fruits or fruit ice cream which is ordinarily used. The fruit gelatin used in ice cream pies is similar to that used in modified aufait ice cream. The pie crusts are about half-inch in thickness, and can be made by hardening vanilla ice cream between to plates. Closed or open pies can be made by this procedure.

The modified ice cream cake is made by placing a lternate layers of ice cream and fruit-flavoured gelatin in cake pans. The gel is the same as that used in modified ice cream pies. It is desirable to have the gel filling for ice cream pies and cakes and modified aufait slightly weaker than that used for gelatin cubes. The pies and cakes can be decorated with whipped cream.

Aufait Ice Cream

Aufait ice cream usually consists of a layer of fruit between two layers of ice cream.

Other Novelties

Variegated or rainbow ice cream is made by mixing several different colour as the product is packaged. The variegated ice cream sundae, and other colourful products packaged in transparent plastic containers have good consumer appeal.

Cassata Ice Cream

This is essentially ice cream on a sponge cake. Hemispherical moulds of aluminium are used in making this ice cream. The outer layer is usually made of chocolate ice cream. Different varieties of ice cream constitute the middle and inner layer. The ice cream which constitutes the outer layer is first filled into the mould (outer mould) from the freezer. Another mould, which is smaller in size, is inserted into the first mould and pressed so that the ice cream occupies the annular space between the two moulds. This ice cream is hardened, and the smaller inner mould is taken out.

Ice cream is now filled again into the mould and another smaller mould of a different size is inserted and pressed lightly. This ice cream layer now forms the middle layer.

The ice cream is hardened and the smaller mould taken out. Now a third variety of ice cream is filled into the outer mould and this ice cream constitutes the innermost layer. The mould is hardened and ice cream is taken out by dipping the mould in slightly warm water. Now the three-layered ice cream is inverted on the sponge cake to which a thin coating of whipped cream has been applied. The whipped cream serves the purpose of an adhesive between the cake and ice cream. The ice cream is also coated with whipped cream to which nuts (usually small pieces of cashew) have been added. This Cassata ice cream is transferred to the cold store or the hardening tunnel so that it becomes sufficiently hard for slicing into small pieces.

Usually the ice cream is cut into 8 pieces of equal size, wrapped in a wax-coated paper and put into corrugated boxes and kept in the cold store until further distribution.

Quiescently Frozen Stick Items

These items include water ice frozen without overrun in a stick and cream on a stick which has ice cream centre with a quiescently frozen outer section.

Water Ice

The following formula is suggested for an ice base (on weight basis) :

Water	85-90 parts
Cane sugar	20-23 parts
Glucose syrup	5-7 parts
Stabilizer	0.25-0.35 parts
Citric Acid	0.35-0.50 parts
Brix	22-24

(i) Weigh the stabilizer carefully and mix it with cane sugar in the ratio 1:3 parts by weight and add to the required amount of water. Then agitate until it is fully suspended. It is necessary to maintain the temperature of the mixture between 60-70°C to fully dissolve the stabilizer.

(ii) Add the remaining amount of cane sugar and the required amount of glucose syrup, and agitate until it is fully dissolved. It necessary, homogenize at 100 bars to obtain homogenous mix.

(iii) Pasteurize at 80-85°C for 20-40 sec and cool the mixture; add citric acid, desired colour and flavour.

(iv) Ageing may not be necessary. But from experience in commercial production, ageing for 4 hr seems to be beneficial in imparting smoother body when gelatin or agar is used as a stabilizer.

Pour the mix into the mould and allow sufficient space in the pockets for expansion during freezing. Place the moulds in the brine tank at -25-30 °C.

On partial freezing, insert sticks into the mould pockets (the water ice should be just sufficiently firm and hard to hold the sticks).

Freezing is usually accomplished in 15-20 min. The frozen sticks are than taken out by immersing the mould in hot water for a few seconds.

For the cream-on-a-stick item, a special filler attachment can be used so that in one operation, a freezer can be used to freeze the ice cream to 100% overrun for the centre, and a second freezer to freezer the ice or sherbet shell to 10-15% overrun for the shell.

Ice Cream Bar Freezer

Ice Cream bar freezers (Fig. 9.5) are available for the production of ice cream, sherbet, ices of any imaginable size and shape.

The sequence of operations followed on the bar freezer is given below :

(i) Filling of ice cream into the moulds.

(ii) Insertion of sticks into the ice cream.

(iii) Freezing of the bars in a cold brine bath at -40°C.

(iv) Defrosting of a thin layer of the bars in a warm brine bath at +25°C.

(v) Extraction of the frozen bars from the moulds.

(vi) Lay-off for packing.

The bar freezer can also be provided with chocolate coating equipment placed after the extractor. It can also be provided with equipment for coating the bars with dry ingredients, nuts, candy, etc. The dry coating equipment is placed after the chocolate coating equipment.

Fig 9.5 ***Ice cream bar freezer for the continuous production of ice cream, sherbet or water ice with sticks,***

Chocolate Bar

Chocolate bars usually consists of Vanilla ice cream stick which has been dipped in chocolate coating. The composition of chocolate coating can be the following (on weight basis)

Chocolate mass	65-70 parts
Coconut oil	27-32 parts
Cocoa butter	1-1.5 parts
Dextrose	1-1.5 parts
Lecithin	0.3-0.4 parts

Refined deodorized coconut oil is added as a thinner, and to increase the covering ability. The quantity of coconut oil will vary with the amount of chocolate mass, higher amount of chocolate mass requiring greater quantity of coconut oil to avoid the excessive viscosity. Coconut oil is preferred since other oils have melting points which are too low for satisfactory use in coatings.

Chocolate Jam Sticks

These are made by coating vanilla ice cream sticks with white chocolate and injecting the vanilla portion with a flavoured syrup or jam base which constitutes the innermost core.

A white chocolate coating is made by adding a thinner, cocoa butter and an emulsifier. Usually coconut oil is added as a thinner and lecithin is added as an emulsifier. An appropriate amount of colour (oil soluble) is added to the coating so that it is characteristic of the flavour added to the syrup or jam base. The total soluble solids content of the syrup or jam base is so adjusted that its freezing point is much lower than the vanilla portion. But the syrup should have a sufficiently high viscosity so that it does not drip while eating. A syrup or jam base can consist of sucrose, glucose syrup, citric acid, stabilizer, water, fruit pulp or concentrate and flavour.

Indigenous Frozen Dairy Products

Kulfi

It is a frozen dessert, characterized, by slight whitish to brownish appearance, compact body, icy texture and nutty, caramel flavour. It is popular in the northern, central and western parts of India. In the traditional process, milk is thickened in a shallow pan with constant agitation. Sugar, nuts, essence and colour are added towards the finishing stages. Concentrated mass is poured into metallic moulds and frozen in a mixture of ice and salt.

In the industrial process the ingredients used are the same as for ice cream—milk, cream, skim milk power, sugar and stabilizer. Water is added to dilute the mixture (not having stabilizer and a small amount of sugar), and the fat: MSNF ratio is maintained at 1.4:1. Usually the fat in the finished product is about 16%. The required quantity of ingredients are taken in an open steam kettle and the contents heated with vigorous agitation. When the mixture has been concentrated approximately two times, the stabilizer blended with little sugar (1:3 parts by weight) is added to the concentrated mix, and the heating and agitation is continued till the mix has been concentrated three times. The concentrated mass is cooled promptly and frozen in a batch freezer to an overrun of 20-30%. Chopped nuts, almonds, pistachio, flavour and colour can be added in the freezer. The frozen mix is transferred immediately into the moulds having freezing pockets. Wooden sticks are inserted and the mix hardened in a brine tank maintained at -23 to -30°C. The mould is then transferred into a tank having lukewarm water to defrost the bars so that they can be easily lifted from the freezing pockets. The bars are wrapped in paper, put into corrugated boxes and placed in cold store until further distribution.

Malai-ka-Baraf

It is popular in the northern and western parts of India. It is similar to kulfi and prepared by freezing a mixture of *malai* (heat desiccated / clotted milk), sugar, nuts and essence. This product has plastic body, crunchy, icy texture, and delicate, nutty and caramel flavour.

Chapter 10

Ices and Sherbets

Ices and Sherbets have become increasingly popular in recent years in the western countries. As these have high cooling characteristics, they are in greatest demand during the summer months, and are also sold in combination with ice cream, specialities and fancy ice cream throughout the year. They account for 6.5% of the frozen desserts produced in the USA. The popular flavours are orange, pineapple, raspberry, lime, lemon and strawberry.

A water ice is a semi-frozen product made of water, sugar, fruit or fruit flavouring, fruit acid, colour and stabilizer. A sherbet is a semi-frozen product having the same ingredients as ice except that it also contains some amount of milk solids.

Ices and sherbets differ from ice cream in the following respects :

(i) Ices and sherbets are not as rich as ice cream. Ices do not contain any fat or serum solids; sherbets contain much less fat and serum solids than ice cream.

(ii) They are much sweeter than ice cream, the sugar content ranging from 25% to 35%

(iii) Have a higher fruit acid content, a pronounced tart flavour, a lower melting point and a coarser texture.

(iv) Have greater cooling effect due to coarser texture and a lower melting point.

The quality of ices and sherbets is affected by the kind and amount of sugar, stabilizer, acidity and overrun.

Sugar

The sugar content is much higher than ice cream, generally ranging from 25 to 35%. To make a good product, it is necessary to control the sugar content and overrun. One of the major problems in the sale of ices and sherbets is the crystallization of sucrose. The crusty surface defect is especially likely to occur when ice or sherbet is exposed to repeated temperature fluctutations in the retailer's cabinets. This can be adequately explained by the following :

In the freezing of ice cream, water separates out as ice, and the unfrozen portion containing lactose, sucrose, etc. becomes more and more concentrated. Eventually, a point is reached where lactose and sucrose remain in solution in a highly supersaturated condition; crystallization of lactose resulting in sandy ice cream will only occur if the lactose content is to high. During the initial stages of freezing, the concentration of sucrose in the unfrozen portion is low, and by the time the unfrozen portion becomes concentrated to a degree of supersaturation for crystallization to occur, the unfrozen portion becomes so viscous that crystallization does not take place at all. Ices and sherbets have a high sugar content, and a lower content of other solids. Thus, even at moderately low temperatures, the sugar in the unfrozen portion exists in a supersaturated state and the viscosity of the unfrozen portion is not sufficiently high to prevent crystallization. Hence, crystallization can be initiated by a sugar crystal or crystal centres from the air or by scraping of the surface. The remedy for this defect lies in reducing the sucrose content. About 20-25% of the sucrose can be replaced with corn sugar (dextrose), invert sugar or corn syrup solids. Corn sugar and invert sugar (dextrose and fructose) have lower molecular weight than sucrose, and their addition will lower the freezing point. Since at any given temperature below the freezing point, there will be less of the water frozen in such mixes their addition would result in a soft product. Corn syrup solids, however, are effective in preventing surface encrustation and also result in a higher freezing point which is nearer to that of ice cream so that the product will have a firmness most suitable for dipping at the usual cabinet temperature of -13 to 16°C.

The amount of sugar used will vary with the degree of sweetness and firmness desired in the finished product. Allowance should be made for the amount of sugar present in the fruit.

Stabilizers

Stabilizers are more important in ices and sherbets than ice cream as these have greater amount of water and a much lower content of serum solids. They assume special significance from the standpoint of body and texture, and a greater danger of syrup drainage. The choice of a stabilizer is largely influenced by

(i) Its effect on body any syrup drainage;

(ii) Its effect on overrun;

(iii) Availability, and

(iv) personal preference and convenience of use.

The various stabilizers used are gelatin, pectin, locust bean gum, guar gum, agar agar, gum Tragacanth, India gum, Methyl cellulose and CMC. All these are effective in imparting smoothness to varying degrees. However, no single stabilizer can satisfactorily meet all the requirements. For instance, though gelatin imparts a smooth texture and is effective in preventing crumbliness and drainage of sugar syrup, it causes excessively high overruns. According to Dahlberg (1926), high grade gums—gum Tragacanth and India gum, when used alone, also cause excessive overrun. He also found that while some gums reduced whipping ability, they tended to yield products which are crumbly and excessively hard on alternate softening and hardening. Desirable body and texture, and whipping characteristics were obtained by using a combination of 0.2% agar-agar and 0.4% gum Tragacanth or India gum. Nowadays, however, stabilizer blends are used in order to obtain maximum advantage from each stabilizer component. Individual stabilizers are blended in different proportions to meet specific requirements of body and texture characteristics. Enough stabilizer should be added to obtain partial gelling at room temperature.

Acidity of Ices and Sherbets

The desired tartness in the finished product is achieved by the addition or citric acid. Citric acid is usually added in the form of a 50% solution. The amount of acid depends of the sugar content, the fruit used and the demands of the consumer. Generally the acidity ranges between 0.35-0.40% (expressed as % lactic acid).

Overrun of Ices and Sherbets

The firmness and dipping qualities of ices and sherbets is also affected by overrun. Overrun in ices is usually 25-35% while for sherbets it is 35-45%.

PREPARATION OF ICES

The following procedure should be used in the preparation of ices

(i) Add sugar and corn-syrup solids to water in the mixing vat.

(ii) Commence agitation and heating, and add 1 part of the dry stabilizer mixed with 4 parts of sugar (by weight) to the mixing vat.

(iii) Continue heating till a temperature of 60-70°C is reached.

(iv) Homogenize at 120 bars and pasteurize at 80-85°C for 20-40 sec.

(v) Cool to 2-4°C. Ageing may not be necessary. But from experience in commercial production, ageing for 4 hr seems to be beneficial in imparting smoother body and texture characteristics. Ageing for 12-24 hr is necessary when agar-agar or gelatin is used as a stabilizer.

(vi) Add the desired quantities of fruit juice / fruit juice concentrate/fruit compounds, flavouring colour and citric acid.

(vii) Freeze the mix to an overrun of 25-35% for cups, bricks, etc., and to approximately 25% for stick confections.

(viii) Harden and store the product.

If fruit pieces form a part of the finished product, these should be added through the fruit freeder when a continuous freezer is used.

The acid should not be added until the mix has cooled. If the mix or part of the mix is heated with the acid, the stabilizer would undergo some hydrolys and lose its effectiveness.

The amount of fruit juice added varies with the intensity of flavour. Artificial flavours and natural extracts are often added to fortify the flavours and make a more uniform product. The amount of fruit, which can be added, depend on the kind of preparation and the variety of fruit used.

Natural and artificial food colours permitted legally by local regulations and which are suggestive of the flavour should be used.

The desired tart flavour is obtained by adding citric or tartartic acid. When neither citric or tartaric acid is available, saccharic acid, phosphoric acid, or lactic acid can be used but these do not give an equally desirable flavour.

The procedure for freezing ices is similar to that of ice cream. Since the presence of very small amount of fat as in sherbets or absence of fat as in ices causes rapid dulling of blades, it is advisable to reserve a freezer for ices and sherbet alone in larger plants. In any case, it is necessary to sharpen scraper blades more frequently to achieve rapid freezing, smaller ice crystals and a smoother product. The temperature of refrigerant should be at least -23^{0}C for obtaining the desired overrun and consistency. Following methods are used for controlling the overrum in a batch freezer :

(i) Overload the freezer, use 30-32 liters mix in a 40-litre freezer.

(ii) Operate the freezer with a colder refrigerant and for a longer time to allow less time for whipping.

(iii) Add less amount of the mix in the freezer (under load the freezer). Use 14-16 litres in a 40 litre freezer. When a limited amount of the mix is placed in a freezer, the dasher will exert very little whipping action as it does not come into contact with the mix which is spread as a thin layer around the freezing chamber by a centrifugal force of the scraper mechanism.

(iv) The beater should be made to idle while the scrapers turn.

Besides the operating conditions described above, it is necessary to select a stabilizer which gives a limited whipping ability consistent with the desirable body and texture characteristics.

The recipe for lemon and strawberry ice are given in Tables 10.1 and 10.2

The body and texture characteristics can be varied to suit different market demands by using suitable hydrocolloid blends. For instance, fresh eating qualities are obtained when locust bean gum is used in combination with pectin, gelatin, and soya protein. A "Chewy" characteristics is imparted by a blend of guar gum, locust bean gum, gelatin, sodium carboxy methl cellulose (CMC) and milk protein.

PREPARATION OF SHERBETS

Sherbets differ from ices in that they contain some amount of milk solids. Homogenized milk, skimmed milk powder, condensed milk or ice cream mix may be used as a source of milk solids. Milk solids enhance the flavour, body and texture of the product and the fat content influences the overrun. Following procedure should be used in the preparation of sherbets.

(i) Add sugar and corn syrup solids to milk in the mixing vat.

(ii) Commence agitation and heating, and add 1 part of the dry stabilizer mixed with 4 parts of sugar (by weight) to the mixing vat.

(iii) Continue heating till a temperature of 60-70°C is reached.

(iv) Homogenize at 190 bars and pasteurize at 80-85°C for 20-40 Sec.

(v) Cool to 2-4°C. Ageing may not be necessary. But under commercial conditions of manufacture, ageing for 4 hr seems to be beneficial in imparting smoother body and texture characteristics. Ageing for 12-24 hr is necessary when agar-agar or gelatin is used as a stabilizer.

(vi) Add the desired quantities of fruit juice / fruit juice concentrate or fruit compound, flavouring, colour and citric acid.

(vii) Freezing is done in the same way as in the case of ices except that the overrun is kept at 35-45%.

(viii) Harden and store the product.

It fruit pieces are used, these should be added through the fruit feeder as in the case of ices. The following points should be borne in mind while making sherbets :

(i) Some stabilizers like gum arabic will coagulate the milk when heated. In such cases, the milk should be pasteurized separately.

(ii) Pasteurization of the mix can be avoided when pasteurized milk products are used.

(iii) In a batch freezer citric acid solution should preferably be added after some ice crystallization has taken place to avoid possible curdling of the milk.

In many ice cream factories, ice cream mix is used as a source of milk solids, being already homogenized and pasteurized it offers the advantage of easy blending with other ingredients. But homogenization at lower pressures can still be necessary in order to achieve proper dispersion of the stabilizer. Like water ices, the body the texture characteristics can be varied to suit different market requirements.

The recipe for orange sherbet is given in Table 10.3

Table 10. 1 Lemon Ice

Ingredients	Amount (in kg)	Total Solids
Cane sugar	19	19
Corn Syrup solids (42 DE)	4	3.8
Stabilizer	0.35	0.35
Lemon juice (concentrate)	2	0.50
Lemon Pieces (compound)	10	5
Water, 50% citric acid solution and colour	64.65	-
Total	100	28.65

Table 10.2 Strawberry Ice

Ingredients	Amount (in kg)	Total Solids
Cane sugar	18	18
Corn syrup solids (42 DE)	4	3.8
Stabilizer	0.35	0.35
Strawberry compund	25	5
Strawberry pieces	12	4.8
Water, 50% citric acid solution and colour	40.65	-
Total	100	31.95

Table 10.3 Orange Sherbet

Ingredients	Amount (in kg)	Total Solids
Cane sugar	18	18
Corn syrup solids (42 DE)	4.7	4.51
Stabilizer	0.35	0.35
Ice cream mix (12% fat, 11% MSNF, 15% sugar)	15	5.74
Orange juice concentrate	7	4.55
Water and 50% citric acid solution	54.95	–
Total	100	33.15

DEFECTS

Flavour

The most common flavour defects include unnatural, excessive or artificial flavour, lack of sweetness due to less sugar or use of improper kind of sugar, development of oxidized or metallic flavour during storage.

Body and Texture

Ices and sherbets should have ingredients in proper proportions to avoid defects which are commonly associated with improperly balanced mixes.

A crumbly body can result from the use of insufficient amount of sugar or improper or insufficient amount of stabilizer. A sticky body is usually caused by excessive amount of stabilizer or sugar. Incorportion of excessive amounts of air yields a "snowy" body, whilst low overrun or insufficient sugar imparts hard body characteristics.

A coarse texture is caused by insufficient amount of sugar or solids, or by drawing at a higher temperature from the freezer. Coarseness can be overcome by increasing the sugar content and by replacing about 25% of the sugar with corn sugar or corn syrup solids. It can also be prevented by using the right amount and kind of stabilizer and by drawing from the freezer at a lower temperature. Depending on the kind of stabilizer used, the mix should be aged for a longer period (12-14 hr ageing may be required) and an adequate amount of stabilizer should be used to cause a partial gelling at room temperature.

Corn sugar or corn syrup solids also provide the additional advantage in preventing the formation of crust which sometimes appears on the surface of ices and sherbets. Surface crust is formed due to the evaporation of moisture from the surface. Very often this defect occurs when sucrose is used alone as a sweetener. Sometimes surface encrustation appears when surcrose crystallizes and water liberated freezes into ice. Surface encrustation may be prevented by using a higher amount of stabilizer or by using corn sugar. Corn sugar prevents surface encrustation by lowering the freezing point of the mix. However, use of corn syrup solids is more beneficial than corn sugar, as it gives a melting point nearer to that of ice cream, so that the product will have the desired firmness at the usual cabinet temperature of -13 to -16 °C. (Considering the depression in freezing point caused by surose as 1, the depression in freezing point caused by the same amount of corn sugar and corn syrup solids (DE 42) is 1.8 and 0.79, respectively).

The defect "bleeding" is due to settling of the sugar syrup to the bottom of the can. The most common causes are excessively high overrun, too high sugar content, inadequate amount of stabilizer and high storage temperature. The remedial measures obviously are proper overrun, using reduced sugar content and using a more effective stabilizer or more stabilizer.

Melt down defects include—melts too fast, does not melt or is curdy.

Colour defects—unevenness due to improperly distributed colour, unnaturalness-not suggestive of the flavour or fruit used in the product.

In recent years, it has been possible to achieve a very high degree of standardization in the manufacture of ice cream on a commercial scale. However, similar efforts are required to commercially produce ices and sherbets of uniform composition and quality.

Chapter 11

Laboratory Tests

It is important to have proper laboratory control for efficient operation and for obtaining ice cream of uniform quality. This constitutes chemical and bacteriological analyses of the ingredients used and the finished product. To avoid undesirable conditions, other samples may also be drawn for chemical and bacteriological examination. Generally, routine testing is done in the plant by its laboratory personnel. For tests which are cumbersome or require a very high degree of precision, arrangements for analyses may be made with a commercial laboratory on the basis of fixed prices per sample or a fixed price per month.

Most of the tests conducted in routine can be bone in a small laboratory containing simple and inexpensive equipment.

Judging Flavour and Aroma

This is the most essential routine test, and is one of the best measures of quality. The aroma should be observed in a place where there are no strong odours, and the observation made immediately after the sample bottles is opened. A small portion of the product is taken into the mouth, allowing, it to warm, and then carefully rolled to the back of the mouth without swallowing any of it. After judging, the portion is delivered into a sink. The next sample may be tested taking care to avoid contaminating the product.

Gerber Test for Fat in Milk and Cream

Determine fat content in milk as described in IS : 1224 (part-I)-1977. Determine fat content in cream as described in IS : 1224 (Part-II)-1977.

SNF and Total Solids in Milk by Lactometer

Determine SNF and total solids in milk as described in IS : 10083-1982.

Analysis of Fat in Ice Cream

The following methods are used for testing the fat content :

(i) Ether Extraction Test

(ii) Gerber Test

Ether Extraction Test

The ether extraction test, most commonly used for the accurate analysis of dairy products, is the Rose-Gottlieb, extraction method. In the industry, a modification of the Rose-Gottlieb extraction method, the mojonnier test is used. The Mojorniner test is accurate and sufficiently rapid to warrant its use in larger plants where each test represents comparatively large batches of the product.

The reagents used are the following :

Concentrated ammonia solution of specific gravity 0.88.

Ethyl alcohol — 98-96% (v/v).

Diethyl ether — specific gravity 0.72 at 25°C, peroxide free.

Petroleum ether — free from residue, specific gravity 0.638-0.660 at 21°C, boiling range 40-60°C.

Preparation of Sample

Let the sample soften at room temperature. As melted fat tends to separate and rise to the surface, it is not advisable to soften the sample by heating on water bath or over flame. Mix thoroughly by pouring back and forth between beakers.

For ice cream containing insolubie particles, melt the product at room temperature or in an incubator at 37°C in a closed container. Transfer entire contents to the mixer (capable of transforming product to fine uniform pulp) and mix until insoluble particles are finely divided. Transfer the mixed sample to a suitable container for convenience in weighing.

Procedure

(1) Using the Fat Extraction Tube or the Rose Gottlieb Method

Weight accurately 4-5g of the sample into the fat extraction tube. Wash the sides of the tube with 2 ml of hot water and mix by gentle swirling. Add 2 ml of concentrated ammonia solution and mix thoroughly but without splashing the contents to the upper part of the tube. Heat in water bath for 20 min at 60°C with occasional shaking. Ammonia is added to make the sample alkaline in order to make the extraction with ether possible. Ammonia also serves the additional purpose of combining with any free lactic acid and in preventing its extraction and inclusion with the fat in the ether layer. Shake the sample well to mix the sample and the ammonia.

Add 10 ml of alcohol. The alcohol makes extraction possible by helping to destroy the emulsion and by making the sample more miscirble with the ether. Shake well to mix thoroughly.

Add 25 ml of ether, close the tube with cork or stopper, which is wetted with water before insertion, and shake vigorously for 1 min. The ether is added to extract the fat; therefore, time and contact with the fat are necessary. One should not shake insufficiently at this stage, as the results are almost certain to be low, due to incomplete extraction.

Add 25 ml of petroleum ether, wash the cork and neck of the tube so that the washings mix into the tube. Replace the cork, again wet it with water, and shake vigorously for 30 sec. Petroleum ether is not added for extracting fat but for precipitating out certain compounds already dissolved by the ether.

Allow the tube to stand until the ethereal layer is clear and completely separated from the aqueous layer, usually for not less than 30 min. Remove the cork and insert the siphon or wash bottle fitting so adjusted for length that the inlet is 2-3 mm above the interface between the ethereal and aqueous layers and transfer the ethereal layer to a suitable weighing flash or dish.

Wash lip and stopper of the extraction tube with a mixture of equal parts of both solvents, and add washings to the weighing flask or dish.

Repeat the extraction of liquid remaining in the tube twice, using 15 ml of each solvent each time.

Evaporate solvents completely on hot plate or steam bath at temperature that does not cause spettering or bumping.

Dry fat in an oven at a temperature of the boiling water and cool the flask to room temperature in a desiccator. Repeat this procedure, until a constant weight is obtained.

Make a blank determination using the specified quantities of reagents throughout and water in place of the mix, and deduct the value found, if any from the apparent weight of fat. A flask, similar to that used to contain fat, could receive the same heating and cooling treatments and could be used as a counterweight.

Some synthetic rubber stoppers may be affected by usual fat solvents and can contribute considerable residue to the blank resulting in high variability in results. Therefore cork stoppers should preferably be used as they give consistently low blank values. If blank is > 0.5 mg, purify or replace reagents.

(2) Using the Majonnier Fat Extraction Flask

In the Mojonnier test, the Rose-Gottlieb extraction is adapted to commercial use, employing the following facilities to make it rapid :

(i) An extraction flask that can be centrifuged to separate the ether layer rapidily, and of such design that the ether layer can be removed conveniently by decantation.

(ii) Aluminium dishes, electric hot plate and vacuum oven for the rapid removal of ether from the fat.

(iii) Water cooled disiccator for rapid cooling of dishes to room temperature.

Procedure

- Mix the sample thoroughly by pouring several times from one container to another.
- Weight a 5 g sample into an extraction flask.
- Add 5-6 ml of water.
- Add 1.5 ml of ammonia and mix thoroughly.
- Asd 10 ml of alcohol, insert cork, and mix by allowing the liquid to flow backward and forward between the two bulbs.
- Allow the tube to cool in cold, running water or by immersing in chilled water.
- Add 25 ml of ethyl ether, insert cork, and shake vigorously for 1 min.
- Add 25 ml of petroleum ether, insert cork, and shake vigorously for 1 min.
- Centrifuge flask at approximately 600 rpm for 45 sec to obtain a clear liquid.
- Examine the flask to see if the junction of the liquid is at the lower end of the narrow neck of the tube. If it is below this, it should be raised by the addition of a little distilled water. Addition of one drop of phenolphthalein indicator aids in demarcating the ether layer from the aqueous layer.
- Carefully decant as much as possible of the supernatant layer into a previously weighed and dried aluminium dish by gradually bringing the cylindrical bulb of the flask into a horizontal position. When a maximum of the supernatant layer has been poured off, wash the outside of the neck of the flask and the cork or stopper with mixed solvent collecting the rinsings in the dish. With the Mojonnier flask in a vertical position, wash the inside of the neck with 4-5 ml of the mixed solvent and decant.
- Repeat the extraction of the mix residue and the subsequent operations twice, using 15 ml of ether and 15 ml of petroleum ether each time.
- The ether is evaporated by placing the dish on the electric hot plate. The temperature of the plate should be such that evaporation proceeds rapidly, but not so hot as to cause spattering. The ether from the first extraction is evaporated while the second extraction is in progress, and when all the ether is gone the dish should be taken off the hot plate, otherwise it will be too hot when the second extraction is added and spattering will result. The ether vapours are removed quite completely by running the suction fan and covering the suction opening and the dishes with a hood.
- When the ether has been evaporated on the hot plate, the dish is placed in the vacuum oven at 57.2^{0}C (135^{0}F) and dried for 5 min under a vacuum of not less than 22 in (55cm).
- The dish is then transferred to the desiccator, and with the motor running to circulate the water through the plate, allow to cool for 7 min before weighing. This is done to cool the dishes rapidly to room temperature.

- The dish and fat are weighed and the weight of the empty dish deducted to obtain the weight of the fat.
- Blank tests should be run on the reagents from time to time. This is done by taking 10 ml of distilled water and using the same procedure as in making a regular test. Any residue found should be deducted from the weight of the fat.
- Reagent blank should have < 0.002 g residue. A negative weight of the reagent blank, however, for a set of samples indicates error, such as the pan not being completely dry before initial weighing or the desiccator not being properly sealed. The cause of negative results should be identified and corrected.
- The percentage of fat is calculated by dividing the weight of fat by weight of the sample, and multiplying by 100.

Gerber Test

Gerber test is less accurate than the ether extraction test for the determination of fat in frozen dessert and mixes. Therefore, it should be restricted only to in-plant production control.

High concentrations of non-fat milk solids, sugars, stabilizers, emulsifirs and homogenizing treatment make vigorous shaking necessary to liberate fat after the addition of reagents. Prolonged action of sulphuric acid and isoamyl alcohol appears to increase the solubility of alcohol in fat, thus often resulting in higher fat determinations than those by the ether extraction method.

Apparatus and reagents

- Gerber butyrometer for ice cream
- Balance having sensitivity at 0.01 g and having a suitable vertical support for the butyrometer.
- Butyrometer support rack to hold butyrometers in a secure, vertical position.
- Centrifuge for butyrometers, standard style, with disc and a trunnion head to rotate at 1100+/- 100 rpm. Trunnion head models are supplied with heaters to maintain the internal temperature at approximately 60°C.
- Check the operating speed of all Gerber centrifuges under full load at monthly intervals, or more frequently, if necessary.
- Reagent dispensers, 10 ml for sulphuric acid, 1 ml for isoamyl alcohol.
- Water bath which is equipped to provide intermittent or constant agitation and to control temperature between 60 to 63°C.
- Diluted sulphuric acid : Prepared by adding 94 parts (by volume) of

sulphuric acid (Sp. gr. 1.82-1.825 at 15.5°C) to 6 parts (by volume) of cold water.

- Isoamyl alcohol (Sp. gr. 0.814-0.816 at 15.5°C)

Preparation of Sample

Prepare the ice cream sample in the same way as for the Ether Extraction Test.

Procedure

Measure 10+/- 0.2 ml of dilute sulphuric acid into an ice cream butyrometer. Place butyrometer in support on balance and preweigh. Weigh 5.00 g of a well-mixed sample into the butyrometer. Remove butyrometer from balance and add 5 ml of water and 1 ml of isoamyl alcohol. Insert lock stopper securely and proceed as with milk, except that, the butyrometer should be centrifuged for 5 min. Read the scale to the nearest 0.2% graduation and record the results. Recentrifuge without inverting the bottle, retemper, and reread the fat column. If the second reading differs by more than 0.2% from the first, the initial shaking was inadequate and the test must be repeated. When the second reading is less than 0.2% above the first, report the result of the first test.

Determination of Total Solids

The methods commonly employed for determining total solids are described as follows :

1. Mojonnier Total Solids Test

The samples used in this test must be small so as to have a thin film of solids in order to make rapid drying possible.

Procedure

- Mix the sample thoroughly by pouring it several times from one container to another.
- Weigh a 1 g sample accurately into a nickel or aluminium total solids dish which has been previously heated for 5 min in a solids oven at 100°C, and then cooled for 5 min in a cooling desiccator.
- Make weighings to the fourth decimal place with cover on the dish. Record the weight of the dish and the weight of the sample.
- Add 1 ml water and tilt the dish in order to spread the mix on a thin film over the entire bottom of the dish.
- Place the dish on the hot plate at 175-180°C, and heat until the residue begins to turn a light brown. Use the contact maker to ensure uniform evaporation.

- Place the dish into the solids vacuum oven at 100°C, and heat for 10 min. under not less than 20 in vacuum.
- Cool for 5 min in the cooling desiccator and weigh the dish and solids. Record the weight

$$\% \text{ Total solids} = \frac{\text{Weight of Solids}}{\text{Weight of Sample}} \times 100$$

2 AoAC Official method (AoAC International, 2000)

Weigh quickly 1-2 g of the sample into a round flat-bottom dish (dish of aluminium or nickel), 5 cm in diameter. Heat on steam bath for 30 min, then, in an air oven at 100°C for 3.5 hr. Cool in a desiccator and weigh quickly to avoid the absorption of moisture.

$$\% \text{ Total solids} = \frac{\text{Weight of Solids}}{\text{Weight of Sample}} \times 100$$

Determination of Acidity in Milk and Cream

Determine acidity in milk and cream as described in IS : 1479 (Part-I)-1960 and IS ; 3509-1966, respectively.

Determination of Acidity in Plain Ice Cream Mix

Like milk or cream, the natural or normal acidity of ice cream mix is due to the milk proteins, mineral salts and dissolved gases. It varies with the percentage of MSNF in the mix. A mix containing 11% MSNF will have a natural acidity of 0.17% to 0.19% (expressed as % lactic acid). A higher MSNF would raise the natural acidity and lower the pH. A mix will have normal acidity if fresh dairy ingredients are used. An acidity above the normal value indicates the presence of developed acidity which is due to the production of lactic acid by bacteria in dairy products. A mix having high acidity will have inferior flavour, high viscosity, low whipping ability, and low stability resulting in possible coagulation during pasteurization.

Determine acidity in ice cream mix as described in IS : 2802-1964.

Determination of Protein in Ice Cream

The protein content in ice cream is determined by the Kjeldahl method as per AoAC Official Method (AoAC International, 2000).

Assessing Protein Stability in Ice Cream Mix

The protein stability is assessed by the quantity of alcohol required to form a precipitate (Arbuckle, 1986).

Specific Gravity of Ice Cream Mix

The specific gravity of ice cream mix at 15.5°C (60°F) can be calculated by using the following formula :

$$\frac{100}{(\text{Fat } (\%)\ 0.9 + \text{Sugar, MSNF, Stabilizer } (\%) / 1.58 + \text{water } (\%))}$$

It is obvious that the specific gravity of ice cream mix will vary with composition. Specfic gravity can also be determined by weighing a known volume of the mix at a known temperature on a gravimetric balance or by means of a hydrometer. Specific gravity of the mix can vary from 1.05-1.12.

Determination of Free Fat in Ice Cream (Free Fat Estimate of FFE Value)

Free fat in ice cream includes the "churned out" fat and the fat not covered by the protein membrane. A solvent is used to extract the free fat. The amount of free fat gives an idea about the level of mechanical treatment applied to the product during aeration / freezing, and storage stability. The melting time and FFE value is normally closely related, a lower FFE value indicating a lower melting resistance and vice versa.

Apparatus and Reagents

- Rotator 30 rpm
- Balance
- 100 ml glass cylinders with lids
- 100 ml conical flasks + pumice dried for 60 min at 105°C.
- Sand bath
- Incubator 105°C
- Heptane

Procedure

Weigh 25.0g frozen ice cream into a 100 ml glass cylinder. Thaw the ice cream samples (takes approximately 2 hr) and fill 30 ml heptane into each glass cylinder. Close the lid and place the glass cylinders on the rotator. Rotate 15 times at a speed of 30 rpm. Wait for a couple of minutes to avoid the mix on the surface, then rotate 10 times. Let the samples stand for approximately 60 min for separation. Transfer the heptane phase into a 100 ml conical flask which has been dried for 1 hr in an incubator at 105°C together with a pumice stone and weighed. Evaporate the heptane phase in a sand bath. Repeat the extraction two times, without however, rotating 10 times as done earlier. After the final evaporation, dry the conical flasks in the incubator at 105°C for 4 hr.

Calculation :

Free Fat = Weight of the flask+fat - weight of the flask

$$\text{Per cent free fat} = \frac{\text{weight of fat} \times 100 \times 100}{25.0 \times y}$$

where

y = percentage of fat in ice cream sample

Chromatographic Analysis

Advancement made in the application of chromatography to carbohydrate analysis has enabled quantitative determination of sugars in ice cream. Sugars like glucose, fructose, sucrose, galactose, lactose, maltose and higher sugars have been resolved on a single chromatographic strip.

Stability to Heat Shock

Use a portion of ice cream in a container and store it for 6 hr each at -20°C, -5°C, -20°C and -5°C. Repeat this cycle daily for 6 days and evaluate the sample for appearance, coarseness of texture, degree of product break-down and conversion to serum.

Meltdown Test and Shape Retention

A rectangular piece of ice cream (125ml) which has been stored at -20°C is placed on a 4 min wire mesh in an atmosphere maintained at 20°C. The wire mesh is placed on top of a beaker and a stop watch is stated. The time when the first drop of ice cream falls into the beaker is noted. The weight of melted ice cream is noted after 15, 30, 45, 60, 75 and 90 min respectively. The result may be stated as g (%) melted ice cream per hr. The residue is examined and the degree of shape retention and appearance is assessed as bad, poor, fair, good or excellent. Photographs of the residue may be taken as a record.

Farrall Homogenization Index

Using a standard medicine dropper add 3 drops of the ice cream mix to 10 ml solution of water and glycerine (3.3 ml glycerine+6.7 ml water). Place the diluted product in a special slide, cover it with a cover glass, and let it set for 5 min. Using an oil immersion lens (x100), count the number of fat globules having a size of over 2 microns in diameter in each of the five fields. Fat globules over 2 microns in size are grouped as 2-2.5, 2.5-3, 3-4, 4-5, 5-6, 6-7, and 7-8 with a K value for each group as 1.4, 2.6, 5.4, 11.4, 21.0, 34.0 and 53.0 respectively. To calculate the Farrall Index, the number of globules counted in each group is multiplied by the K value and the values obtained are added. For example, if an examination of five fields show three globules 2-2.5 in size, two globules 2.5-3 and one globule 4-5, the Homogenization Index would be 20.8, i.e. the sum of (3x1.4, 2 x 2.6 and 1 x 11.4) Ideally for efficient homogenization, the Farrall Index should not exceed 7.

Measurement of Viscosity

Pipette Method

This method is used for comparing the flow time of different mixes, and also for comparing the flow time of mixes of the same composition on different days.

For comparison, a mark is made on an arbitrary place below the bulb of a measuring pipette of 50-100 ml capacity. The sample to be tested is tempered to a standard temperature in the range 15 to 20°C. The pipette is tempered by putting water at 15 to 20°C into the pipette. Record the time in seconds required to discharge the sample to the lower mark for water and then for the sample being tested for comparison purposes.

Borden Flow Meter Method

Border Flow Meter is available from the Borden Co, Columbus, Ohio, the USA. The tube-out type is used for determining the viscosity of ice cream mix. The instrument and the ice cream mix to be tested are tempered to 18 to 20°C. The sample is placed in the instrument after mixing it gently, and the excess is allowed to flow out of the overflow tube. The time (in seconds) that a continuous stream of the mix flows the instrument is recorded as the flow time and can be used for comparison purposes.

Viscosity of ice cream mix may be measured in absolute units. Measurements in absolute values are valuable in indicating whether there are other factors which influence the behavior of the mix.

Brookfield Viscometer

This instrument is used for measuring the viscosity of ice cream mix. It is available from Brookfield Engineering Laboratories, Inc., Massachusetts, USA.

The Brookfield viscometer is of the rotational variety. It measures the torque required, to rotate an immersed element (the spindle) in a fluid. The spindle is driven by a synchronous motor through a calibrated spring; the deflection of the spring is indicated by a pointer and a dial. By utilizing a multiple speed transmission and interchangeable spindles, a variety of viscosity ranges can be measured, enhancing the versatility of the instruments.

For a given viscosity, the viscous drag, or resistance to flow (indicated by the degree to which the spring winds up) is proportional to the speed of rotation of the spindle, and is related to the size and shape of the spindle.

The drag will increase as the spindle size and / or rotational speed increases. It follows that for a given spindle geometry and speed, an increase in viscosity will be indicated by an increase in the deflection of the spring. For any viscometer model, the minimum range is obtained by using the largest spindle at the highest speed; the maximum range by using the smallest spindle at the slowest speed.

Calculation

To obtain viscosity in centipoise (m Pas), the dial reading is multiplied by a factor. The factor varies with the spindle speed (rpm). Factors for different viscometer models, speed and spindle number can be obtained from the manufacturer. For instance, if a measurement is made at 50 rpm and spindle No. 1 of model RV1 is used, the factor for this speed, spindle combination is 2. If the dial reading is 40, then—

Viscosity in centipoise (m Pas) = Dial reading x factor

= 40 x 2 = 80 centipoise.

Microsopic Examination of ice Cream Texture

The ice cream is hardened at -26°C for 48 hr before texture measurements are made. The ice cream should be kept in the frozen state whilst viewing under the microscope. This is best done by employing a cold stage. This requires a supply of liquid nitrogen or a method of cooling nitrogen gas. The magnification required is in the region of x40 to x200.

The method described by Sztehlo (1994) can be used. For determining the ice crystal size, the easiest and simplest method involves taking a small sliver of ice cream using a scalpel and spreading it slightly on the microscope slide. The ice crystals can be separated by placing a cover slip on top and pressing down whilst moving the cover slip from side to side using the scalpel butt. Several slides should be prepared from a number of areas within the sample. The image quality is enhanced by using an immersion fluid of refractive index similar to the fat and matrix, thus rendering them invisible. Typically used fluids are ethyl acetate, white spirit and 1-pentanol-kerosene. The ice crystal size and distribution can be determined by image analysis either directly from the image or by following the recording through photomicrography / video, or by comparison against a standard photograph.

For determining the air cell size, a small sliver of ice cream is placed on a slide. Two drops of a high viscosity medium (such as glycerol) containing sodium dodecyl sulphate are pipetted on to the sliver. This has the effect of melting the ice cream to some extent, preventing air cell coalescence. A cover slip is slowly placed over the sliver (taking great care not to introduce additional air cells) and a thin layer of well dispersed air cells is obtained. Air cell size and distribution can be calculated by the same method as previously described for ice crystal.

Test for Ammonia Leaks

Leakage of ammonia in pipes, compressor heads and valves can be easily detected in the following manner (Arbuckle, 1986).

A phenolphthalein-treated ammonia test paper (ammonia test paper purchased from refrigeration companies) is passed along the ammonia pipes, valves, or compressor head suspected of leaks. If there is a leak, the paper turns pink where it comes in contact with the escaping ammonia. Similarly, leakage of ammonia in brine or cooling water can be detected as follows : Half-fill a tumbler with suspected brine or cooling water and add about 1/8 teaspoonful of dry caustic soda. Cover it with a piece of glass. Insert right under the cover, but not in the solution, a small strip of the phenolphthalein-treated paper. Leakage of ammonia in brine or cooling water is indicated by a pink discolouration after a few minutes.

Surface Tension

The drop method can be used for comparison purposes. A tube of uniform bore is used, and the number of drops of the sample falling per unit time is compared with that of water.

Precise and accurate determination of surface tension is made using a tensiometer. In the tensiometer, a platinum ring is connected to a sensitive balance and the force (in dynes) required to pull the ring from the iiquid is measured. The surface tension of water is 72-73 dynes / cm while the normal range for the ice cream mix is 48-53 dynes / cm.

Chapter 12

Cost and Merchandising

In recent years, the merchandising of ice cream has become highly competitive and the profit margins have been greatly reduced. Marketing methods have also changed extensively. The ice cream manufacturer is required to adapt these changes to be assured of a dependable market for his product. However, sufficient information on costs and merchandising of ice cream and related product in India is not available. Detailed studies in this area have been done in the US and European countries. In the US, Baumer and Jacobson (1969) carried out detailed studies on economics and marketing of frozen desserts. Their studies covered demand, electricity, consumption patterns, competition among ice cream and related products, and competition from other dessert and snacks. They concluded that ice cream consumption responds immediately to price change, and that a price increase leads to a decrease in consumption by a proportional amount. Demand analysis suggested that an industry average price increase of 10% would result in a reduction of consumption by 8%. They concluded that while ice cream has generally been thought of as a dessert, it has taken on increased importance in the US as a snack food in the past few years; that about 50% of the ice cream and related products is being consumed as snacks and 45% as a dessert; and that price competition from other desserts and snacks would likely become more intense in the future. Consequently, price changes might be expected to result in greater changes in ice cream consumption, as increased volumes are mass merchandised through large retail outlets in the form of a snack.

Analysis of Costs

Different items that contribute to the cost of ice cream and related products are given below :

1. Ingredient and packaging material costs.
2. Manufacturing Costs :
   - (a) Labour
   - (b) Supplies
   - (c) Repairs
   - (d) Depreciation
   - (e) Steam, power, refrigeration
   - (f) Light, water
   - (g) Taxes, insurance
   - (h) Miscellaneous

3. Selling Costs :
   (a) Salaries
   (b) Automobile and travelling
   (c) Advertising and Publicity
   (d) Miscellaneous
4. Delivery costs :
   (a) Labour
   (b) Air-conditioned van, truck supplies and expenses
   (c) Dry ice
   (d) Repairs
   (e) Depreciation
   (f) Rent, freight and expenses
   (g) Taxes, insurance and miscellaneous
   (h) Excise duty
5. Administrative costs :
   (a) Salaries ad wages
   (b) Supplies and miscellaneous
   (c) Taxes and insurance

The main cost items and their percentage are given below :

These are generally applicable to the ice cream industry in India.

Ingredients and packaging material costs	40-47%
Manufacturing costs	14-17%
Selling costs	10-13%
Delivery costs	8-11%
Administrative costs	18-22%

Hence, it is clear that ingredient and packaging material costs constitute only 40-47% of the total cost. To the lay man, who may have some conception of the cost of ingredients used in making ice cream but no conception of the other costs, it might appear that the business of manufacturing and distributing ice cream is exceedingly profitable. No doubt, this incomplete knowledge of the industry and the resulting expectations of large profits has promoted the establishment of more ice cream plants in the country. The competition has also resulted in increased cost to the consumer because of increased selling and advertising costs.

Ingredients and Packaging Material Costs

The ingredient cost of the ice cream varies with the composition of the product, overrun, quality standards, and distance from sources of raw materials. When the composition of the product has been fixed and a more or less definite quality standard has been adopted, the cost of ingredients can be kept at the lowest possible figure by judicious buying. Since the constituents can be selected from a wide variety of ingredients (e.g. serum solids from any one concentrated product like plain condensed milk, sweetened condensed milk or skimmed milk powder; cane or beet sugar, fat from cream or butter, etc.), the buyer should be thoroughly familiar with the various raw materials and their effect on quality. This requires a sound knowledge of the dairy industry.

Manufacturing Costs

The manufacturing cost can be kept to a minimum by

(i) having the investment in plant and equipment in proper relation to the actual production;

(ii) Maintaining equipment in an efficient condition;

(iii) By convenient arrangement of the plant; and

(iv) By proper management.

The necessity for a proper relation between fixed investment and volume of sales is evident, but this business principle is very commonly overlooked. The urgent necessity for increasing sales, so that the overhead expenses are spread over a larger volume, lead to consequences that have an unfavourable effect not only on individual concern, but also on the entire industry. Frequently, the consequences for the ice cream industry are as follows :

(i) Selling costs are increased by the extra sales effort and by the various concessions that are made to buyers.

(ii) Delivery costs are increased by taking on many small dealer and by greatly extending delivery routes. To some extent, other manufacturers in the territory and forced to deviate somewhat from sounder business practices and consequently, their selling and delivery costs are also increased.

(iii) Losses also increase because of bad debts which have to be "written off".

The total annual gallonage should be used as a basis for arriving at the highest permissible investment in plant and equipment. The factor that should be used in making such an estimate will vary with certain conditions and with locality. A large manufacturer may have a larger investment in proportion to production than a smaller enterprise, because greater production justifies the use of automatic and semi-automatic machinery which increases the investment considerably, but also decreases the labour costs.

It is necessary to have suitable equipment as also a conveniently arranged plant. The maintenance of the equipment in its most efficient condition is frequently neglected. The important sources of added costs through neglect of equipment are :

1. Inefficient firing of the boiler and not maintaining it in proper condition for the maximum evaporation of water per kg of fuel.
2. Neglect of leaky cylinder and faulty homogenizing valves resulting in
(a) Reduced capacity and increased power consumption, and
(b) Imperfect homogenization resulting in slower whipping and increased power and labour, besides, of course, a coarser product.
3. Scraper blades dull or poorly aligned in the freezer with the result that freezing is slower, and power consumption and labour at the freezers is increased, and also, a coarser product is obtained. Coils covered with frost necessitate lower pressures on the "low side" of the compressor to maintain the desired low temperature, under such conditions the refrigerating unit operates less efficiently and power consumption is greater for the same amount of refrigeration.

Selling Expenses

The question of efficient selling constitutes practically a separate problem in each community and must be studied as such. The size of the community, the type of dealers, and consuming public, and competitive conditions must be considered. A brief outline of the various selling methods will be given in a later section.

Delivery Expenses

The delivery expenses in the case of ice cream are high because of the very nature of the product. The necessity for refrigerating in transit and the comparatively small sales at each delivery stop, are the main reasons for the high delivery expense. The dealer who sells only a small of ice cream is generally recognized as a source of increased delivery expense. A sales policy which minimizes delivery expenses, especially on account of small dealers, should be adopted.

Administrative Expenses

The main item of expense under this head consists of the salaries of the administrative and technical staff. These expenses are susceptible to considerable variations, according to the salaries drawn by the administrative officers, who are frequently also the owners or part owners of the business.

SELLING AND ADVERTISING METHODS

The effectiveness of the method depends upon the proficiency with which it is executed and varies with the locality and the type of consuming public.

Most of the leading ice cream companies have adopted 'intensive distribution' strategy for selling of ice cream. The prime idea of this strategy is, "Ice cream should be available anywhere any time". There is a current trend to have stockist or distributors indifferent regions. The distributors supply ice cream to dealers located in different cities. Both the stockists ranges from 6 to 10%. The profit margin for the dealer may be as high as 20 to 30%. The profit margin for the manufacturer is influenced by the cost of raw and packaging material, labour, distribution, and fixed overhead. Usually, while calculating the cost escalation factor on account of anticipated increase in the cost of raw materials, the cost of packing materials is also taken into consideration by the ice cream manufacturer.

Most of the leading ice cream manufacturers in India that stockists or dealers have their own deep freeze facilities. Some dealers buy deep freezers from the manufacturers. In that case, the manufacturer could provide guarantee for as long as seven years for the compressor. Also, servicing of the machinery is chargeable and is made compulsory. Sometimes the management at its discretion provides deep freeze facilities to dealers whose sales outlets are located at strategically important points against a nominal deposit. The manufacturer also provides facilities like signboard, danglers, stickers, posters to its stockists and dealers.

The concept of selling ice cream in pushcarts is now obsolete; pushcarts have the inherent limitation of accommodating low volume of product and less number of varieties. As compared to this, selling of ice cream through parlours has been a tremendous success in some cities.

Advertising

Two general type of advertising have been used for ice cream—educational publicity stressing its nutritional and health appeal, and advertising of a particular make of ice cream. The latter method seeks to increase the consumption of ice cream, in general, and each manufacturer, who contributes to such advertising expects to get his due share of the increase. Since the nutritive value of ice cream as a food is now well established, the product is rarely given educational publicity.

The usual channels for advertising are radio, television or television sponsored programmes, organizing social programmes, print-newspaper, magazines, signboards, billboards, posters, calendars, window and counter displays.

Some manufacturers also give high-powered advertisement and publicity to specific varieties of flavours. Such advertisement is aimed to create good will for the product, and by its content repetition seeks to induce the buying public to ask for that particular product.

Retailing Ice Cream

The selling of ice cream through stores devoted chiefly to the sale of ice cream has greatly increased. The success of retailing involve favourable location of the store, greater prominence of display in the store, greater variety of products offered and the featuring of specials; emphasis on the freshness of the product.

The majority of stores located in the residential section but near the shopping districts. In selecting such a location parking conditions should be considered; if they are normally crowded due to nearby movies, etc. the location should be avoided. Closeness to institutions is desirable, since it helps sales especially during the time of the year when sales are normally low.

Most ice cream manufacturers nowadays are adopting the parlour route in ice cream marketing. The ice cream parlours not only prove to be ideal leisure joints but also help in socialising.

Dipping Losses

The dipped package usually refer to carry-out packages filled by the retailer who dips the hardened ice cream from a bulk package in his cabinet and presses it into the new container. It is best to press the ball of ice cream gently on the side of the new package, e.g. a cone with the outside of the dipper bowl, pressing just enough to make it stick, but not enough to spoil its shape or to break the cone. The dispenser should learn quickly at what temperature ice cream would dip or cut easily and still not be so soft as to spoil the texture and cause shrinkage. He would get this "feel" for dipping only by practice.

It is well known that the volume of ice cream after dipping is less than the volume before dipping. This decrease in volume is due to air being compressed or expelled from the ice cream with a corresponding loss in overrun. It is impossible for the retailer to sell the same volume of ice cream that the receives from the manufacturer as he sustains what is known as a dipping loss several factors affect dipping losses among which are overrun composition and dipping temperature. These factors were studied in detail by Bierman (1926) whose findings still offer valuable information.

The number of servings, which the ice cream dealer can dip from a container of ice cream, is influenced by the percentage overrun. This is shown in Table 12.1. The percentage of dipping loss increases as the overrun of the ice cream increases.

Table 12.1 How Overrun Affects Dipping Losses

Average Overrun	Dealer Dips from 20 Quart Containers	Average Dipping Loss	Weight per Quart	
			Before dipping	After dipping
Per cent	Quarts	Per cent	Ounces	Ounces
60.3	16.96	15.18	22.95	27.05
80.6	15.37	23.14	20.37	26.52
100.8	14.07	29.66	18.30	26.25
118.6	13.45	32.76	16.81	25.14
Average	14.96	25.18	19.61	26.24

Source: Marshall and Arbuckle, 1996

The dipping temperature also influences the number servings, which can be dipped from a container of ice cream. The effect of dipping temperature on losses is shown in Table 12.2.

Table 12.2 How Dipping Temperature Affects Dipping Losses and Weight per Quart

Dipping Temp	Average Overrun Per cent	Dealer Dips From 20-Quarts Containers Quarts	Average Dipping Loss Per cent	Weight per Quart Before Dipping Ounces	After Dipping Ounces
3 to 8° F (-13.3 to -16.1C)	90	15.33	23.35	19.34	25.72
9 to 16° F (-8.8 to -12.7°C)	90	14.65	26.75	19.34	26.82
17 to 20°F (-6.6 to -8.3°C)	90	15.86	20.70	19.34	24.46

Source: Marshall and Arbuckle, 1996

From the tables it is evident that the most desirable overrun for dipping is 80-100%. The percentage of dipping loss increases as the overrun of the ice cream increases. Moreover, minimum dipping loss occurs at a dipping temperature of -6.6 to -8.3°C. However, ice cream at this temperature is soft and this can spoil the texture. Therefore, if dipping losses are to be kept at a minimum, ice cream of average composition (15% sugar) should be dipped at -13.3°C or lower. The dipping temperature should be varied inversely; 0.5-0.8°C for each 1% difference in sugar content and to make dipping practical at -13.3°C or lower, the ice cream should contain approximately 90% overrun.

The proper dipping temperature is determined by different factors. It must be low enough to keep dipping losses to minimum, and yet, afford easy dipping. This is influenced by the overrun and composition, especially the sugar content of the product.

There is only slight effect of composition on dipping losses when compared to the effect of dipping temperature and overrun. The dipping losses in ice cream of high fat content are slightly less than in average or low fat ice cream. The dipping loss in ice cream of high MSNF content is greater than in ice cream of low MSNF content, when dipped at the same temperature. This is due to the increased lactose content introduced in the mix when the MSNF is increased. Ice cream with a high sugar content has a greater dipping loss than icecream containing a lower sugar content unless the dipping temperature is varied so as to give equal hardness to the ice cream; the dipping loss then would be approximately the same, regardless of the sugar content.

Studies indicate that two factors influence the weight of ice cream dipped. One of these is the resistance offered by the ice cream which prevents the expulsion of air. The second factor is the amount of force applied to push the dipper into the ice cream.

Dipping temperature of -13.3°C or lower, an overrun of 80-90% and ice cream of an average composition all tend to keep dipping losses at a minimum and maintain uniformity in the portion of ice cream dispensed.

Bulk vs Packaged Ice Cream

The consumers' choice between bulk and packaged ice cream intimately concerned with the question of shrinkage and weight per litre. Many consumers feel that they commonly obtain more weight in bulk ice cream dished into carry-out packages at the parlours. If there is no difference in price, the consumer is quite likely to prefer the bulk product for reasons of economy.

The view that packaged ice cream should be sold at a lower price has not been generally adopted. Packaged ice cream has distinct advantage over bulk ice cream. The package is neater in appearance and permits more attractive servings. Moreover, as packaged ice cream is not dished, it is at a lower temperature and in a better condition for serving when it reaches home. Some manufacturers give a concession on the weight in packaged ice cream; the overrun for packaged ice cream might be 15-20% lower than for bulk ice cream. Some manufacturers make no distinction in overrun; this position, however, cannot be justified moreover, they cannot expect to build up any sizeable business on the packaged product.

The cost of packaging and the lower overrun necessitate a higher price per litre to the dealer and a smaller profit margin, than in the case of the bulk product. However, the dealer should be willing to handle the packaged product at a higher price since he incurs no loss from shrinkage in the case of the packaged product, and requires less time in selling it.

ICE CREAM PARLOUR

Retailing ice cream directly to customers through ice cream parlours offer tremendous opportunities to increase the volume of sales. At the parlours, ice cream can be served in several tempting flavours by combining with different toppings, syrups, nuts or whipped cream. The items generally prepared and served at the parlour are the cone, the soda, the sundae, the milk shake, the banana split, the parfait and novelty items. The parlours should have a pleasant atmosphere and an ambience that suggests cleanliness and sanitation.

The success of a parlour depends on the quality of service rendered by its personnel. For efficient functioning, thorough training is necessary for all its employees. The men and women at the counter should be courteous, cheerful, dignified and quiet and give quick, gracious service. Persons handling and serving ice cream should be hygiene-conscious and constantly observe sanitary details. Hygienic habits include well groomed hair, neat and clean uniforms, clean hands and trim finger nails. In order to attract customers, ice cream, toppings and syrups used should be of high quality. The staff should be adept in making different items and should serve variously flavoured and coloured ice creams in the most attractive manner. They should also have the necessary experience and skill in dipping ice cream most economically.

The parlour route for retailing should be adopted when there is sufficient capital for investment in large storage facilities and an appropriate arrangement for customer servicing. If properly equipped and efficiently managed with perfectly trained personnel, parlours can be a truly profitable venture.

Chapter 13

Plant Economics of Ice Cream Stabilizer

Capacity	=	300000 Kgs/Annum
LAND & BUILDING (Land Area 500 Sq.mts)	=	Rs. 5,60,000.00

PLANT & MACHINERY

1. Pulverizer
2. Micropulverizer
3. Mixing machine
4. Screening machine
5. Air Blower
6. Conveyor system
7. Automatic bag forming filling and sealing machine
8. Miscellaneous machine

FIXED CAPITAL

1. LAND & BUILDING	Rs. 5,60,000.00
2. PLANT & MACHINERY	Rs. 6,85,000.00
3. OTHER FIXED ASSETS	Rs. 1,40,000.00
TOTAL	Rs.13,85,000.00

RAW MATERIALS

1. Alginates
2. Carragheenan gums
3. Locust bean gums
4. Agar - Agar
5. Modified food starch
6. Guargum (Food Grade)
7. Carboxymethyl cellulose
8. Disodium phosphate
9. Oxostearin solid

TOTAL WORKING CAPITAL/MONTH

1. RAW MATERIAL		Rs. 27,59,500.00
2. SALARY & WAGES		Rs. 43,200.00
3. UTILITIES & OVERHEADS		Rs. 67,500.00
	TOTAL	Rs. 28,70,200.00

TOTAL CAPITAL INVESTMENT

TOTAL FIXED CAPITAL		Rs. 13,85,000.00
TOTAL WORKING CAPITAL FOR 3 MONTHS		Rs. 86,10,600.00
	TOTAL	Rs. 99,95,600.00

TURN OVER/ANNUM

By Sale of 300000 kgs of Ice cream stabilizer	Rs. 4,20,00,000.00

PROFIT SALES RATIO = Profit / Sales x 100 = 15%

RATE OF RETURN = Operating profit / T.C.I x 100 = 61%

BREAK EVEN POINT (B.E.P) = 25%

Chapter 14

Plant Economics of Ice Cream & Ice-Candy

Capacity =

1.	BIG CUP 100 GM	6,00,000
2.	SMALL CUP 50 GM	9,00,000
3.	ICE CREAM BAR 50GM,	50,000
4.	ICE CANDY BAR 50 GM,	50,000

LAND & BUILDING (Land Area 400 sq.mt.) = Rs. 3,30,000

PLANT & MACHINERY

1. Milk Storage S.S. Tank
2. Freon compressor
3. Brine tanks (Freezers)
4. Homogenizer
5. Blending tank
6. Lab. Equipment
7. Baby Boiler
8. Misc. Equipments & Accessories

FIXED CAPITAL

1. LAND & BUILDING	Rs. 3,30,000.00
2. PLANT & MACHINERY	Rs. 2,24,500.00
TOTAL	Rs. 5,54,500.00

RAW MATERIALS

1. Fresh Milk
2. Fat Cream
3. Sugar
4. Stabilizer, colour essences, Chemicals dry fruits

5. Big Cup
6. Small Cup
7. Sticks for bar
8. Ice blocks for trolleys

TOTAL WORKING CAPITAL/MONTH

1. RAW MATERIAL		Rs. 3,05,625.00
2. SALARY & WAGES		Rs. 26,040.00
3. UTILITIES & OVERHEADS		Rs. 76,000.00
	TOTAL	Rs. 4,07,665.00

TOTAL CAPITAL INVESTMENT

TOTAL FIXED CAPITAL		Rs. 5,54,500.00
TOTAL WORKING CAPITAL FOR 2 MONTHS		Rs. 8,15,330.00
	TOTAL	Rs.13,69,830.00

TURN OVER/ANNUM

1. By sale of Big cup 6,00,000
2. Small Cup 9,00,000
3. Ice Cream bars 4,50,000
4. Ice Candy bar 4,50,000

TOTAL Rs. 74,25,000.00

PROFIT SALES RATIO = Profit / Sales x 100 = 31%

RATE OF RETURN = Operating profit / T.C.I x 100 = 167%

BREAK EVEN POINT (B.E.P) = 25%

Chapter 15

Plant Economics of Instant Ice Cream Mix

Capacity	=	150000kg/Annum
LAND & BUILDING (Land 250 Sq.mt)	=	Rs. 5,80,000.00

PLANT & MACHINERY

1. Double cone dry blender or mixer
2. Sugar Grinding machine
3. Sieving machine
4. Laboratory testing equipments
5. Automatic pouch, weighing, filling and sealing machine

FIXED CAPITAL

1. LAND & BUILDING	Rs. 5,80,000.00
2. PLANT & MACHINERY	Rs. 4,30,000.00
3. OTHER FIXED ASSETS	Rs. 1,40,000.00
TOTAL	Rs. 11,50,000.00

RAW MATERIALS

1. Milk powder
2. Sugar ground
3. Starch gelatinized
4. Stablizer guargum powder
5. Flavour
6. Colour
7. G.M.S
8. Packing materials

TOTAL WORKING CAPITAL/MONTH

1. RAW MATERIAL		Rs. 5,09,090.00
2. SALARY & WAGES		Rs. 49,125.00
3. UTILITIES & OVERHEADS		Rs. 45,200.00
	TOTAL	Rs. 6,03,415.00

TOTAL CAPITAL INVESTMENT

TOTAL FIXED CAPITAL		Rs.11,50,000.00
TOTAL WORKING CAPITAL FOR 3 MONTHS		Rs.18,10,245.00
	TOTAL	Rs. 29,60,245.00

TURN OVER/ANNUM

By sale of 150000 kgs. of Ice cream mix powder in 100 gms. packs Rs. 90,00,000.00

PROFIT SALES RATIO = Profit / Sales x 100 = 11%

RATE OF RETURN = Operating profit / T.C.I x 100 = 33%

BREAK EVEN POINT (B.E.P) = 56%

Chapter 16

Plant Economics of Ice Cream of Different Flavours

Capacity	=	300000 Kgs/Annum
LAND & BUILDING (Land area 500 sq.mt)	=	Rs. 12,75,000.00

PLANT & MACHINERY

1. Milk storage tank
2. Mixing tank
3. Homogenizer
4. Milk Heating tank
5. Brine making tank
6. Ice Cream Whipping tank
7. Ice Cream filling machine
8. Brine Solution Chiller
9. Ice Cream Refrigeration Unit
10. Pipes, Pumps, Valves, and other requirements
11. Laboratory testing equipments

FIXED CAPITAL

1. LAND & BUILDING	Rs.12,75,000.00
2. PLANT & MACHINERY	Rs.16,60,000.00
3. OTHER FIXED ASSETS	Rs.10,75,000.00
TOTAL	Rs.40,10,000.00

RAW MATERIALS

1. Milk Powder
2. Sugar
3. Milk fat

4. Stabiliser
5. Flavour, Chocolate Powder & different flavour
6. Colour
7. Cardboard packs

TOTAL WORKING CAPITAL/MONTH

1. RAW MATERIAL		Rs.15,51,875.00
2. SALARY & WAGES		Rs. 70,250.00
3. UTILITIES & OVERHEADS		Rs. 1,02,000.00
	TOTAL	Rs.17,24,125.00

TOTAL CAPITAL INVESTMENT

TOTAL FIXED CAPITAL		Rs.40,10,000.00
TOTAL WORKING CAPITAL FOR 1 MONTH		Rs.17,24,125.00
	TOTAL	Rs.57,34,125.00

TURN OVER/ANNUM

By sale of Ice Cream of different flavour 300000 Kgs. — Rs. 2,85,00,000.00

PROFIT SALES RATIO = Profit / Sales x 100 = 23%

RATE OF RETURN = Operating profit / T.C.I x 100 = 115%

BREAK EVEN POINT (B.E.P) = 24%

Chapter 17

Plant Economics of Cone For Softy Ice Cream

Capacity = 1500000 Nos./Annum

LAND & BUILDING (Land Area 400 sq. mt.) = Rs. 8,25,000.00

PLANT & MACHINERY

1. Mixing Machine.
2. Hand operated baking machine
3. Dies
4. Miscellaneous Equipment such as balance, trays etc.

FIXED CAPITAL

1. LAND & BUILDING	Rs. 8,25,000.00
2. PLANT & MACHINERY	Rs. 1,08,000.00
3. OTHER FIXED ASSETS	Rs. 75,000.00
TOTAL	Rs.10,08,000.00

RAW MATERIALS

1. Maida
2. Starch
3. Lecithin
4. Refined oil
5. Food colour
6. Antioxidant
7. Flavour, Vanilla, Chocolate

TOTAL WORKING CAPITAL/MONTH

1. RAW MATERIAL		Rs.	9,887.50
2. SALARY & WAGES		Rs.	8,875.00
3. UTILITIES & OVERHEADS		Rs.	25,550.00
	TOTAL	Rs.	44,312.50

TOTAL CAPITAL INVESTMENT

TOTAL FIXED CAPITAL	Rs. 10,08,000.00
TOTAL WORKING CAPITAL FOR 3 MONTHS	Rs. 1,32,937.50
TOTAL	Rs. 11,40,937.50

TURN OVER/ANNUM

By sale of 15,00,000 ice cream
Flavoured Cones. Rs. 12,00,000.00

PROFIT SALES RATIO = Profit / Sales x 100 = 37

RATE OF RETURN = Operating profit / T.C.I x 100 = 39%

BREAK EVEN POINT (B.E.P) = 47%

Chapter 18

Plant Economics of Ice Cold Flavour Tea

Capacity = 7500000 Pouch/Annum

LAND & BUILDING (Land Area 500 Sq. Mt.) = Rs. 13,50,000.00

PLANT & MACHINERY

1. Drum Mixer
2. Sugar Grinder
3. Automatic Weighing, Filling & Pouch Packing Machine
4. Laboratory Equipments
5. Misc. Equipments Electrical Fittings & others

FIXED CAPITAL

1. LAND & BUILDING	Rs. 13,50,000.00
2. PLANT & MACHINERY	Rs. 9,55,000.00
3. OTHER FIXED ASSETS	Rs. 8,25,000.00
TOTAL	Rs. 31,30,000.00

RAW MATERIALS

1. Sugar
2. Instant Tea Powder
3. Dry Powdered Flavour
4. Citric Acid
5. Vitamin-C (Ascorbic Acid)
6. Plastic Pouches Cardboard boxes,Carrugated Cartons, Adhesive tapes
7. Laboratory Chemicals

TOTAL WORKING CAPITAL/MONTH

1. RAW MATERIAL	Rs.11,75,000.00
2. SALARY & WAGES	Rs. 1,57,500.00
3. UTILITIES & OVERHEADS	Rs. 1,69,400.00
TOTAL	Rs.15,01,900.01

TOTAL CAPITAL INVESTMENT

TOTAL FIXED CAPITAL	Rs. 31,30,000.00
TOTAL WORKING CAPITAL FOR 3 MONTHS	Rs. 45,05,700.00
TOTAL	Rs. 76,35,700.03

TURN OVER/ANNUM

By sale of ice tea mix of different flavour in 18 gm pouches	Rs. 3,00,00,000.00

PROFIT SALES RATIO = Profit / Sales x 100 = 34%

RATE OF RETURN = Operating profit / T.C.I x 100 = 131%

BREAK EVEN POINT (B.E.P) = 26

Chapter - 19

Suppliers of Ice Cream Making Machinery

VCS India Pvt. Ltd.
Mr. Hasmukh Gajjar
No. 96/7, Behind Shiv Estate,
Opposite Ravirandal Society,
Near Jasodanagar Cross Road,
N. H. No. 8, C. T. M.
Ahmedabad - 380026,
Gujarat, India
Mobile:
+(91)-9825023410
+(91)-9375523410
Telephone:
+(91)-(79)-25893038
+(91)-(79)-25890128
Fax:
+(91)-(79)-25893038

New National Refrigeration Engineering Company
Mr. Zuber Hawa / Mr. Azhar/ Mr. Irshad (Owner)
No. 1256/3-4, Opposite Amdupura Petrol Pump, Naroda Road
Ahmedabad - 380025,
Gujarat, India
Mobile:
+(91)-9825693796
+(91)-9909820546
+(91)-9979204673
Telephone:
+(91)-(79)-22203773

Mitora Machinex Pvt. Ltd
Mr. Mihir Patel (Owner)
Plot No. 2903, Phase-4, GIDC, Vatva
Ahmedabad - 382 445,
Gujarat, India
Mobile:
+(91)-9825050144
Telephone:
+(91)-(79)-25840204
+(91)-(79)-25842636
+(91)-(79)-40083559
Fax:
+(91)-(79)-25842636

Sakthi Engineering
Mr. M Shanmugam / Mrs. Sakthi Maheshwari (Partner)
No. 20, 2nd Floor, Bharathi Nagar, Ganapathy
Coimbatore - 641006,
Tamil Nadu, India
Mobile:
+(91)-9150136807
+(91)-8643096918
Telephone:
+(91)-(422)-2136807
Email:
diamondshanmugam2015@gmail.com
diamondshanmugam2015@yahoo.com

SAS Bakery Equipments
Mr. V. V. Shaji (Chairman & Managing Director)
No. 763, R. C. Road, Rajevgandhi Nagar, Bommanahalli
Bengaluru - 560068,
Karnataka, India
Mobile:
+(91)-7204549036
+(91)-8123619283
Telephone:
+(91)-(431)-2740482

Matrix Kitchen Makers
Mr. Mir. Mohd. Faheemuddin (Manag-ing Director & CEO)
No. 945, 1st Main Road, 6th Cross Road, Near Shreya Hospital, Kengeri Satellite Town
Bengaluru - 560060,
Karnataka, India
Mobile:
+(91)-9880229452
+(91)-9632112221

Saini Engg. Works
Mr. Avtar Singh (Owner)
Plot No. 359, Industrial Area, Phase - IX, S. A. S. Nagar

Mohali - 160 062, Punjab, India
Mobile:
+(91)-9316450028
+(91)-9023568366

VCS India Pvt. Ltd.
Mr. Hasmukh Gajjar (Managing Director)
No. 96/7, Behind Shiv Estate, Near Raviran-dal Society, Near Jasodanagar Cross Road, N. H. No. 8, C. T. M.
Ahmedabad - 380026, Gujarat, India
Mobile:
+(91)-9825023410
+(91)-9375523410
Telephone:
+(91)-(79)-25893038
+(91)-(79)-25890128
Fax:
+(91)-(79)-25893038

Devi Airconditioning Engineering
Mr. Jignesh Shah (Partner)
A - 52, Adarsh 2nd, Industrial Estate, Behind Ashish Manga-lam, Cinema, Odhav
Ahmedabad - 382 415, Gujarat, India
Mobile:
+(91)-9377740253
+(91)-9898231594
Telephone:
+(91)-(79)-32200034
Fax:
+(91)-(79)-22890604
Email:
deviair2005@gmail.com

Mitora Machinex
P. No. 2903, PH.-4, GIDC, Vatva
Ahmedabad - 382445, Gujarat, India
Telephone:
+(91)-(79)-25840204
Website:
http://www.mitoramachinex.in

Om Engineering
Mr. Hitesh Panchal (Owner)
No. 242, Pushkar Industrial Estate, Ph. 1, Gidc, Vatva, Near Torrent Power, Opposite Macon Zone
Ahmedabad - 380016, Gujarat, India
Mobile:
+(91)-9824356739
+(91)-9924135432
Telephone:
+(91)-(79)-65135432

PWS Engineers Pvt Limited
Mr. Panchal (Brand Manager)
P.B. No. 62, Panchal Estate, Near Madhubhan Resort, Anand - Sojitra Road
Anand - 388001, Gujarat, India
Mobile:
+(91)-9099579747

Kunal International
Mr. Mahendra Jituri (Proprietor)
No. 19, 1st Floor, Lucky Paradise Complex, Opposite ICICI Bank, 22nd Cross, 8th Floor, Main 3rd Block, Jaya Nagar
Bengaluru - 560011, Karnataka, India
Mobile:
+(91)-9844041280
Telephone:
+(91)-(80)-22455685
Fax:
+(91)-(80)-26532449

Hakimi Tin
Mr. Ibrahimji Dosaji Vaid
Bedi Para, Girnari Street, Near Patel Vadi, Bhawnagar Road
Rajkot - 360001, Gujarat, India
Mobile:
+(91)-9824915683
+(91)-9879072552
+(91)-9879072952
+(91)-8460885552
Telephone:
+(91)-(281)-2490661

A. K. Bhavnagarwala & Co.
Mr. Shabbir
No. 158, Bhavani Peth
Jalgaon - 425001, Maharashtra, India
Mobile:
+(91)-9423185452
Telephone:
+(91)-(257)-2236952

+(91)-(257)-2237852
Website:
http://www.akbjalgaon.com

Soosham Foods Limited
Mr. Dhruvit Kakkad
A-402, Malica Apartments,
Opp. Nakoda Hospital,
60 Feet Road,
Bhayandar West
Mumbai - 401101,
Maharashtra, India
Mobile:
+(91)-9869270103
Telephone:
+(91)-(22)-28183635

Vino Technical Services
Mr. N. Srinivasan (Prop.)
No. 29/1, Mahathma Gandhi Road,
N. K. Palayam Post
Coimbatore - 641033,
Tamil Nadu, India
Mobile:
+(91)-9994435262
+(91)-9585535261
Telephone:
+(91)-(422)-2272559
Email:
sales@smartpumps.co.in
srinivasan@smartpumps.co.in
marketing@smartpumps.co.in
service@smartpumps.co.in

Sap Techno Trade Pvt. Ltd.
Mr. Mazhar Shaikh (Director)
Shop No. 5/6, NB Arcade, Pune-Bombay Road, Akurdi
Pune - 411035,
Maharashtra, India
Mobile:
+(91)-9890095121
+(91)-9767222111
+(91)-9490753171
+(91)-9822660782
Telephone:
+(91)-(20)-65303168
Fax:
+(91)-(20)-27125155

Eskimo Refrigeration Industries
Mr. Anil. S. Upalaikar (CEO)
S. No. 85/1,
Shree Shankar Nagar,
B-Building,
Ground Floor,
Poud Road, Kothrud
Pune - 411038,
Maharashtra, India
Mobile:
+(91)-9822403226
+(91)-9822206070
Telephone:
+(91)-(20)-25381934,
+(91)-(20)-25382124
Fax:
+(91)-(20)-25381934

Best Engineering Technologies
H.No.5-9-285/13,
Plot No.69/A, Rajiv Gandhi Nagar,
I.E, Kukatpally,
Hyderabad - 500 037
A.P. India.
Telephone:
040-23070231
040-23077478
Mob:
+(91)-9391057812
Website:
www.bestengineeringtechnologies.com

Om Metals And Engineers
Mr. Raju Baravkar (CEO)
S. R. No. 5,
Ekata Housing Society,
Bapujibuwa Nagar,
Thergaon
Pune - 411033,
Maharashtra, India
Mobile:
+(91)-9272228397
+(91)-9850846493
+(91)-8888827833
Telephone:
+(91)-(20)-65300457

JD Tech Projects
Mr. Jesudas Medidi (Director)
No. 4, Jhansi Enclave,
Bhagyanagar Colony,
Kukatpally
Hyderabad - 500072,
Andhra Pradesh, India
Mobile:
+(91)-9490753171
+(91)-8626083476
+(91)-9491922777
+(91)-9849205209
Telephone:
+(91)-(40)-23700361
+(91)-(40)-23063216
Fax:
+(91)-(40)-23816496

Akshar Industries
Mr. Ghanshyam Patel / Ghanshyam H. Patel (Director)
No. 94-C, Shankar Estate,
Near Reva Bhai Estate,
C. T. M., Amraiwadi
Ahmedabad - 380026,
Gujarat, India
Mobile:
+(91)-9327060160
+(91)-9375260160
+(91)-9601600699
Telephone:
+(91)-(79)-25860149

Shrikrishna Engg. Co.
Mr. Krishna More (CEO)
D-90, MIDC, Ambad
Nashik - 422 009,
Maharashtra, India
Mobile:
+(91)-9422255381
+(91)-9850682899
+(91)-7350010092
Telephone:
+(91)-(253)-2381114

Food & Biotech Engineers India Private Limited
Mr. Sanjeev Kumar
Chaprola Road, Prithla,
Tehsil- Palwal
Faridabad - 121 102,
Haryana, India
Mobile :
+(91)-9312069945
+(91)-8376808249
Telephone:
+(91)-(1275)-262157
+(91)262158/262259
Fax No. :
+(91)-(1275)-262259
Email Id :
info@foodbiotech.co.in

Magnam Netlink Pvt. Ltd.
Mr. A.K. Bhattacharya / Mr. Mahesh Chandra (Director)
No. 303,
Earth Complex, Extension Tower-X1,
Akshar Chowk,Behind Yamaha Showroom,
Munjh Mahuda,
Vadodara 390020,
Gujarat, India
Vadodara - 390020,
Gujarat, India
Mobile:
+(91)-9824059803
Telephone:
+(91)-(265)-2340357
+(91)-(265)-2974001
Fax:
+(91)-(265)-2340357
Email:
info@magnam.in
akbhattacharya@magnam.in
info@fbfind.in

Jaya Industries, Kolkatta
Mr. Pinak Pani Bhattacharya
Mr. Pinaki Pani Bhattacharjee (Partner)
No. 543, Jessore Road, Dum Dum
Kolkata - 700028,
West Bengal, India
Mobile:
+(91)-9231694285
+(91)-9433005594
+(91)-9830469278
Telephone:
+(91)-(33)-25600361
+(91)-(33)-25513568
Fax:
+(91)-(33)-25799337

Raj Refrigeration
Mr. Arun Kumar
Plot No. 3, KH, No.31/18, Meera Enclave,
Main Bus Stand, Near Pradhan Dharam Kanta, Ranhola Village
New Delhi - 110001,
Delhi, India
Mobile:
+(91)-9811276720
Website:
http://www.rajrefrigeration.com

MANN Ventures
Contact Person : Surinder Singh
Address : Plot No. 103,
Sector 25,
Ballabgarh
Faridabad,
Haryana - 121 004 (India)
Mobile:
+91-8105688471

Smart Pumps
Mr. R. Packiaraj (Prop)
S.F. No. 184/2, MG Road,
N. K. Palayam P. O.
Coimbatore - 641033,
Tamil Nadu, India
Mobile:
+(91)-9994435261

Telephone:
+(91)-(422)-6552261
+(91)-(422)-2271261

Sanjivan Industries Private Limited
Mr. Sandeep Jayram Sarfare (Director)
A - 13, Karimsheth Industrial Estate,
Wagdevi Nagar,
Near Vaishali Nagar,
Dahisar East
Mumbai - 400068,
Maharashtra, India
Mobile:
+(91)-9820998248
+(91)-9987187747
+(91)-9869080944
+(91)-9892322333
Telephone:
+(91)-(22)-28966414

Pasteur Engineering Co. Private Limited
Mr. Setu Samanta
No. 15/8/A,
The Mall Road,
Dum Dum
Kolkata - 700080, West Bengal, India
Mobile:
+(91)-9830056050
Telephone:
+(91)-(33)-25593015

Dairy Tech India
Mr. B. S. Rawat (CEO)
El-31/5, J- Block, M. I. D. C., Bhosari
Pune - 411026,
Maharashtra, India
Mobile:
+(91)-9822028137
Telephone:
+(91)-(20)-65101272
+(91)-(20)-65330399
Fax:
+(91)-(20)-27128100
+(91)-(20)-30628100

Unitech Services
Mr. Ajay Gupta
No. 439, Industrial Area, Phase- 9
Mohali - 160062, Punjab, India
Mobile:
+(91)-9417272702
Telephone:
+(91)-(172)-5095508
+(91)-(172)-2230100
Website:
http://www.unitechservicesindia.com

Star Enterprises
Mr. Sandeep Tarade (Proprietor)
Radhakrishna Nagar,
Nashik-Pune Road,
Bhosari
Pune - 411039,
Maharashtra, India
Mobile:
+(91)-9922682324

Master Food Tech
Mr. Ibrahim Pathan (Manager)
S. No. 232/2,
Pune-Nasik Road,
Atlas Compound,
Opposite Rupee Co. Operative Bank,
Bhosari,
Pune - 411039,
Maharashtra, India
Mobile:
+(91)-9822027910

YSM Biotech International
Mr. S. M. Mishra (Managing Partner)
UL - 30, EF - 3 Mall,
Plot No.-12, Sec - 20 A
Faridabad - 121006,
Haryana, India
Mobile:
+(91)-9810005609
+(91)-9990016952
+(91)-9990016153
Telephone:
+(91)-(129)-2220669
Fax:
+(91)-(129)-2220669
Email:
info@ysmbiotech.com

Repute Engineers Private Limited
12/23 D-1 Block
MIDC Chinchwad,
Pune - 411 019.
Maharashtra, (India)
Mobile:
+(91)-9422020943
Telephone:
+(91)-(20)-27481687
Telefax :
+(91)-(20)-27481368
Email:
info@reputeindia.net
Visit Us :
www.reputeindia.com

Chapter - 20

Suppliers of Raw Materials

Vinic Lifesciences Private Limited
Mr. Salvin Shah
Revin House 57, Shiv Kumud Society,
Between Akota Garden and Gold's Gym,
Akota.
Vadodara - 390007,
Gujarat, India
Mobile:
+(91)-9898337133
Telephone:
+(91)-(265)-2353291
+(91)-(265)-2341346
Website:
http://www.viniclife.com

C L Trading Company
Mr. Vishal Sindhwani /
Mr. Jitender Kumar
Community Center,
No. 20,
Pankaj Chamber,
Opposite Central Bank,
Lawrence Road,
Industrial Area
New Delhi - 110035,
Mobile:
+(91)-9873344590
Telephone:
+(91)-(11)-47055406

Gujarat General Food Chem Pvt. Ltd.
Mr. Chottubhai Koradia
Mr. Sadrubhai Koradia
(Director)
No. 427,
Arun Chambers,
Opposite Chokkha Bazar, Kalupur
Ahmedabad - 380001,
Gujarat, India
Mobile:
+(91)-9879892823
+(91)-9825141763
+(91)-9979892824
Telephone:
+(91)-(79)-22136595
+(91)-(79)-22130225
Fax:
+(91)-(79)-22172802

FLAVOURS

Hardik Corporation
Mr. Mehul Shah (Prop
A7, Shayona Golden Estate, Old
Maheshwari Mills,
Behind Advance Mill,
Shahibaugh
Ahmedabad - 380004,
Gujarat, India
Mobile:
+(91)-9375544645
+(91)-9825244645
Telephone:
+(91)-(79)-25623842
+(91)-(79)-25623838
Fax:
+(91)-(79)-25623842

Bakewell Products
Mr. Rajkumar Punjabi
(Manager)
Tenement No. 3, Old Barrack No. T/ 58,
Chembur Colony,
Chembur
Mumbai - 400 074,
Maharashtra, India
Mobile:
+(91)-9820261159
+(91)-9820994295
Telephone:
+(91)-(22)-25206264
+(91)-(22)-24136439
Fax:
+(91)-(22)-25206264

Concept Flavours & Fragrances Pvt. Ltd.
Mr. Ramachandran Baskar (Director)
No. 7/7,
South Patel Nagar
New Delhi - 110 008,
Delhi, India

Mobile:
+(91)-9717613341
+(91)-9312217242
Email:
conceptflavours@gmail.com

Omkar Herbals
Mr. D.N Kishore (Managing Director)
No. 26-M, Abhinandan Nagar, Near M. R. 10, Sukhliya
Indore - 452010,
Madhya Pradesh, India
Mobile:
+(91)-08447563253
+(91)-9301503838
+(91)-9617006638
Telephone:
+(91)-(731)-4024338
Fax:
+(91)-(731)-4024338

Raunak Enterprises
Mr. Rakesh Paryani (CEO)
Raunak House,
Q40-41,
Jai Mata Di Compound,
Thane Bhiwandi Road,
Kalher Thane
Mumbai - 421302,
Maharashtra, India
Mobile:
+(91)-9920024454
+(91)-9322292822
+(91)-9260709643
Telephone:
+(91)-(22)-25822526
Fax:
+(91)-(22)-25822526

INVERT SUGARS

Rahul Sugar Products
Mr. Rahul Gupta (Director)
LG-CS-18 & 19,Ansal Plaza,Sec-1,Vaishali
Ghaziabad - 201010,
Uttar Pradesh, India
Mobile:
+(91)-9412217957
Telephone:
+(91)-(120)-4247184
+(91)-(120)-4247185
Fax:
+(91)-(120)-4247185

ICE CREAM IMPROVER

C L Trading Company
Mr. Vishal Sindhwani / Mr. Jitender Kumar
Community Center, No. 20, Pankaj Chamber, Opposite Central Bank, Lawrence Road, Industrial Area
New Delhi - 110035,
Delhi, India
Mobile:
+(91)-9873344590
Telephone:
+(91)-(11)-47055406

ICE CREAM CUPS

GMP Plastics
Mr. G Masilamani
No. 30, 1st Cross, Ragavendra Nagar, Kurumbapet
Pondicherry - 605009,
Pondicherry, India
Mobile:
+(91)-9345429389
Telephone:
+(91)-(143)-2645070
Website:
http://gmpplastics.wordpress.com

JMS Plast
Mr. Swpneel Gupta
No. 37, Industrial Area, Indore Road
Khandwa - 450001,
Madhya Pradesh, India
Mobile:
+(91)-9893330401

A. G. Auto & Thermo-plast
Mr. Balbir Singh (CEO)
F - 282,
DSIDC Bhawana Industrial Area,
Sector - 5
New Delhi - 110039,
Delhi, India
Mobile:
+(91)-9560250193
+(91)-9212434393
Email:
agthermoformers@gmail.com
balbiraccount@yahoo.com

Varsha Packaging Industries
Mr. Hiren Soni (Managing Director)
No. 29/ A-30/ A, Industrial Area, Rau
Indore - 453331,
Madhya Pradesh, India
Mobile:
+(91)-9617771777
+(91)-9425313993
Telephone:
+(91)-(731)-2538899

Indevco Group
Mr. V. Rajagopalan
Srinivasa Nilayam No. 6, Venkatesapuram, 2nd Street, Kottivakkam
Chennai - 600 041, Tamil Nadu, India
Telephone:
+(91)-(44)-24929736
Website:
http://www.indevcogroup.com

Vandanaa Paper Products
Mrs. Vandana Padmanaban (Managing Director)
Lakshmi Industrial Area, Sipcot, Phase I, Next To Uma Maheswari Mills
Hosur - 635126, Tamil Nadu, India
Mobile:
+(91)-9986026484
+(91)-9986036484
Telephone:
+(91)-(4344)-400478
Fax:
+(91)-(4344)-400474

Jebas Exports
Mr. S. Jebastine
Mr. Thomas Sam (Managing Partner)
No. 11/1, Main Road, Near Govt. Hospital, Somanur
Coimbatore - 641668, Tamil Nadu, India
Mobile:
+(91)-8012108609
+(91)-9442233645
+(91)-7502612313
+(91)-9788830345
Telephone:
+(91)-(421)-2333644
Email:
jebasexports@gmail.com
jebastine@jebasexports.com
info@jebasexports.com
enquiries@jebasexports.com

Axiler Impex
Mr. V. Raja
No. 133,
Sri Venkatachalapathy Complex, 1st Floor, Avinashi Road, Civil Aerodrome Post, Sitra
Coimbatore - 641014, Tamil Nadu, India
Mobile:
+(91)-9942242405

Kashi Enterprise (A Unit Of Kashi Pack Care)
Mr. Keval Chothani
Mr. Keval Chothani
Mr. Vipul (Proprietor)
F 106,
Krish Residency, Nikol
Ahmedabad - 382350, Gujarat, India
Mobile:
+(91)-9722228009

Ftek Pondy
Mr. G Masilamani
No. 602/4, Mariamman Koil Street, Pannakuppam, Kandamangalam
Villupuram - 605602, Tamil Nadu, India
Mobile:
+(91)-9345429389
Telephone:
+(91)-(413)-2645070

Mr. Vicky Jain
Survey No.168/1, Machohalli Village, (Near Vani School) Magadi Main Road,
Bangalore - 560 091, Karnataka, India.
Email :
info@colorflex.in, colorflex10@gmail.com
Mobile:
+(91)-9886332878
+(91)-9886297870

Meru Industries
Mr. Koushik Jain
Mr. Rahul Jain (Partners)
Yusuf Processors, 235, Real Estate Compound, Near Bansidhar Mill, P. O Narol, Narol
Ahmedabad - 382405, Gujarat, India
Mobile:
+(91)-9840674504
+(91)-9840671200
Telephone:
+(91)-(44)-25291223

Thoran Paper Products
Mr. Prashanth CS / Mr. Prashanth (General Manager- Marketing)
Plot No. A / 17,
Road No. 12,
Industrial Park,

Nacharam
Hyderabad - 500076,
Andhra Pradesh, India
Mobile:
+(91)-8377802682
+(91)-8106944040
+(91)-8008191940
+(91)-9490791940
Telephone:
+(91)-(40)-27172652
+(91)-(40)-27170443
+(91)-(40)-20081402
Fax:
+(91)-(40)-27172652

P S Paper Products
Mr. Anil Tuteja (Owner)
20/23, Old Market,
Near Kali Mata Mandir,
West Patel Nagar
New Delhi - 110 008,
Delhi, India
Mobile:
+(91)-9810026296
Telephone:
+(91)-(11)-25884891
+(91)-(11)-25884899
+(91)-(11)-42484296
Email:
anilkumartuteja@gmail.com

Jupiter Paper Tech
Mr. Devin Patel
164, Vijay Estate,
Behind Bhikshuk Grun,
Odhav
Ahmedabad - 382 415,
Gujarat, India
Mobile:
+(91)-9904696894

Jay Mangal Industries
Mr. Sachin Madhogaria
Mr. K.N Madhogaria
(Partner)
D 1503, DSIDC, Narela
Industries Complex
New Delhi - 110040,
Delhi, India
Mobile:
+(91)-9818336999
+(91)-9350505849
+(91)-9311123985
Telephone:
+(91)-(11)-47563985

Jallan Polypack India Pvt Ltd
Mr. Susanta Bhaumik
(Assistant Manager)
Plot No. 8 C, KIADB
Industrial Area, Attibele
Anekal Taluk
Bengaluru - 562107,
Karnataka, India
Mobile:
+(91)-9880501432
Telephone:
+(91)-(80)-25720749

Vibrant Nature
Mr. S. Ramakrishnan
(Manager)
No. 13/ 4, 3rd Cross
Street, Kasthurbai
Nagar, Adyar, Next To
Nalli
Chennai - 600020,
Tamil Nadu, India
Mobile:
+(91)-9940024372
Telephone:
+(91)-(44)-43201616

V. R. Laminations Private Limited
No. 1-10-122/19,
Ashok Nagar Street
No. 10
Hyderabad - 500037,
Andhra Pradesh, India
Mobile:
+(91)-9849025506
Telephone:
+(91)-(40)-27653248
+(91)-(40)-27603456
+(91)-(40)-27668730

V. R. Laminations Private Limited
No. 1-10-122/19,
Ashok Nagar Street
No. 10
Hyderabad - 500037,
Andhra Pradesh, India
Mobile:
+(91)-9849025506
Telephone:
+(91)-(40)-27653248
+(91)-(40)-27603456
+(91)-(40)-27668730

Hi-Life Labels
218 Palladam Main
Road,
Veerapandi Post,
Tiruppur - 641605,
Tamil Nadu, India
Mobile:
+(91)-9150444390
Telephone:
+(91)-(421)-2210382
+(91)-(421)-2214382
Website:
http://www.hilife
labels.in

Pal Industries
Mr. Tushar Kothari
No. 75,
GIDC, Ganeshpur
Modasa - 383315,
Gujarat, India

Mobile:
+(91)-9898179848
Telephone:
+(91)-(2774)-242081
+(91)-(2774)-243082
Website:
http://www.icecreamcones.in

City Polymers
Mr. Rajesh Mittal (Owner)
F-28, Sector-1,
Bawana Industrial Area
Delhi - 110036, India
Mobile:
+(91)-9810092449

Rajeswari Paper Products
Mrs. Rajeswari
No. 4/382,
Backside To Hotel Mathoos, Swaminathan Nagar, 3rd Main Road,
Kottivakkam
Chennai - 600 041,
Tamil Nadu, India
Mobile:
+(91)-9884024791
Telephone:
+(91)-(44)-24487696
Website:
http://www.rajeshwaripaperproducts.com

Sri Vari Paper Products
Mr. Ravi Desigan
No. 16, 8th Street,
Krishna Nagar, West Tambaram
Chennai - 600045,
Tamil Nadu, India
Mobile:
+(91)-9382899553
Telephone:
+(91)-(44)-22397160

KR Printographs
Mr. Kalirajan Rajan
No. 2/2184/3,
Deivanai Nagar,
Vishwanatham Road,
Sivakas,
Virudhunagar District
Sivakasi - 626123,
Tamil Nadu, India
Mobile:
+(91)-9843079476
Telephone:
+(91)-(4562)-278776
Website:
http://www.krprintographs.com

Green India Exports
Mr. R K Raghunandan
No. 90, Palghat Road,
Pollachi - 641001,
Tamil Nadu, India
Mobile:
+(91)-9787709119
Telephone:
+(91)-(4259)-224827
Website:
http://www.greenindiaexports.com

ICE CREAM STICKS

Rupali Traders
Mr. Pramod More (Proprietor)
No. 290/1, Ghorpade Peth,
Near Hotel 7 Loves
Pune - 411042,
Maharashtra, India
Mobile:
+(91)-9370035406
+(91)-9326664646
+(91)-9922356666
+(91)-9422035406
Telephone:
+(91)-(20)-26451613
+(91)-(20)-30425406
Fax:
+(91)-(20)-26449862

Trade Centre
Mr. R. H. Shah
No. 9, Bombay Mutual Building, 3rd Floor,
Sri PM Road
Mumbai - 400001,
Maharashtra, India
Telephone:
+(91)-(22)-22693908
+(91)-(22)-22665463
Website:
http://www.dtechbiz.com

Realtime Enterprises
Mr. Kumaravel M Sambandan
No. 2/139, 1st Floor,
Mount Poonamallee Road,
Ayyappanthangal
Chennai - 600 056,
Tamil Nadu, India
Mobile:
+(91)-9894610922
Telephone:
+(91)-(44)-65738253

Kapgroup India Limited
Mr. Kuldeep Duggal
A-31/4, Mayapuri

Industrial Area, Ph - I
New Delhi - 110064,
Delhi, India
Telephone:
+(91)-(11)-28112454
+(91)-(11)-28115789
Website:
http://www.kapgroup.huematrix.com

Alka Manufacture Company Pvt Limited
NO. 102, Vithalwadi, Kalbadevi Road
Mumbai - 400 002, Maharashtra, India
Telephone:
+(91)-(22)-22402610
+(91)-(22)-32564087
Website:
http://www.ezeeproducts.com

Tag Overseas
Mr. Manish
C 1/10,
Ranapratap Bagh
Delhi - 110007, Delhi, India
Mobile:
+(91)-9899690003

Amul Ice Cream
Gujarat Cooperative Milk Marketing Federation,
PO Box 10, Amul Dairy Road
Anand - 388 001, Gujarat, India
Telephone:
+(91)-(2692)-258506
+(91)-(2692)-258507
Website:
http://www.amulicecream.in

Nilkamal Rangoli Store
Mr. Mitul Rangwala / Mr. Mukund (Partner)
Baranpura Main Road, Opposite Champagali, Near Chokhandi Char Rasta
Vadodara - 390001, Gujarat, India
Mobile:
+(91)-9427592964
+(91)-9426024402
Telephone:
+(91)-(265)-2414339

Pawan Traders
Mr. Roshan Rohra
Shop No. 479, Main Road, Near Satya Sai Complex, Ulhasnagar
Mumbai - 400001, Maharashtra, India
Mobile:
+(91)-9322888542

Ice Cream Stabilizer

Gujarat General Food Chem Pvt. Ltd.
Mr. Chottubhai Koradia
Mr. Sadrubhai Koradia (Director)
No. 427,
Arun Chambers,
Opp Chokkha Bazar, Kalupur
Ahmedabad - 380001, Gujarat, India
Mobile:
+(91)-9879892823
+(91)-9825141763
+(91)-9979892824
Telephone:
+(91)-(79)-22136595
+(91)-(79)-22130225
Fax:
+(91)-(79)-22172802

Om Sri Foods
Mr. L. Nandagopal (Prop)
No. 11/5/2, C.K.P. Koil Street, Choolai
Chennai - 600012, Tamil Nadu, India
Mobile:
+(91)-9003071467
+(91)-7845421573
+(91)-9940649949
+(91)-9789989706
Telephone:
+(91)-(44)-42865001
Victory Essence Mart
Mr. Hemanth Kumar
No. 3, Nalband Lane
A. S. Char Street Cross
Bengaluru - 560053
Karnataka, India
Mobile:
+(91)-9844456974
Telephone:
+(91)-(80)-41225464
+(91)-(80)-22873872

EIRI PROCESS TECHNOLOGY BOOKS

07 Technology Of Modern Rice Milling And Basmati Rice

08 Hand Book Of Goat Farming

09 Floriculture Hand Book (Flowers Growing Technology)

10 Aloe Vera Cultivation, Processings, Formulations And Manufacturing Technology

11 Poultry Farming, Hatchery and Broiler Production

DAIRY FARM, MILK PROCESSING AND ICE CREAM

01 Hand Book of Dairy Formulations, Processes & Milk Processing Industries

02 Milk Processing And Dairy Products Industries

03 Hand Book Of Dairy Farming to Produce Milk with Packaging

04 Hand Book Of Ice Cream Technology And Formulae

05 Hand Book Of Milk Processing Dairy Products And Packaging Technology

06 Dairy Farming for Milk Production Technology

07 Commercial Dairy Farming with Project Profiles

HERBS & MEDICINAL CULTIVATION

01 Herbs, Medicinal & Aromatic Plants Cultivation

02 Aushidhi And Sungndhit Paudho Ka Vaysayik (Hindi)

03 Hand Book Of Aromatic & Medicinal Plants And Biodiesel (Jatropha)

04 Hand Book Of Medicinal & Aromatic Plants (Cultivation, Utilisation & Extraction Processed)

FOOD & AGRO PROCESSING, PRESERVATION, SNACK FOOD, DEHYDRATION, FRUIT BEVERAGE, POTATO, MAIZE, MEAT PROCESS

01 Fruits & Vegetables Processing Hand Book

02 Fruit Beverage & Processing With Mango

03 Food Processing & Agro Based Industries

04 Manufacturing Technology of Snacks Food, Namkeen, Pappad & Potato Products

05 Preservation & Canning Of Fruits and Vegetables

06 Hand Book of Food Dehydration & Drying

07 Meat Processing & Meat Products Hand Book

08 Technology of Food Preservation & Processing

09 Hand Book of Food Packaging Technology

10 Agro Based & Processed Food Products

11 Potato & Potato Processing Technology

12 Technology of Maize & Allied Com. Products

13 Technology of Food Processing Industries

14 Technology of Sweets (Mithai) with Formulae

15 Modern Technology of Frozen Food Products

16 Technology of Water and Packaged Drinking water

17 Complete Hand Book on Frozen Food Processing and Freeze Drying Technology

18 Technology of Sweets (Mithai), Namkeen and Snacks food with Formulae

19 Complete Book on Banana Cultivation, Dehydration, Ripening, Processing, Products and Packaging Technology

EIRI PROCESS TECHNOLOGY BOOKS

20 Technology of Chicken Meat and Poultry Products
21 Agro Food Processing and Packaging Technology
22 Modern Technology of Tomato Processing and Dehydration (Ketchup, Juice, Paste, Puree, Soup and Drying)
23 Modern Technology of Agro Processing and Food Packaging Products with Project Profiles
24 Start Your Own Coffee and Coffee Processing

SOAPS & DETERGENTS

01 Household Soap. Toilet Soap & Other Soap
02 Profitable Small Scale Manufacture Of Soaps & Detergents
03 Synthetic Detergents With Formulations
04 Modern Technology of Acid Slurry, Surfactants, Soap and Detergents with Formulae

ORGANIC FARMING AND FOOD

01 Hand Book Of Organic Farming And Organic Foods With Vermi-Composting And Neem Products

FISH FARMING & FISHERY PRODUCTS

01 Hand Book Of Fish Farming And Fishery Products

COSMETIC (SYNTHETIC & HERBAL)

01 Cosmetics Processes & Formulations
02 Herbal Cosmetics & Beauty Products With Formulations
03 Profitable Small Scale Manufacture Of Cosmetics (Synthetic & Herbal)
04 Hand Book Of Synthetic & Herbal Cosmetics (How to Make Beauty Products)
05 Technology Of Herbal Cosmetics & Toiletries Products With Formulae

OIL AND FATS

01 Hand Book of Oils, Fats And Derivatives With Refining & Packaging Technology
02 Technology of Oilseeds Processing, Oils & Fats and Refining

ESSENTIAL OILS & AROMATIC

01 Essential Oils Manufacturing & Aromatic Plants
02 Modern Technology Of Essential Oils
03 Technology Of Perfumes, Flavours & Essential Oils
04 Essential Oils Processes & Formulations

PERFUMES AND FLAVOURS

01 Hand Book Of Flavours & Food Colourants Technology
02 Hand Book Of Perfumes & Flavours
03 Hand Book of Perfumes With Formulations
04 Technology Of Perfumes, Flavours & Essential Oils
05 Hand Book Of Flavours Technology

BUILDING MATERIALS & CHEMICALS

01 Technology Of Building Materials & Chemicals With Processes

EIRI PROCESS TECHNOLOGY BOOKS

Complete Hand Book Of Ayurvedic & Herbal Medicines)

STEEL, S.S., NON FERROUS METALS, ROLLING MILL

01 Modern Technology of Non Ferrous Metals and Metal Extraction

02 Processing Technology of Steels and Stainless Steels

03 Modern Technology of Rolling Mill, Billets, Steel Wire, Galvanized Sheet, Forging & Castings

04 Manufacturing Technology of Non-Ferrous Metal Products

WOOD, VENEER, PLYWOOD, PARTICLE, BOARD, FIBREBOARD, BAMBOO & FOREST PRODUCTS

01 Modern Technology Of Wood, Veneer, Plywood, Particle Board, Fibreboard, Bamboo & Forest Products

BIO GAS PRODUCTION

01 Modern Technology of BIOGAS Production

WASTE BASED PRODUCTS INCLUDING INDUSTRIAL, AGRICULTURE, MEDICAL, MUNICIPALITY, ORGANIC & BIOLOGICAL

01 Technology Of Products From Wastes Industrial, Agriculture, Medical, Municipality, Organic & Biological

02 Products from Waste Technology Handbook

FOOD CHEMICALS, FOOD ADDITIVES, PIGMENTS, AROMA, SWEETENERS AND FOOD EMULSIFIERS

01 Technology of Food Chemicals, Pigments and Food Aroma Compounds

02 Modern Technology of Food Additives, Sweeteners and Food Emulsifiers

SOYBEAN

01 Technology of SOYBEAN Products with Formulae

02 Technology of Soya Milk, Tofu, Hydrlyzate and allied Soyabean Products with Project Profiles

EIRI Multiple Project Reports in CD ROM

01 92 New Lucrative Project Reports In Cd

02. 45 Infotech/It, Hospitality, Hospital, College, School & Club

03. 23 Profitable Construction Projects

04. 56 Agro Based & Food Processing Projects

05. 52 Food, Dairy, Bakery, Confectionery & Snacks Foods

06. 45 New Chemicals & Allied Project Reports

07. 100 Profitable Plastic, Polymers & Allied Projects

08. 44 Textile, Garments, Hosiery & Allied Products In Cd

09. 23 Dairy Farming (Buffalo & Jersey Cow, Dairy Products & Other Milk Processing Ind.

10. 42 Paper, Pulp & Paper Converting Products Reports

EIRI Multiple Project Reports in CD ROM

11. 31 Essential Oils, Perfumes, Flavours & Aromatic Compounds
12. 28 Surgical And Disposable Medical Projects
13. 36 Profitable Printing & Allied Projects Reports
14. 63 Profitable Packaging & Allied Project Reports
15. 99 Profitable Printing & Packaging
16. 42 Electroplating, Anodizing & Allied Projects
17. 31 Profitable Plantation & Cultivation Projects
18. 55 Profitable Products From Agro And Other Industrial Wastes
19. 35 Profitable Gums, Adhesives, Sealants And Resins Projects
20. 54 Paint, Varnish, Solvents, Lacquers, Resins, Enamel, Pigments, Thinners & Powder (54 Project Reports In Cd)
21. 43 Iron, Steel, Casting, Fabrication, Wire Drawing & Rolling Mills Projects
22. 26 New Educational Projects (Schools, Colleges, Training/ Management Institute, Hostels Etc.)
23. 12 Mosquitoes Preventive Projects (Coils, Mats, Liquids, Agarbatti, Nets, Spray Etc.)
24. 21 Bakery And Allied Products
25. 67 Rubber And Rubber Goods Industries
26. 37 Aluminium And Aluminium Based Industries
27. 14 Potato And Potato Based Industries
28. 50 Electrical, Electronics And Computer Based Industries
29. 52 Cosmetics (Herbal & Synthetics) Technology Projects (52 Project Reports)
30. 10 Molasses Based Lucrative Projects
31. 24 Fruits/Veg. & Allied Food Dehydration Projects
32. 7 Power Plant Projects (Thermal, Hydro, Solar, Wind Energy And Lignite Coal Based)
33. 35 New Profitable Industries
34. 160 New Export Oriented And Profitable Projects (160 Project Reports In Cd)
35. 5 Ginger & Ginger Processing Industries
36. 13 Fish Farming And Fishery Products
37. 6 Agarbatti And Allied Projects
38. 28 Fruit Juices, Food Dehydration And Allied Products
39. 9 Tea Plantation And Processing Based Industries
40. 14 Roasted/Salted Cashew Nuts, Almonds, Namkeens, Spices Projects
41. 23 Injection Moulded Plastic Products (23 Project Reports)
42. 38 Biofertilizer, Biofuel, Enzyme, Organic Farming & Manure, Protein And Allied Lucrative Projects
43. 10 Maize & Corn Processing Projects
44. 11 Profitable Solar & Solar Based Products
45. 11 Infotech/It Projects
46. 42 Hospitality, Building Material, Power Steels, Alcohol & Other Food Products
47. 24 Soap & Detergents (Scouring Powder, Toilet Cleaner, Laundry Soap, Detergent Cake & Powder, Toilet Soap, Enzyme Based Detergents, Phenyl & Soap Coated Paper)
48. 10 Coconut And Coconut By Products
49. 22 Alcohol, Beer, Imfl, Country Liquor, Wine & Other Related Projects

EIRI Multiple Project Reports in CD ROM

50. 30 Chemicals, Mechanicals, Packaging & Other Profitable Projects
51. 43 Automobile Parts, Gears, Polish, Petrol Pump, Components, Service Station & Other Accessories Projects
52. 23 Canning, Dehydration. Dairy, Jatropha, Fish Other Profitable Projects
53. 83 Export Oriented Units (100% Eou/Eou) Projects
54. 6 Lucrative Projects On Thinners (In Cd Rom)
55. 10 Leather Tanning Garments, Footwear, Chemicals, Adhesive & Goods Industries
56. 25 Ayurvedic/Herbal Pharmacy & Cosmetic Products
57. 63 Multi Crores Profitable Projects (From 1 Crore To 50 Crores Above Projects)
58. 28 Multi Crores Profitable Projects (From 10 Crores To 50 Crores Projects)
59. 16 Multi Crores Profitable Projects (From 50 Crores & Above)
60. 19 Multi Crores Profitable Projects (From 1 Crore To 10 Crores Projects)
61. 9 Wheat And Wheat Projects In Cd
62. 24 Lubricating Oils, Greases, Break Oil, Bitumen, Transformer Oil, Reclamation Used Engine Oils, Cutting Oils Projects In Cd
63. 75 Entertainment, Infotech, Educational, Management, Hospitality & Ware House Projects (75 Project Reports In Cd)
64. 46 Projects On Infrastructure, Real Estate, Hotels, Hospitals, Hospitality, School, Colleges, Clubs, Resorts & Construction Based Projects In Cd. (24 Project Reports In Cd)
65. 8 Mango And Mango Based Projects In Cd Rom
66. 29 New Profitable 1.5 Cr. To 3 Cr. Projects In Cd (29 Project Reports In Cd)
67. 100 Food Processing & Agro Based Profitable Projects
68. 212 Highly Demandable Profitable Projects in Cd
69. 20 Copper and Copper Based Industries
70. 52 Small Scale 25 To 50 Lakh Investment Projects
71. 25 PVC (Poly Vinyl Chloride) and PVC Based Profitable Projects (25 Project Reports in Cd)
72. 57 Small Scale 50 Lakh to 1 Crore Investment Projects (57 Project Reports in Cd)
73. 19 Rice Husk, Bagasse and Molasses Based Profitable Projects (19 Project Reports in Cd)
74. 9 Poultry Farming, Chicken Processing and Hatchery Projects

ENGINEERS INDIA RESEARCH INSTITUTE

4449, Nai Sarak, Main Road, Delhi - 110006 (India)

Ph: +91-11-23918117, 23916431, 45120361, 23947058, 64727385

* E-Mail: eiribooks@yahoo.com & eiriprojects@gmail.com

*Website: www.eiriindia.org & www.industrialprojectreports.com